Fictional Genders

Fictional Genders

ROLE & REPRESENTATION
IN NINETEENTH-CENTURY
FRENCH NARRATIVE

DOROTHY KELLY

UNIVERSITY OF NEBRASKA PRESS

LINCOLN AND LONDON

Publication of this book was assisted by a grant from
The Andrew W. Mellon Foundation.

A slightly different version of the section "Representation's Others:
Séraphîta, the Fantastic, and Undecidable Gender" appeared in *Literature
as Philosophy/Philosophy as Literature,* edited by Donald G. Marshall (Iowa
City: University of Iowa Press, 1987). Permission to use this material has
been given by the University of Iowa Press.

Library of Congress Cataloging-in-Publication Data

Kelly, Dorothy, 1952–
Fictional genders : role and representation in nineteenth-century French
narrative / Dorothy Kelly.
p. cm.
Bibliography: p.
Includes index.
ISBN 0-8032-2718-3 (alk. paper)
1. French fiction—19th century—History and criticism. 2. Sex role in
literature.
3. Narration (Rhetoric). 4. Feminism and literature—France—
History—19th century. I. Title.
PQ653.K4 1989   843'.7'09353—dc19
88-20653
CIP

For Paul

CONTENTS

PREFACE

S ECURE AND stable notions of gender identity are hard to find in nineteenth-century French prose. The problems of gender identity and sexuality are apparent from the René of Chateaubriand to the Raoule of Rachilde, and these problems often act as catalysts that set the plot in motion or as a focus for the main conflict in a text. *Fictional Genders* aims to explore first the inner workings of gender in texts by authors who are usually thought of as realist and then, briefly, the relation of this realist gender identity to its other, fantastic and decadent, counterparts. The methodology is eclectic: using thematic, structuralist, poststructuralist, psychoanalytic, and feminist theories and techniques, I analyze both male and female characters through close readings of the following texts: Stendhal's *Le Rouge et le noir;* Flaubert's *Madame Bovary;* Rachilde's *Monsieur Vénus;* and Balzac's "Le Chef d'oeuvre inconnu," *La Cousine Bette, Eugénie Grandet, Le Lys dans la vallée,* "Une Passion dans le désert," *Sarrasine,* and *Séraphîta.* I also refer, in more general terms, to other texts by these same authors.

Even though this book deals with both male and female gender identities, it must end with a discussion of femininity because it is the notion of the feminine which is most problematic and which, as a consequence, often problematizes male identity, even identity itself. There seems to be an essential incompatibility between realism and the feminine, which is the subject of the conclusion.

I have attempted to refer to English editions of theoretical texts whenever possible. If no reference to an English edition is given, the translation is my own: when the French version of the theoretical text is particularly rich or ambiguous, I have supplied it either in the text itself or in a note. Since cutting out fragments of an English translation of a literary text to match up with the French quotation usually produces an incomprehensible fragment, I have translated the literary texts myself, with the exception of the dated technical vocabulary of *Madame Bovary,* which I gleaned from Paul de Man's edition and translation (and have so noted when these passages appear). In my translation of the literary texts, I have tried to remain as literal as possible, without severely deforming the meaning, to retain the literal flavor of the original French version. Thus, for instance, although the French words *dominer* and *passion* in Balzac and the word *félicité* in *Madame Bovary* might sometimes find a better rendition in a less literal form, I have used *dominate, passion,* and *felicity* because, in my analysis, the force of the repetition of these words in different contexts is more important than a slight change in the nuance of their meaning. In quotations from the French and other sources, new paragraphs are indicated by a paragraph mark rather than by indentation.

I would like to thank the following for their help and support: the Boston University Humanities Foundation, the Humanities Foundation Society of Fellows, and the director, Bill Carroll, for granting me a fellowship that provided me with the time necessary for the writing of a major portion of this work; Jeff Kline, for his help and suggestions; Yolande Grandvaux, for her advice on some of the more difficult translations; Patsy Baudoin, who introduced me to the remarkable works of Rachilde; my colleagues at the *Nineteenth-Century French Studies* Conferences, who discussed much of this work with me; and finally the members of the Modern Foreign Languages and Literatures Department of Boston University, for their numerous suggestions and discussions.

Dorothy Kelly

Fictional Genders

INTRODUCTION

The

APORIA OF GENDER

On entre dans
cette allée par une porte bâtarde, surmontée d'un écriteau sur lequel est
écrit: MAISON VAUQUER, et dessous: "Pension bourgeoise des deux
sexes et autres."–HONORÉ DE BALZAC, *Le Père Goriot.* / *One enters this
alley through a door topped by a sign on which is written* MAISON VAUQUER,
and below that "Bourgeois Pension for the two sexes and others."

IN THE opening pages of *La Cousine Bette,* the text's eponymous heroine
appears in a description that is certainly not a coded litany of ideal
feminine beauty:

> Paysanne des Vosges, dans toute l'extension du mot, maigre, brune,
> les cheveux d'un noir luisant, les sourcils épais et réunis par un
> bouquet, les bras longs et forts, les pieds épais, quelques verrues
> dans sa face longue et *simiesque,* tel est le portrait concis de cette
> vierge. / *A Vosges peasant woman, in every sense of the word: skinny, dark;
> with shiny black hair, thick eyebrows joined in the center in a tuft, long and
> strong arms, wide feet, a few warts on her long,* simian *face: such is the
> concise portrait of this virgin.* [1]

Strong arms, large feet, thick eyebrows, warts: this seems more like a
portrait of man—a rather ugly man—than that of a woman. To complicate Bette's androgyny, she loves one of those blond, slight, sensitive
Balzacian artists, who himself seems more feminine than masculine.
Masculine woman loves feminine man in a chiasmic structure made
explicit in the text:

Quoique Steinbock eût vingt-neuf ans, il paraissait, comme certains blonds, avoir cinq ou six ans de moins, et à voir cette jeunesse, dont la fraîcheur avait cédé sous les fatigues et les misères de l'exil, unie à cette figure sèche et dure, on aurait pensé que la nature s'était trompée en leur donnant leurs sexes. (p. 107) / *Although Steinbock was twenty-nine, he seemed to be, as certain blond young men, five or six years younger; and seeing his youthful countenance, whose freshness had been faded by the fatigue and wretchedness of exile, alongside her hard, dry face, one might have thought that nature had erred in giving them their sexes.*

Their odd friendship, called a "mariage de cette énergie femelle et de cette faiblesse masculine" (p. 110) ("marriage of this female energy and this masculine weakness") is decidedly comic, and, of course, the handsome Steinbock does not love Bette but eventually marries Hortense, a conventionally feminine beauty. The androgynous couple is never allowed to form; but for a moment, the question, Who is the man and who the woman? arises. *

This chiasmus of gender in *La Cousine Bette* is not an isolated one; it recurs over and over in nineteenth-century French fiction, and it will be one of the central concerns in the analyses to follow. When one comes upon so many masculine women and feminine men, the very nature of masculinity and femininity comes into question. Thus the comical rhetorical question of Bette's and Steinbock's genders becomes more serious (as Paul de Man shows, rhetorical questions have this effect sometimes[2]), as it gives expression to one of the most disturbing complexities of modern times: what is a man, what is a woman, and how can we tell the difference? The undecidability of gender illustrated by the Balzac text evinces an unsettling modern aporia, for sometimes we cannot decide one way or the other. *Fictional Genders* explores various manifestations of this aporia in realist, fantastic, and decadent texts, as well as in the works of three important modern theorists.

The most persistent structure in this analysis will be one which manifests itself in the Bette/Steinbock couple. Their gender relation has two structural moments: the first is that of aporia and ambiguity when the two genders cannot be distinguished from each other; the second is a repositioning of the genders into their original, traditional definitions when Steinbock marries Hortense. A double trajectory of gender identity is created: a radical questioning of gender accompanied by a conservative return to tradition (these two "moments" do not necessarily have to appear in this temporal order: they can be reversed or simultaneously present). In this introduction, this double trajectory of gender identity will be examined in the important theoretical texts of Sigmund Freud, Jacques Lacan, and Jacques Derrida, while we look at their theories as *texts,* which themselves pose certain literary problems relating to gender identity. With these problems in mind, the main body of the book will study the problematic double trajectory of gender identity in texts by Stendhal, Balzac, Flaubert, and Rachilde.

*

It is with Freud and the advent of psychoanalysis that a real theory of gender aporia and of a gender identity not based simply in biology finds its home. Freud begins an investigation of female sexuality by showing how we take for granted the difference between the sexes and the importance of gender difference in the way we categorize other human beings: "When you meet a human being, the first distinction you make is 'male or female?' and you are accustomed to make the distinction with unhesitating certainty."[3] One of the most important implications of Freud's work, however, is the undermining of that certainty, for in raising the question of human sexuality and its relation to human identity, he also raises the lid of a Pandora's box from which escape unsettling questions concerning the very nature of sexuality and gender. His investigation of the importance of the Oedipus complex in the development of human sexuality leads him to reflect upon the different directions taken by the complex in males and females and thus to ponder the natures of masculinity and femininity. This very investigation of gender identity is a radical and far-reaching step, for it presupposes that gender identity is not biological: "What constitutes masculinity or femininity is an unknown characteristic which anatomy cannot lay hold of" (Freud, "Femininity," p. 114). Our inability to ground gender in biology, in the real physical world, is a disturbing problem indeed, for it renders problematic a denotative, representational definition of gender.

Since gender does not exist as a physical given, Freud says that it is a process of development: "Psycho-analysis does not try to describe what a woman is—that would be a task it could scarcely perform—but sets about enquiring how she comes into being, how a woman develops out of a child with a bisexual disposition" (Freud, "Femininity," p. 116). The genderization of the human being is thus the process by which two different impulses, both present in bisexuality, are later polarized and separated, so that an individual is allowed to manifest only one or the other, even though traces of the effaced gender can and do reappear.[4] This notion of bisexuality (which I will study as aporia in the textual analyses) is, as Jonathan Culler has noted, "one of the most radical contributions of psychoanalysis," one that explodes any true polarization of gender.[5]

Bisexuality undermines gender opposition in two ways. On the one hand, as an anatomical concept, it is that which prevents biological gender distinction: "In every normal male or female individual, traces are found of the apparatus of the opposite sex" (Freud, *Three Essays on the Theory of Sexuality, SE,* 7:141). But more important, bisexuality is also a psychoanalytic concept: "Each individual seeks to satisfy both male and female wishes in his sexual life" (Freud, *Civilization and Its Discontents, SE,* 21:106n); "Both in male and female individuals masculine as well as feminine instinctual impulses are found" (Freud, "A Child is Being Beaten," *SE,* 27:202). Thus neither physical nor mental characteristics can clearly distinguish between the sexes, and the genders blend together in an uncanny aporia.

Sketchy and scattered throughout his work, Freud's writings on bisexuality are unclear, and they never cohere into a solid psychoanalytic theory, as Freud himself admits: "The theory of bisexuality is still surrounded by many obscurities and we cannot but feel it as a serious impediment in psychoanalysis that it has not yet found any link with the theory of the instincts" (Freud, *Civilization and Its Discontents,* p.106n). As Freud points out, one of the difficulties encountered in the analysis of bisexuality stems from its very nature as a heterogeneous concept. Since bisexuality undermines the traditional definitions of male and female, one can no longer speak coherently about those concepts. The problem is one of terminology, of language: "It is essential to understand clearly that the concepts of 'masculine' and 'feminine', whose meaning seems so unambiguous to ordinary people, are among the most confused that occur in science. It is possible to distinguish at least three uses. 'Masculine' and 'feminine' are used sometimes in the sense of activity and passivity, sometimes in a biological, and sometimes, again, in a sociological sense" (Freud, *Three Essays,* p.219n). This linguistic confusion in the definition of the terms *masculine* and *feminine,* the circulation of their meanings in different symbolic systems, reinforces the confusion inherent in bisexuality itself. The problem of gender identity thus becomes one of symbolic meaning, of rhetoric, and of metaphor.

[4]

But the path of Freud's argument takes that double trajectory, and gender identity does not remain in such an uncanny, aporetic state. Freud seems to have difficulty accommodating his radical understanding of gender and shies back from it, retreating to a more familiar, secure, and less threatening position. Bisexuality, originally proper to both sexes, evolves into a property of the woman: "First of all, there can be no doubt that the bisexuality, which is present, as we believe, in the innate disposition of human beings, comes to the fore much more clearly in women than in men" (Freud, "Female Sexuality," *SE*, 21:227–28). In another example, Freud states that men and women share an original similarity (which means, in the context of this particular passage, that the woman is first masculine and feminine, is bisexual), but that later this similarity turns into genderized difference: "Something which both sexes have in common has been forced, by the difference between the sexes, into different forms of expression." What both sexes share is their common valorization of the phallus: "The two corresponding themes are in the female, an *envy for the penis*—a positive striving to possess a male genital—and, in the male, a struggle against his passive or feminine attitude to another male." Thus the common theme changes from the initially more radical similarity between the sexes into the "repudiation of femininity" (Freud, "Analysis Terminable and Interminable," *SE*, 23:250), the desire for a penis in the female and a clear and simple repudiation of femininity in males. Somehow the similarity between the sexes turns into a denigration of femininity.

Freud retreats in another place from the concept of a heterogeneous state of bisexuality first by asserting that one must not equate the masculine with the active and the feminine with the passive, for both active and passive apply to both sexes, and then by making that very equation himself even as he says one must not make it: "These wishes represent active as well as passive impulses; if we relate them to the differentiation of the sexes which is to appear later—though we should avoid doing so as far as possible—we may call them masculine and feminine" (Freud, "Femininity," p. 120). In the context of Freud's text, this is specifically in relation to the girl, but the boy also, of course, has bisexual wishes: "Even in boys the Oedipus complex has a double orientation, active and passive, in accordance with their bisexual constitution; a boy also wants to take his *mother*'s place as the love-object of his *father*—a fact which we describe as the feminine attitude" (Freud, "Some Psychical Consequences of the Anatomical Distinction between the Sexes," *SE*, 19:250).

Furthermore, although both boy and girl share the same sexual activities, Freud insists upon calling them male activities for two reasons: first, they are active, and second, he interprets clitoral sexuality as masculine sexuality (he views the clitoris as an inferior penis). Even as he says that there is no distinction between the sexes at this infantile stage, he calls libido masculine:

> The auto-erotic activity of the erotogenic zones is, however, the same in both sexes, and owing to this uniformity there is no possibility of a distinction between the two sexes such as arises after puberty. So far as the auto-erotic and masturbatory manifestations of sexuality are concerned, we might lay it down that the sexuality of little girls is of a wholly masculine character. Indeed, if we were able to give a more definite connotation to the concepts of "masculine" and "feminine", it would even be possible to maintain that libido is invariably and necessarily of a masculine nature. (Freud, *Three Essays*, p. 219)

> There is only one libido, which serves both the masculine and the feminine sexual functions. To it itself we cannot assign any sex; if, following the conventional equation of activity and masculinity, we are inclined to describe it as masculine, we must not forget that it also covers trends with a passive aim. (Freud, "Femininity," p. 131)

Disavowing the conventional, social distinctions between masculine and feminine as active and passive, Freud still falls back on them; and although he asserts that libido has no sex, he calls it masculine (this male ownership of the rights to desire will appear again and again in the texts studied). The second moment of the double trajectory thus manifests itself when gender identity can return to conventional notions of its definition.[6]

Thus from the radical theory of bisexuality we end up with a familiar repetition of the cultural clichés of woman as passive, man as active. This swerve in Freud's argument reveals a conservative trend in his works in the sense that gender difference ultimately returns to the biological difference between the sexes when the woman seems to be castrated in physical fact. The man has a penis and the woman is castrated; she must acknowledge, as Freud says, "the fact of her castration" (Freud, "Female

Sexuality," p. 229; in German: "die Tatsache seiner Kastration").[7] Freud's inevitable return to the biological echoes his inevitable return to the prostitutes described in his article "The Uncanny" and the inevitable return of certain metaphors of gender identity in the texts discussed in Chapter 2, in which "fallen women" play an important part.

The point of the intersection of these two opposing trajectories, the point of the collision between the revolutionary and conservative forces in Freud's texts on bisexuality, is a crucial one, which, when analyzed in detail, reveals certain structures and themes intrinsic to the investigation of gender. As Freud pursues the investigation of the different ways in which gender is determined in boys and girls, he elaborates a coherent, dramatic, and convincing story of the establishment of the boy's sexuality and sexual objects. The boy's journey to his gender identity, though perilous, is continuous: "During the phase of the normal Oedipus complex we find the child tenderly attached to the parent of the opposite sex, while its relation to the parent of its own sex is predominantly hostile. In the case of a boy there is no difficulty in explaining this. His first love-object was his mother. She *remains* so" (Freud, "Female Sexuality," p. 225; emphasis added). Freud has no difficulty in explaining male sexual development because it is continuous and logical. Female sexuality, however, tells a different story:

> With the small girl it is different. Her first object, too, was her mother. How does she find her way to her father? How, when and why does she detach herself from her mother? We have long understood that the development of female sexuality is complicated by the fact that the girl has the task of giving up what was originally her leading genital zone—the clitoris—in favor of a new zone—the vagina. But it now seems to us that there is a second change of the same sort which is no less characteristic and important for the development of the female: the exchange of her original object— her mother—for her father. The way in which the two tasks are connected with each other is not yet clear to us. (Freud, "Female Sexuality," p. 225)

Woman's access to gender and to sexuality is unclear, illogical, and involves semirhetorical exchanges and substitutions of love-objects, supplementary tasks, incompleteness; it tells a discontinuous, circuitous story. Female sexuality poses a rhetorical problem of interpretation to Freud, a linguistic riddle against which "throughout history people have knocked their heads" ("Über das Rätsel der Weiblichkeit haben die Menschen zu allen Zeiten gegrübelt) (Freud, "Femininity," p. 113).[8]

If we use Freud's methods of interpretation on his own text, we may understand one of the reasons why female sexuality poses this problem. Just after he mentions this riddle of the nature of femininity, Freud quotes a stanza from a Heine poem:

Häupter in Hieroglyphenmützen,
Häupter in Turban und schwarzem Barett,
Perückenhäupter und tausend andre
Arme, schwitzende Menschenhäupter. ("Femininity," p. 113)
Heads in hieroglyphic bonnets,
Heads in turbans and black birettas,
Heads in wigs and thousand other
Wretched, sweating heads of humans.

These verses, in conjunction with Freud's text, conjure up an epic vision of autonomous, detached heads marching through the ages and multiplying endlessly as they confront the question of woman. In the essay "The Uncanny" Freud interprets the symbolic meaning of the multiple, detached heads as a phallic symbol, which, when doubled and multiplied, becomes a representation of and, at the same time, a guard against castration (like a fetish): "For the 'double' was originally an insurance against destruction to the ego, an 'energetic denial of the power of death,' as Rank says; and probably the 'immortal' soul was the first 'double' of the body. This invention of doubling as a preservation against extinction has its counterpart in the language of dreams, which is fond of representing castration by a doubling or multiplication of the genital symbol."[9] This fetishistic representation is threatening: the multiple heads are detached and represent castration. Female sexuality poses a problem, for it seems to threaten the very nature of masculinity with castration; by manifesting its bisexuality, female sexuality threatens to contaminate the male with femininity. But at the same time, the fetish is reassuring because Freud guards against the threat of castration by multiplying the male symbols of heads, as well as by seeing in the woman the passive, incomplete double of man, by seeing the woman as the illogical detour that leads back to man. As soon as the threatening images of female sexuality and bisex-

[8]

uality arise in Freud's investigation of gender identity, they are covered over with a fetishistic reassertion of masculine, active primacy, with conventional and reassuring gender definitions (however ambiguous those definitions might be). [10]

But to conjure up the myriad heads, Freud also conjures up poetry, Heine, and literature. Feminine sexuality seems to refer to textuality as if the raising of a problematic gender identity had something to do with texts, just as in the investigation of bisexuality, Freud refers to a problem of language, and in the investigation of female sexuality, he confronts the rhetorical substitutions involved in woman's desire. Freud's texts thus again relate feminine identity to rhetoric.

Lacan's development of Freud's thought links sexuality explicitly to textuality: specifically, Lacan defines the phallus as the signifier that orders the difference between the two genders. The concept of the phallus is extremely difficult in Lacan's writings (as are all Lacanian concepts) mainly because it has somewhat contradictory functions, again a double trajectory of conservative and radical meanings. If for Freud the problem posed by bisexuality stems in part from language, for Lacan the obscurity of the concept of the phallus stems in part from the difficult nature of Lacan's own ambiguous and polysemous language, as if the problem language poses suddenly becomes the center of attention.

The phallus for Lacan implies a certain similarity between the sexes, as does Freud's notion of bisexuality. The "radical phallus" is the signifier representing the human being's insertion into language, into the symbolic, and the alienation which that insertion brings with it (no such terminology occurs in Lacan; I use it to distinguish between several conflicting meanings of the phallus in his works). It is, in a sense, the signifier of signification, "the privileged signifier," "itself a sign of the latency with which any signifiable is struck," "the signifier intended to designate as a whole the effects of the signified, in that the signifier conditions them by its presence as a signifier." [11] For Lacan, too, gender relates to the rhetorical, to the symbolic, to the linguistic.

The signifying process gives rise to a certain alienation because, since humans speak, their needs must be expressed in language by demands, and that very deviation of need through demand leaves, one could say, something to be desired:

> Let us now examine the effects of this presence [as a signifier]. In the
> first instance, they proceed from a deviation of man's needs from the

fact that he speaks, in the sense that in so far as his needs are subjected to demand, they return to him alienated. This is not the effect of his real dependence . . . but rather the turning into signifying form as such, from the fact that it is from the locus of the Other that its message is emitted. ¶ That which is thus alienated in needs constitutes an *Unverdrängung* (primal repression), an inability, it is supposed, to be articulated in demand, but it re-appears in something it gives rise to that presents itself in man as desire (*das Begehren*). (Lacan, "Signification," pp. 285–86)

For Lacan, the radical phallus is an empty structural term signifying this juncture of language with desire. The phallus signifies a certain constitutional incompleteness of humans (desire) brought about because they speak: "Man cannot aim at being whole (the 'total personality' is another of the deviant premises of modern psychotherapy), while ever the play of displacement and condensation to which he is doomed in the exercise of his functions marks his relation as a subject to the signifier. The phallus is the privileged signifier of that mark in which the role of the logos is joined with the advent of desire" (Lacan, "Signification," p. 287). Thus the radical phallus is, from this first perspective, the constitutional lack in all subjects, male or female (a corollary of the split of the subject manifested in the mirror stage). [12]

The radical phallus implies a similarity between the sexes in another way in the role that it plays in the Oedipus complex. In the Lacanian version of the complex, the child (of either sex) recognizes that the mother desires, that there is "lack in the place of the Other": [13] "It is this desire of the Other as such that the subject must recognize" (Lacan, "Signification," p. 288). For Lacan, then, it is not simply that the child desires the mother, but in addition that the child desires to be the object of that desire (one meaning of the phrase "man's desire is the *désir de l'Autre* [the desire of the Other]). [14] The phallus thus first represents this object of the other's desire (what Jacqueline Rose terms the imaginary phallus). The child finds, however, that the mother desires something else (the father, the symbolic phallus); therefore, the child cannot be the object of the mother's desire: "The object of human desire is the object of desire of the other, and desire is always the desire for something else (for that which is missing from the primordially lost object)." [15] Desire cannot be satisfied, and a third space is inserted into the mother-child couple, as Rose says: "The duality of the relation between mother and child must be broken, just as the analytic relation must be thrown onto the axis of desire. In Lacan's account, the phallus stands for that moment of rupture. It refers mother and child to the dimension of the symbolic which is figured by the father's place" (Mitchell and Rose, p. 38). Again, the phallus as radical phallus represents a certain lack, an impossible plenitude that constitutes all subjects and not, as the term would imply, a real plenitude that constitutes the male.

That other, conservative trajectory taken by Lacan's argument emerges, however, when the phallus plays the role of ordering the difference between the sexes, of determining gender. The biological difference between male and female bodies, the penis and its absence, is seized upon, says Lacan, as that which is most easily visible, that which stands out in desire: "It can be said that this signifier is chosen because it is the most tangible element in the real of sexual copulation" (Lacan, "Signification," p. 287); the phallus becomes the "real phallus" (this term does exist in Lacan and means "what in reality he [the subject] may *have* that corresponds to this phallus" (Lacan, "Signification," p. 289). [16] What is important is that the child sees that the mother does not have either the real phallus, the penis, or the object of her desire, the "radical" phallus: "This test of the desire of the Other is decisive not in the sense that the subject learns by it whether or not he has a real phallus, but in the sense that he learns that the mother does not have it" (Lacan, "Signification," p. 289).

What separates the two sexes, then, is that the lack, the incompleteness of the phallus, is projected symbolically onto the woman, who does not have this phallus, and she comes to represent, as Lacan says, "not all": "When any speaking being whatever lines up under the banner of women it is by being constituted as not all that they are placed within the phallic function." [17] Conversely, man, who has what corresponds to the real phallus, is on the side of the all: "It is through the phallic function that man takes his inscription as all." [18] The biological difference then comes to symbolize gender difference and becomes our conventional understanding of gender identity. What must be emphasized in Lacan (and what distinguishes his views from those of Freud in some of Freud's statements, as, for instance, when castration appears to be a "fact") is that the absence of the woman's phallus is always already symbolic, the notion of lack itself being symbolic, a construct of language. As Rose says:

Sexual difference is then assigned according to whether individual subjects do or do not possess the phallus, which means not that anatomical difference *is* sexual difference (the one as strictly deducible from the other), but that anatomical difference comes to *figure* sexual difference, that is, it becomes the sole representative of what that difference is allowed to be. It thus covers over the complexity of the child's early sexual life with a crude opposition in which that very complexity is refused or repressed. The phallus thus indicates the reduction of difference to an instance of visual perception, a *seeming* value. (Mitchell and Rose, p.42)

This symbolic nature of gender identity is clearly illustrated in a relatively early Lacan essay, "The Agency of the Letter in the Unconscious or Reason since Freud,"[19] in which he shows how gender identity is essentially the taking up of a position, the assumption of a role that exists in a cultural and historical text. Saussure's juxtaposition of the word *tree* with a picture of a tree is replaced by Lacan with two identical restroom doors (behind which the same functions are served) labeled as "men" and "women." Obviously men and women are not the doors themselves, nor what lies behind them. There is no physical, literal determination of gender here; rather, the meaning of gender must take shape on the symbolic, rhetorical plane of relations between signifiers and their texts (cultural here), and it entails an assumption of a position: "Any speaking being whatever is inscribed [s'inscrit] on one side or the other" (Lacan, "A Love Letter," p.150; French from Lacan, *Encore,* p.74). Gender also poses a problem of representation because the door does not directly represent gender in a simple relation. Rather, for Lacan, this assumption of gender identity becomes the assumption of a role when one acts one's part; it is a "masquerade," a "comedy," something that "masks," something whose role is "to seem" (Lacan, "Signification," pp.289–90). One's biological sex may or may not correspond to the gender position that one occupies, and, as Bette and Steinbock show, males and females can align themselves on either side of the symbolic divide.

For Lacan, as for Freud, then, man seems easy to define, he becomes the "all," but woman cannot be defined, she is "not all"; we must cross out the word *the* in *the woman:* "It is this that defines the . . . the what?—the woman precisely, except that *The* woman can only be written [s'écrire] with *The* crossed through. There is no such thing as *The* woman, where the definite article stands for the universal. There is no such thing as *The* woman since of her essence—having already risked the term, why think twice about it?—of her essence, she is not all" (Lacan, "God and the

[12]

Jouissance of ~~The~~ Woman," p.144; French from Lacan, *Encore,* p.68). Woman does not exist, in the sense that all representations and definitions of her must be situated in the already phallic, symbolic system, and the woman (as the man for that matter) conceived of in the phallic system is a fiction, a fantasy (the woman as the "objet petit a"). But any woman outside the system is inconceivable precisely because concepts themselves belong to the symbolic, to language.

Lacan, in his later writing, does not leave it at this, however, but speaks also of a *jouissance* of the woman "beyond the phallus," in the place of the Other, outside the phallic system. One must be careful not to elevate this other *jouissance* into a transcendental signifier but must view it as the radical nature of the concept of the Other: "Might not this *jouissance* which one experiences and knows nothing of, be that which puts us on the path of ex-istence?" (Lacan, "God and the *Jouissance* of ~~The~~ Woman," p.147). The woman then becomes that which relates to the undermining of the totalization of the phallic system's truth: "The Other is not only this place where truth falters [balbutie]. It is worth representing [Il mérite de représenter] what the woman necessarily relates to" (Lacan, "A Love Letter," p.151; French from Lacan, *Encore,* p.75). She exposes the fraud of the phallus, the fraud of the distinction between the sexes: "The description of feminine sexuality is, therefore, an exposure of the terms of its definition, the very opposite of a demand as to what that sexuality should be" (Mitchell and Rose, p.44). She is thus a symptom that exposes the Other, is that which "dallies [se bécotte] with the unconscious."[20]

Thus Lacan's arguments, too, have a double trajectory, for the phallus has two contradictory significations: one being man's symbolic plenitude and woman's symbolic lack, and the other being the shared lack that underlies the real phallus and problematizes gender differences. Furthermore, in Lacan's writings, feminist pronouncements stand side by side with a reenactment of Freud's phallocentrism; and Lacan, significantly, calls the radical lack that constitutes all subjects the "phallus," a word with unquestionably masculine associations. Lacan uses this phallocentric term knowingly: he manipulates the conjunction of phallocentrism and that which undermines it (the radical phallus itself), plays on the aporia created by their co-presence, and confuses the system with its deconstruction. He defines the nature of woman as nonknowledge and man as knowledge both to mime and repeat the phallic repressive system, but also to make fun of it and himself, since, as male, he can occupy only the position of a misguided knowing: "There is woman only as excluded by the nature of things which is the nature of words, and it has to be said that if there is one thing they themselves are complaining about enough at the moment, it is well and truly that—only they don't know what they are saying, which is all the difference between them and me" (Lacan "God and the *Jouissance* of ~~The~~ Woman," p. 144).[21]

Lacan points out that any attempt to know gender difference leads one to the nonknowledge of woman's place. Gender is this aporia, the contradiction involved in the assumption of one's sex: "There is an antinomy, here, that is internal to the assumption by man (*Mensch*) of his sex: why must he assume the attributes of that sex only through a threat—the threat, indeed, of their privation? . . . This is not the only *aporia*, but it is the first that the Freudian experience and the metapsychology that resulted from it introduced into our experience of man" (Lacan, "Signification," pp. 281–82; emphasis added). One confronts the aporia of gender, its enigma, the woman who lies beyond phallic logic.

This enigma leads to deconstruction, to what one might call the philosophy of aporia, in which in particular Jacques Derrida's work links aporia to gender. Deconstruction implicates gender identity very obviously in the analysis of the system of dichotomous oppositions which form philosophical thought. Western philosophical tradition rests upon a powerful foundation of opposing couples, among which that of man/woman is a special case, as Hélène Cixous illustrates:

Activity/passivity
Sun/Moon
Culture/Nature
Day/Night

Father/Mother
Head/Heart
Intelligible/Palpable
Logos/Pathos
Form, convex, step, advance, semen, progress.
Matter, concave, ground—where steps are taken,
holding- and dumping-ground.

$$\frac{\text{Man}}{\text{Woman}}$$

Always the same metaphor: we follow it, it carries us, beneath all its figures, wherever discourse is organized.[22]

[14]

Here the positioning of the term *Man* above the term *Woman* reveals the important hierarchical nature of this dichotomy: "In a classical philosophical opposition we are not dealing with the peaceful coexistence of a *vis-à-vis,* but rather with a violent hierarchy. One of the two terms governs the other (axiologically, logically, etc.), or has the upper hand."[23] This hierarchical ordering will be another of the persistent structures to recur in the analyses that follow.

This initial step of Derrida's strategy, the isolation of dichotomous oppositions, is not radical but conservative in the sense that it starts within the system itself, studying the existing state of things without destroying it. But deconstruction takes a radical turn, has itself a reverse double trajectory, for it pursues this logic to its illogical conclusions by following the path of arguments into an inevitable area of nonsense, of aporia. This logical impossibility is often revealed in a textual system when a particular duality, crucial to the logical functioning of the system, no longer constitutes a clear opposition. The essence of the subordinate term (and thus that which distinguishes one term from the other) shows itself to be a necessary part of the privileged term (for example, the supplement added to the whole is essential to the concept of the whole). Or the aporia arises when each term of the opposition reveals that the claims of the other are wrong (*parole* and *langue* as both being necessary for the origin of language but also as negating each other's original nature), or when a crucial term in a system proves to be undecidable (hymen, pharmakon).[24]

This illogical core of the male/female duality is studied by Derrida in several contexts, one of which is a criticism of psychoanalysis, and particularly of Lacan's "Séminaire sur la lettre volée." Here Derrida denounces the phallocentric aspect of Lacan, using it, as Barbara Johnson points out, as a straw man for Lacan by not taking into account the more radical side of his writing.[25] In "The Purveyor of Truth," Derrida's criticism focuses on the phallus and castration as ordering the difference and the hierarchy between the sexes, the phallus being man's plenitude and the woman's lack being her castration. Derrida claims that Lacan simply reverses the traditional philosophical strategy that places plenitude (presence, truth, and so on) at the center by replacing it with a central lack: "The lack has its place."[26] The castration of the woman at the center, as truth, thus assures the proper meaning of the phallus: "Castration is what contracts (constriction of the ring) to bring the phallus, the signifier, the letter or the fetish back to their oikos, their familiar dwelling, their proper place" (Derrida, "Purveyor of Truth," p.63). The signifier-phallus becomes the irreducible center of the system, turns into the signified, the whole truth. This exactly corresponds to Lacan's own analysis of the phallic system, in which man occupies the position of the all.

Derrida shows, however, that, in the Poe text analyzed by Lacan, the undecidability introduced by its textuality and its rhetoric (framing, doubling, and the like) undermines the primacy of the phallus and its indivisibility and undermines any primacy or mastery. Derrida then hints at a different and contradictory meaning of this castration-truth in which the phallus would not be whole, would not permit mastery, but would instead partake of the "truth as essential dislocation and irreducible parcelling" (Derrida, "Purveyor of Truth," pp.62–63). This essential dislocation corresponds to Lacan's notion of the radical phallus (not discussed by Derrida), to the notion of the essential dislocation of the human subject by desire and language (like Derrida's *différance*, it defers and distances plenitude). Irreducible parceling corresponds to the space present in the subject, the necessary split, the impossible unity and wholeness of the speaking human being.

Thus instead of being the place that assures the proper, the place of origin, the grounding of the system, castration, in Derrida's view, *"does not take place. . . . is no longer determinable."*[27] What reveals this undecidability of castration is the woman's place: " 'Woman'—her name made epoch—no longer believes in castration's exact opposite, anti-castration, than she does in castration itself" (Derrida, *Spurs*, p.61). Whereas for Lacan, one aspect of woman adheres paradoxically to castration and another undermines it,[28] for Derrida, the woman adheres paradoxically to neither one—she takes an undecidable, aporetic stance.

Gender, then, is undecidable for Derrida; the distinction between the sexes is impossible: "There is that one cannot cut through to a decision between the two contrary and recognized functions of the fetish, any more than between the thing itself and its supplement. Any more than between the sexes."[29] Derrida shows that the systematization of gender in a hierarchical opposition entails a moment of aporia, an illogical place where the system can be shown to undo itself. In Derrida's theory, then, traditional gender concepts are studied and assumed, but, when one follows their logic to its conclusions, gender self-destructs.

Derrida, even more than Lacan, links gender to texts and rhetoric; as Sarah Kofman says, he sexualizes texts, showing that the *"Aufhebung* is very precisely the relation of copulation and the sexual difference" (*Glas*, p. 111)[30] and how texts become the locus of the playing out of genderization. Derrida also textualizes sex, showing the textual, differential basis of gender identity, for the polarity male/female becomes a special case of the repeated polarization of textual structures which house their own undoing: "But this opposition (Signified/Signifier), just as all oppositions moreover, the sexual opposition in particular, by regular occurrence, is compromised, each term divided into two sticking to the other."[31]

This rhetorization of gender leads us to three literary problems that emerge from readings of these theoretical texts and from the Bette/Steinbock couple; these literary problems will organize my studies of the literary texts in the chapters to follow. The first of these literary problems to be considered, one that is perhaps the most important in Freud's (and consequently in Lacan's) theories, is the role of social institutions in the formation of gender identity. For Freud, the place of the child in the social institution of the family and the child's relation to its male and female parents help to mold the child's gender identity. By *institution* I mean the notion that the state and the other social, cultural, and political institutions that govern us and direct our way of life are discourses, in the sense that a discourse is an abstract order of concepts that forms and informs people. William C. Dowling summarizes this notion of a discourse-institution:

> The figure in the immediate background is Foucault, whose general point might be illustrated by considering a modern science like physics as a discourse. What this means, first, is that physics as an abstract order of concepts, rules, problems, etc., has the power to make or constitute people what they are: if I wish to become a physicist I can do so only by internalizing the system of rules and concepts called physics, and then when I "speak as a physicist" it is really this same system of rules and concepts speaking through me. Then, second, the "discourse of physics" has the power to create social and even physical institutions: physics departments, conferences, journals, laboratories, etc., all are *generated by* physics as an abstract conceptual order.[32]

The institution of the family, for example, has its own evolving set of rules and concepts, and this "discourse" certainly forms and informs everyone in a particular culture. Post-structuralist theories go so far as to say that everything is formed and informed by discourse in a very general sense, as Jonathan Culler explains: " 'Il n'y a pas de hors texte' in that the realities with which politics is concerned, and the forms in which they are manipulated, are inseparable from discursive structures and systems of signification, or what Derrida calls 'the general text' " (Culler, *On Deconstruction*, p. 157). It is in this general text that the Lacanian subject is defined, is given a place. There identity is born: "Thus the subject, too, if he can appear to be the slave of language is all the more so of a discourse in the universal movement in which his place is already inscribed at birth, if only by virtue of his proper name" (Lacan, "The Agency of the Letter," p. 148).

In Chapter 1, I will investigate the relation of gender to two institutions that play an important role in nineteenth-century texts: class structure in the works of Stendhal, whose novels are often seen as investigations of class relations; and family structure in two novels, *La Cousine Bette* and *Eugénie Grandet,* by Balzac, which often weave family conflicts into their more general problematics. The following questions will be asked: How do family structures help to determine gender identity in the nineteenth century and in its fictions? Do class distinctions relate to gender distinctions? What is the general relation between gender and institutions in these texts?

The second literary theme I will study is the linguistic, rhetorical problem involved in the definition of gender identity. As we have seen, the assumption of female gender identity in Freud's theory involves semirhetorical substitutions, and the feminine becomes associated with the rhetorical. Furthermore, in Freud's tendency to fall back to the clichés of activity and passivity, we see again the rhetorical nature of gender identity, in the sense that a cliché is a mechanized metaphor, a "figure multipliée à l'infini" ("figure multiplied infinitely").[33] In Lacan's texts, the restroom doors provide a telling metaphor for the symbolic, rhetorical nature of gender identity; in Derrida, the "textuality" of Poe's work undermines a phallocentric gender identity. Chapter 2 will look at certain metaphors and clichés of femininity in three works by Balzac, who has often been thought to incarnate in his heroines a certain Romantic rhetoric of femininity.[34] The following questions will be asked of the three texts, *Le Lys dans la vallée,* "Une Passion dans le désert," and *Sarrasine:* How does female gender identity relate to rhetoric in these texts? How does female differ from male gender identity? What is the logic behind certain metaphors of femininity in these texts?

The third literary theme is the problem of the nonreferentiality of gender identity. Freud's claim that gender identity is not biological, is not defined in any final way in the physical world, poses problems of representation and reference: How can we represent gender identity if it does not have a biological referent? What is the relation of gender identity to representation and to realism? How do nonrealist texts represent gender identity? To answer these questions, I will study the relation of gender to representation in Flaubert's texts and its relation to the decadent and fantastic genres in works by Rachilde and Balzac. The answers to be found there lead to my conclusion on realism and gender identity.

These three literary themes of institutions, rhetoric, and representation will organize my analysis of gender in these nineteenth-century literary texts, which very often link the problem of gender identity to one of the text's major conflicts. One could speculate on various historical reasons for the preponderance of this problem in nineteenth-century French fiction: it could be owing to the emergence of organized feminism in France in the nineteenth century; or to the obvious (and recognized) injustice of the Civil Code in regard to women's rights and to the consequent questioning of these rights and of the status of woman. Or it could be imputed to the "digestion" of the tenets of equality espoused by the revolution in the preceding century: there was, of course, a document called the "Déclaration des droits de la femme et de la citoyenne" ("Declaration of the rights of woman and the female citizen"), although by the end of the year 1793, its author, Olympe de Gouges, had been guillotined and advocates of women's rights were being silenced. Another contributing factor might be the growing ranks of women wage earners, whose work outside the home changed the family, economic, and social roles of women (in 1866, almost 35 percent of the total labor force was composed of women).[35] Julia Kristeva explicitly links the emerging feminism of the late nineteenth century to radical changes in the literary, political, and social structures of the time: "The texts which belong to what is called the 'literary avant-garde' have been breaking out in western culture since the end of the nineteenth-century, at the same time as the crises of the state, of the family, and of religion. They seem to me to be a kind of symptom of a vast upheaval of western society, in which woman's struggle is inscribed."[36]

Michel Foucault might well impute the growing importance of gender in literature to the general tendency to put sex into discourse.[37] In any case, it is clear that a certain double trajectory exists in the overall picture of the woman's role in nineteenth-century France, for as the Civil Code institutionalized the economic and familial powerlessness of women, it also made evident their unequal status and influenced the formation of French feminism: "Sexual difference was enshrined in the new legal codes, which not only weakened women's position relative to men's but also, ironically, helped shape feminist consciousness by making unmistakably visible the significance of sex as a status category" (Moses, p.x).

The primary analytical method of this study, however, is not historical and sociological, and its primary function is not to determine the causes of this literary phenomenon. Indeed, as we will see in the analyses in Chapter 2, these literary texts give us an implicit warning about historical interpretation that sees literature as a mere reflection of the historical realities of the times. I will, nevertheless, give some historical background on the everyday life of the nineteenth century and on the gender roles played by men and women, most notably in Chapter 1 on the institutions of family and class.

Whatever the causes of gender aporia, its symptoms appear with unfailing frequency in the literature of the period immediately preceding and overlapping with Freud's, and it is the literary, textual problem of gender that will be the main focus of this book. My analytical methods will be modern yet heterogeneous: the critical tools used in this study vary from Freudian to post-modern, from thematic to feminist. The main critical stance is, however, what one might call deconstructive *feminism*. I have placed the word *feminism* in italics to differentiate it from American feminism, which appears to be a more activist search for an authentic female discourse or identity. The italics serve also to align my stance with one aspect of French feminism, which tends to approach feminist problems from a theoretical direction and rejects the label "feminism," because, as an "ism," it represents another belief system to be evaluated. Thus my study differs from Peggy Kamuf's *Fictions of Feminine Desire,* Nancy K. Miller's *The Heroine's Text,* and Naomi Schor's *Breaking the Chain,* in that those critical texts investigate the feminocentric text and look for the specificity of woman's place, for as yet overlooked implications of the depiction of women in fiction.[38] Rather than centering on one or the other of male or female positions, however, I begin from a more global perspective so as to examine the differential, moving relation between the two genders and the problems involved in the construction of the gender identity of both sexes.

I shall not, of course, do an exhaustive rereading of each primary text (an impossible task) but rather, by working through a specific and limited problematic in each text, I shall bring my conclusions to bear on the more traditional readings of these texts and on the central problems of nineteenth-century narrative. I have given a larger place to the works of Balzac in this book because gender identity relates to several different literary problems in the enormous corpus of his works, whereas for Stendhal, Flaubert, and Rachilde, gender relates more generally to one particular problem in the more limited corpus of their works.

Of the three theoretical texts on gender, Freud's is closer in spirit to the texts studied here, for when the aporia of gender meets up with a conventional, secure meaning, Freud chooses meaning, the conservative moment of the double trajectory. Gender versus meaning is, again, a dichotomous relation, according to Lacan: "Everything implied by the analytic engagement with human behavior indicates not that meaning reflects the sexual but that it makes up for it."[39] Text-sex, the problem of gender identity, gets covered over by meaning, logic, phallocentrism, unity, and so on. Freud retreats from his investigation of gender to a preexisting definition of gender as active/passive: meaning makes up for gender aporia. This falling back from aporia may be what distinguishes a modern Freud from a post-modern Derrida and Lacan, who continue to confront aporia head-on, to "knock their heads" against its enigma when Freud retreats. In the texts studied here there is almost always this falling back to preexisting meaning, but in each text there is a moment when meaning falters, when the aporia of gender shows through. It is only in Chapter 3 that we encounter texts that make a literal aporia of gender their subject.

It is this shock of the confrontation of gender and meaning, the shock of the system's encounter with its own undoing, that I wish to study in the following pages. My aim, as Freud understood his, cannot be to determine what is woman and what is man, but to understand the process of genderization in texts, the ideologies behind these constructions, the strategies involved in their elaboration, and the effects of gender polarization and chiasmus on the textual systems. My starting point must necessarily be traditional thematic and rhetorical images of gender identity, but a study of their construction and deconstruction takes us beyond tradition. If hysteria is the confusion of gender polarities (the assumption of multiple identities) and paranoia the reinforcement of gender polarization (the denegation of bisexuality), then this book is the study of the clash between these two trajectories.[40]

ONE

Gender

AND INSTITUTIONS

STENDHAL'S GENDER
CLASSES

La question
de ce que nous sommes, une certaine pente nous a conduits, en quelques
siècles, à la poser au sexe. —MICHEL FOUCAULT, *La Volonté de savoir.* / *The
question of what we are; a certain path has led us, in a few centuries, to ask it of
sex.*

SINCE THE ordering of French society in the nineteenth century into
different social and economic classes was clearly a social, political, and
economic "institution" that classified and organized people, our question
must be, Do these class distinctions relate to gender distinctions in
nineteenth-century French fiction? To investigate the relation of class
difference to gender difference, we turn to the novels of Stendhal, about
whose works, as F. W. J. Hemmings says: "A realization of class difference
and, what was more important, of class conflict, was one of Stendhal's
principal bequests to the French novel."[1]

The general image of class structure in nineteenth-century France—
that of a three-tiered society composed of a weakened aristocracy; a
powerful, diverse, and expanding bourgeoisie; and a threatening working
class—is being complicated by current historians. Some actually feel the
need to drop the notion of the bourgeoisie altogether because the term has
been used in so many conflicting ways (economic, political, cultural,
ideological) that it no longer has meaning. Rather than the term *bour-*

geoisie they prefer *new middle class.*[2] Others divide the class alliances of the latter part of the nineteenth century into the *classes possédantes* (propertied classes), which actually include part of the *paysannerie* (peasantry), as well as certain economic groups of the bourgeoisie and of the aristocracy; the *classe ouvrière* (working class); and the *bourgeoisie financière* (financial bourgeoisie); thus seeming to reorganize the previous three-tiered concept.[3]

If historians disagree over the exact denomination and alliances of specific classes, they do seem to agree that the notion of class in nineteenth-century France is complex and confusing because society was in the midst of a long process of change (accelerated by the French Revolution and Napoleon)[4] from an aristocratic or late feudal society to a market society, from the *ancien régime* to the modern, from a rigid hierarchical society of order based on land and accumulated wealth to a more fluid capitalist society based on wealth from industry. This transition was not smooth, of course: for instance, the nobility retained its social influence even if it lost its economic clout.[5] As nineteenth-century novels show so well, the two *régimes* coexisted and conflicted in a double trajectory: consider Rastignac's system of noble values in conflict with his economic and social reality and Julien Sorel's code of honor at times in conflict with his *arrivisme.*

Whatever the definition of class, it is clear that Stendhal's novels make class conflict and change the center of their problematics. As so many readers have noted, *Le Rouge et le noir* turns around Julien's social climb through the ranks of the "old" aristocratic order: a *paysan,* he scrambles over the provincial bourgeoisie and aristocracy to move up to the heights of Parisian nobility. This elevation is symbolized in an almost humorous way by his climbing a ladder inside the church at Besançon and into his lovers' windows. The peasant Lamiel, called by Henri Martineau a "female Julien," also rises rapidly through the ranks, moving from peasant circles to noble ones.[6] In the context of Julien's ladder climbing, Fabrice del Dongo, in *La Chartreuse de Parme,* appears to be a negative image of Julien and Lamiel when he, a noble, succeeds in climbing *down* from his high position in the prison tower. This descent (which is a purely practical one for Fabrice, who needs to escape the constant threat of poisoning) could be seen to symbolize the degradation of society in post-Napoleonic Europe, particularly that of noble society, which is thematized in the opening pages of the novel. Nobility has changed, has "descended" in the Parma court, whose members make their future dependent on the "intrigues d'une femme de chambre" ("the intrigues of a chambermaid") and whose prince worries about "ce que va me dire mon valet de chambre français quand je lui conterai ma défaite" ("what my French valet will say to me when I tell him about my defeat").[7] If, on the one hand, Fabrice's constant disguises as various characters belonging to classes lower than his own symbolize perhaps this "lowering" of the aristocracy, on the other hand, when Fabrice is rich and successful as an aristocratic ecclesiastic he is completely unhappy and clearly can find no acceptable place in that sphere. His decided preference for his tower prison and his retreat to the "Chartreuse" at the end of the novel figure a rejection of the confused social structure of his world and a discovery of a new personal and moral, although tragic, superiority. Lamiel, described significantly in the context of gender as having a courage "plus humain que féminin" (p. 1018) ("more human than feminine"), likewise finds no place in society: bored with aristocratic codification, disgusted by the grossness of her aunt and uncle, and offended by the overly polite, hypocritical Madame Anselme, she becomes the mistress of an outlaw in the projected end of the novel, the mistress of someone outside of the social structures of her world.

Even though Stendhal's works are clearly political novels about class struggle and change, no one has as yet really questioned the curious link between this class struggle and the "sexual politics" of the novels: for instance, the link between climbing into lovers' windows and social climbing in *Le Rouge et le noir*. Quite simply, for Julien sex is a kind of politics, a policy of action that aims at particular ends, as Julien himself expresses when he refrains from embracing Mathilde in order to ensure her seduction: "Ses bras se raidirent, tant l'effort imposé par la *politique* était pénible. Je ne dois pas même me permettre de presser contre mon coeur ce corps souple et charmant, ou elle me méprise et me maltraite" ("His arms grew stiff, so painfully difficult was the effort imposed on him by his 'politics.' I must not even let myself press this lithe and charming body to my heart, or she will despise and mistreat me").[8]

It would be tempting to justify the substitution of personal for political struggle by saying that, in the world of the novel, love affairs are more palatable than those of the state. Certainly Stendhal was well aware of that fact when he wrote in *Armance* (and similarly in other texts): "La politique venant couper un récit aussi simple, peut faire l'effet d'un coup de pistolet au milieu d'un concert" ("Politics cutting in on such a simple story can have the effect of a pistol shot in the middle of a concert").[9] But a closer look at the relation between class war and sex war reveals that things are not quite so straightforward in Stendhal's novels. Even though the male protagonists in his novels do battle with women, more often than not they and the women work together against the social rules of the time: in *Le Rouge et le noir* Madame de Rênal and Mathilde, Amanda in the café of Besançon, the nameless woman in the inn who takes in Julien and gives him a meal and advice. In *La Chartreuse de Parme,* the women continually save Fabrice's life: Clélia, the Flamande, when he is imprisoned early in the novel, the vivandière at Waterloo, the woman and her daughters in the inn who care for his wounds, and especially the powerful intriguer Gina, who so clearly foretells to him that he should speak "avec plus de respect . . . du sexe qui fera votre fortune; car vous déplairez toujours aux hommes" (*La Chartreuse de Parme,* p. 51) ("with more respect . . . of the sex that will make your fortune, for you will always displease men").

The multiple women who help Julien and Fabrice find a literary counterpart in the numerous scenes in Stendhal's novels in which "multitudes" of women are portrayed. In *Le Rouge et le noir* these groups of women often relate to sexual fantasy for Julien:

> Alors il songeait avec délices qu'un jour il serait présenté aux jolies femmes de Paris, il saurait attirer leur attention par quelque action d'éclat (p. 239). La moitié de la population monta sur les toits. Toutes les femmes étaient aux balcons (p. 311). Il récita: sa mémoire se trouva fidèle, et ce prodige fut admiré avec toute la bruyante énergie de la fin d'un dîner. Julien regardait la figure enluminée des dames; plusieurs n'étaient pas mal (p. 349). Autour de la table, que les gens venaient d'apporter toute servie, se trouvaient sept à huit femmes fort nobles, fort dévotes, fort affectées, âgées de trente à trente-cinq ans. (p. 466) / *So he dreamed with delight that one day he would be introduced to the pretty women of Paris; he would be able to attract their attention by some brilliant action. . . . Half of the population went up on the roofs. All the women were on the balconies. . . . He recited: his memory served him well, and this prodigy was admired with all the noisy energy of the end of a dinner. Julien looked at the flushed faces of the ladies; some of them were not bad looking. . . . Around the table, which the servants had just brought already set, were seven or eight women, very noble, very devout, very affected, between thirty and thirty-five years old.*

In *La Chartreuse de Parme,* Fabrice looks down from the church tower and sees "une quantité de jeunes filles vêtues de blanc et divisées en différentes troupes" (*La Chartreuse de Parme,* p.174) ("a number of girls dressed in white and divided into several groups"); his joy in this scene of imprisonment, linked with the sight of young women, prefigures his happiness in the prison tower and his love for Clélia. Fabrice also notices upon his return to his hometown, "Beaucoup de charmantes petites filles que Fabrice avait laissées à l'âge de onze ou douze ans étaient maintenant des femmes superbes" (*La Chartreuse de Parme,* p.177) ("Many charming little girls whom Fabrice had left at the age of eleven or twelve were now magnificent women"). In the feminocentric novel *Lamiel,* we again see several groups of women: "Un choeur de soixante jeunes filles bien pensantes, formées et exercées par M. l'abbé Le Cloud, chanta les antiennes choisies (p.884). Une trentaine de femmes lavaient du linge à ce bassin (p.895). Lamiel fit la fâcheuse rencontre de quatre ou cinq vieilles femmes du village" (p.903) ("A choir of sixty right-thinking young ladies, formed and trained by M. l'abbé Le Cloud, sang the selected anthems. . . . Thirty or so women were washing linen in this basin. . . . Lamiel unfortunately met up with four or five old women of the village"). It is not surprising that, in a novel whose heroine traverses the social order, some of these groups of women should appear threatening.

This overriding presence of groups of women in Stendhal's novels will be studied by investigating the role women and groups of women play in Julien's class climbing. In three scenes in *Le Rouge et le noir* the link between these groups of women and Julien's social climb becomes involved with much larger issues because these scenes represent three forces of subjugation in the text: the church (the *chapelle ardente*), the law (in the courtroom scene), and finally the political and industrial (the mayor's factory).

Just before the first of these scenes to be discussed, Julien enters the bishop of Agde's chambers and sees him making odd gestures in front of a mirror. It eventually dawns on Julien that the bishop is practicing his benedictions so as to make a good impression on the public later, and Julien understands the hypocrisy and ambition underlying these actions. The very dark room, "une immense salle gothique extrêmement sombre, et toute lambrissée de chêne noir" (p.314) ("an immense, extremely dark gothic room, completely paneled in black oak"), represents Julien's naïveté and incomprehension (he had, at first, no idea what the bishop was doing) as well as the hidden underside of the church's manipulative actions.

From this somber underside of the church, where its machinations are visible, Julien climbs to the dazzling spectacle of the "chapelle ardente" (a kind of mortuary chamber), where innumerable candles illuminate a gilded room and where twenty-four pretty young women kneel before the bishop of Agde:

Devant la porte étaient réunies à genoux vingt-quatre jeunes filles, appartenant aux familles les plus distinguées de Verrières. Avant d'ouvrir la porte, l'évêque se mit à genoux au milieu de ces jeunes filles toutes jolies. Pendant qu'il priait à haute voix, elles semblaient ne pouvoir assez admirer ses belles dentelles, sa bonne grâce, sa figure si jeune et si douce. Ce spectacle fit perdre à notre héros ce qui lui restait de raison. En cet instant, il se fût battu pour l'inquisition, et de bonne foi. La porte s'ouvrit tout à coup. La petite chapelle parut comme embrasée de lumière. On apercevait sur l'autel plus de mille cierges divisés en huit rangs séparés entre eux par des bouquets de fleurs. L'odeur suave de l'encens le plus pur sortait en tourbillon de la porte du sanctuaire. La chapelle dorée à neuf était fort petite, mais très élevée. Julien remarqua qu'il y avait sur l'autel des cierges qui avaient plus de quinze pieds de haut. Les jeunes filles ne purent retenir un cri d'admiration. On n'avait admis dans le petit vestibule de la chapelle que les vingt-quatre jeunes filles, les deux curés et Julien. (pp. 318–19) / *Outside the door were kneeling in a group twenty-four young ladies belonging to the most distinguished of the families of Verrières. Before opening the door, the bishop knelt down in the middle of the young ladies, all of whom were pretty. While he was praying aloud, they did not seem able to admire enough his beautiful lace, his grace, his face so young and so sweet. This spectacle made our hero lose whatever reason he still possessed. At that instant, he would have fought for the Inquisition, and in good faith. The door opened suddenly. The little chapel appeared as if ablaze with light. One saw on the altar more than a thousand candles divided into eight rows, which were separated by bouquets of flowers. The pleasant scent of the purest incense flowed out in swirling clouds through the door of the sanctuary. The newly gilded chapel was quite small, but very high. Julien noticed that on the altar there were candles that were more than fifteen feet high. The young ladies could not keep back a cry of admiration. They had*

let into the small vestibule of the chapel only the twenty-four young women,
the two curés, and Julien.

Because we have seen the bishop's machinations, we understand that he is using this spectacle, along with his elegant clothing and handsome appearance, to seduce the young women's imaginations (a seduction that becomes suggestively sexual when they let out a cry of admiration after the description of the fifteen-foot candles). Having perfected his gestures in the mirror, the bishop can now enjoy the fruits of his labors in the admiring gaze of the twenty-four beautiful young women. Julien, impressed with the spectacle, the beautiful young women, and the bishop's power, succumbs to the seduction in a different way: he becomes willing to do battle for the church. Julien's seduction hints also at an erotic component, for when he looks for the statue of Saint Clément, he can see it only through the sensual crook of the naked arm of one of the girls: "Ce fut alors seulement que Julien, collé contre la porte dorée, aperçut, pardessous le bras nu d'une jeune fille, la charmante statue de saint Clément" (p. 319) ("It was only then that Julien, standing close to the gilded door, saw, under the bare arm of one of the girls, the charming statue of Saint Clément"). After this scene, the scope of seduction grows even broader to include an entire class of people (Julien's original class): "Les paysans étaient ivres de bonheur et de piété. Une telle journée défait l'ouvrage de cent numéros des journaux jacobins" (p. 318) ("The peasants were drunk with happiness and piety. One such day undoes the work of one hundred issues of Jacobin papers").

This affiliation of church, power, and seduction appears again several times after this episode. In one instance, the abbé de Frilair takes a somewhat sadistic pleasure in exercising his power over the young, attractive Mathilde, who desperately needs his help:

J'ai ma revanche! pensa-t-il. Enfin, voici un moyen de conduire cette petite personne si décidée; je tremblais de n'y pas réussir. L'air distingué et peu facile à mener redoublait à ses yeux le charme de la rare beauté qu'il voyait presque suppliante devant lui. Il reprit tout son sang-froid, et n'hésita point à retourner le poignard dans son coeur. . . . Si Mathilde n'avait pas semblé si jolie à M. de Frilair, il ne lui eût parlé aussi clairement qu'à la cinq ou sixième entrevue. (pp. 660–61) / *I have my revenge! he thought. At last, here is a way of*

*manipulating this young woman who is so resolute; I trembled at the thought
of being unsuccessful. Her distinguished manner, of one who seemed not
easily led, doubled in his view the charm of the rare beauty which he saw
almost entreating him. He resumed his controlled attitude, and did not
hesitate one bit to turn the dagger in her heart. . . . If Mathilde had not
seemed so pretty to M. de Frilair, he would not have spoken this clearly to her
until their fifth or sixth meeting.*

Furthermore, when Madame de Rênal gives herself over to the church
after her affair with Julien, her confessor gains so much power and
influence over her that he convinces her to write the damning letter to
Monsieur de La Mole, and they set in motion Julien's demise. Significantly, Julien shoots her in a church, which, as Geneviève Mouillaud has
suggested, is a rival that seduces her, for it takes her love away from
him. [10]

The men of the church thus use their religious power as a political tool
to dominate, most often to dominate women. One's gender, then, represents a certain political position in the text. It also becomes clear that, in
all of these incidents, the church's power of seduction victimizes a person
of the other gender: Julien. One cannot forget that at his trial he is
condemned for *religico*-political reasons: Frilair and Valenod use Julien's
case to accomplish certain goals, and Valenod uses his influence to retali-
ate for past offenses and to revenge himself on Julien. All of these scenes,
then, link women and Julien in their common victimization or seduction
by the church's power.

Yet in these scenes Julien occupies a strange intermediate position. In
the chapel scene, Julien, naïve and seduced like the young women and the
peasants, also represents the seducer, the church (more or less), as he
stands dressed in his cassock. To complicate his position further, Julien
strongly identifies with the very young bishop, yet he never does so
completely, for his spurs, representing the Napoleonic hero as opposed to
the religious parvenu, peek out beneath his cassock. In short, Julien
belongs to two opposing realms at once, an aporia echoed throughout the
novel. Being neither peasant nor noble, neither priest nor layman, Julien
has no real place. Because he differs from the other men, he is somewhat
identified with women, yet he is not completely on their side either.

To understand Julien's ambiguous link to the women's political position, we must turn to the second scene in the trio, the courtroom drama at
the end of the text:

Mais bientôt toute son attention fut absorbée par douze ou quinze jolies femmes qui, placées vis-à-vis la sellette de l'accusé, remplissaient les trois balcons au-dessus des juges et des jurés. En se retournant vers le public, il vit que la tribune circulaire qui règne au-dessus de l'amphithéâtre était remplie de femmes: la plupart étaient jeunes et lui semblèrent fort jolies; leurs yeux étaient brillants et remplis d'intérêt. . . . ¶ Les témoins furent bien vite entendus. Dès les premiers mots de l'accusation soutenue par l'avocat général, deux de ces dames placées dans le petit balcon, tout à fait en face de Julien, fondirent en larmes. . . . ¶ L'avocat général faisait du pathos en mauvais français sur la barbarie du crime commis; Julien observa que les voisines de madame Derville avaient l'air de le désapprouver vivement. Plusieurs jurés, apparemment de la connaissance de ces dames, leur parlaient et semblaient les rassurer. . . . ¶ On apporta des rafraîchissements à l'avocat et à l'accusé. Ce fut alors seulement que Julien fut frappé d'une circonstance: aucune femme n'avait quitté l'audience pour aller dîner. . . . ¶ Le jury ne revenait point, et cependant aucune femme ne quittait la salle. (pp.672–75) / *But soon all his attention was absorbed by twelve or fifteen pretty women who, seated across from the bench of the defendant, filled the three galleries above the judges and the jury members. When he turned toward the public, he saw that the circular gallery above the courtroom was full of women; most of them were young and seemed to him quite pretty; their eyes were shining and filled with interest. . . . ¶ The witnesses testified quickly. At the very first words for the prosecution uttered by the advocate general, two of the ladies sitting in the small gallery, directly across from Julien, broke down in tears. . . . ¶ The advocate general used contrived pathos in bad French to speak of the barbarity of the crime that had been committed; Julien observed that the women sitting next to Madame Derville appeared to disapprove strongly. Several members of the jury, who seemed to know these ladies, spoke to them and appeared to reassure them. . . . ¶ Refreshments were brought to the lawyer and to the defendant. It was only then that Julien was struck by one circumstance: not one woman had left the session to dine. . . . The jury did not return, and yet not one woman left the room.*

One must wonder why Julien is of such great interest to the women of the town. The answer, as is almost always the case with Julien, is somewhat paradoxical. Most obviously, Julien is attractive (he has always succeeded with women) and he again *seduces,* both because of his looks and because of his romantic adventures: "Toutes les dames de la ville voulaient assister au jugement; on criait dans les rues le portrait de Julien" (p.670) ("All the ladies of the city wanted to go to the trial; Julien's portrait was being sold in the streets").

But the women desire more: they want to know the outcome of Julien's trial. The verdict obviously means something to them in particular, for they all remain to the very end of a trial that continues after two o'clock in the morning. When one considers this scene with gender in mind, the position of the women in the courtroom stands out. One group of women sits isolated in the circular gallery above the amphitheater, and the other group of twelve to fifteen pretty women sits facing Julien, in a mirrorlike position mentioned twice in the text. Julien and the groups of women mirror each other in another sense: both are isolated, whether physically or symbolically, from the groups of men, the judges and the jury (women were, in fact, prohibited from many legal rights[11]). Julien furthermore feels contempt for these men: "Il s'était senti pénétré d'un mépris sans mélange pour tous les hommes qui assistaient au jugement" (p.673) ("He was penetrated by an unmitigated contempt for all the men who were present at the trial"). Thus a sympathy and equivalence are established between the women and Julien in their relation to the law and to authority.

Of course, in this text (as in all nineteenth-century texts) men control law and authority and have power, here over Julien's life. He is governed by a sequence of men: his father, the abbé Chélan, Monsieur de Rênal, the abbé Pirard, and Monsieur de La Mole. All wield a life-threatening power, symbolized here when Monsieur Pirard glares at Julien with "un air à lui arracher le peu de vie qui lui restait" (p.378) ("a look which threatened to snatch from him the tiny bit of life that remained in him"). These men of authority do dispense with Julien's life, for they succeed in doing away with him: Monsieur de La Mole, Valenod in his defiance of Frilair, the men of the jury, and even Julien himself.

A revealing representation of the men's authority and of Julien's subjection to it appears in the strange episode in which he accompanies Monsieur de La Mole to a secret political gathering that conspires to reinforce the monarchy and the power of the aristocracy. Here Julien, a totally subservient outsider, finds himself in the midst of a large group of anonymous, powerful men (paralleling the scenes with anonymous, power*less* women). Julien merely copies down what they say. Prohibited from participating in the event, he does not even understand their ultimate purpose, which is, ironically, to reinforce the established social structures that destroy him in the end. At two other times, physically large, powerful men dominate Julien: first, his giant brother (p. 232) and second, the giant men of Besançon: "La haute stature de ces hommes, leurs épaules arrondies, leur démarche lourde, leurs énormes favoris, les longues redingotes qui les couvraient, tout attirait l'attention de Julien" (p. 370) ("The large stature of these men, their round shoulders, their heavy gait, their enormous sideburns, the long frock-coats covering them, all this attracted Julien's attention").

Julien's powerless position in relation to the men in his life parallels the women's powerless position in life as a whole. In particular, Madame de Rênal's subservience to her husband resembles the servitude of harem women, except that Madame de Rênal's is worse: "Une odalisque du sérail peut à toute force aimer le sultan; il est tout-puissant, elle n'a aucun espoir de lui dérober son autorité par une suite de petites finesses. La vengeance du maître est terrible, sanglante, mais militaire, généreuse: un coup de poignard finit tout. C'est à coups de mépris public qu'un mari tue sa femme au XIXe siècle; c'est en lui fermant tous les salons" (p. 343) ("An odalisque in a seraglio can love the sultan with all her heart; he is all-powerful, she has no hope of surreptitiously stealing his authority by means of a series of small, wily tricks. The vengeance of the master is terrible, bloody, but martial, generous: a dagger thrust ends all. It is with the blows of public contempt that a husband kills his wife in the nineteenth century; it is by having all the doors of the drawing rooms closed to her"). This parallel could explain the identification of women and Julien in the courtroom scene.

On the one hand, Julien willingly submits to this law and authority: "—J'ai donné la mort avec préméditation, lui dit Julien; j'ai acheté et fait charger les pistolets chez Un Tel, l'armurier. L'article 1342 du Code pénal est clair, je mérite la mort, et je l'attends" (p. 646) ("'I killed with premeditation,' Julien said to him; 'I bought the pistols and had them loaded at So-and-so's, the gunsmith's, store. Article 1342 of the Penal Code is clear, I deserve death, and I await it'"). Similarly, when he discovers that he is to be a father, he immerses himself in the patriarchal system and becomes maniacally ambitious, losing sight of the more idealistic standards he had set for himself before his success. He thus ironically belongs to the group of men who kill him.

On the other hand, although Julien would seem to contribute actively to the system that dominates him, he also rebels against this male authority and power: again he occupies the place of aporia. He hates his father and rejects his father's name, he rejects paternal, and thus patriarchal, authority, and instead of playing that game, he turns to sexual politicking. He constantly looks for or is given a new father, whether it be Monsieur de La Mole: "J'ai retrouvé un père en vous, monsieur" (p.444) ("I have found a father in you, Sir"), or the father in his fantasy of being the bastard son of a rich man: "Serait-il bien possible, se disait-il, que je fusse le fils naturel de quelque grand seigneur exilé dans nos montagnes par le terrible Napoléon?" (p.641) ("Could it really be possible, he asked himself, that I am the natural son of some great nobleman exiled to our mountains by the terrible Napoleon?").[12] Several of Stendhal's other protagonists also question parental power and authority: Fabrice seems to go further in the rejection of the father since he is the son of a French soldier; Lamiel is an orphan; and Armance has lost her parents. Julien's new father represents a new identity for him, and he almost becomes the son-in-law of Monsieur de La Mole; he does, for a short while, become noble, rich, and even a soldier (all his dreams come true). He escapes the repressive social identity of his birth and crosses the social barriers between class levels. Perhaps this is why the gaze of the women becomes so significant at Julien's trial, for his temporary escape from his social plight could figure the possibility of theirs.

But, of course, he is condemned, as he says to the jury, for breaking the paternal-patriarchal social law:

"Messieurs, je n'ai point l'honneur d'appartenir à votre classe, vous voyez en moi un paysan qui s'est révolté contre la bassesse de sa fortune. Mais quand je serais moins coupable, je vois des hommes qui, sans s'arrêter à ce que ma jeunesse peut mériter de pitié, voudront punir en moi et décourager à jamais cette classe de jeunes gens qui, nés dans une classe inférieure et en quelque sorte opprimés par la pauvreté, ont le bonheur de se procurer une bonne éducation, et l'audace de se mêler à ce que l'orgueil des gens riches appelle la société. ¶ "Voilà mon crime, messieurs, et il sera puni avec d'autant plus de sévérité, que, dans le fait, je ne suis point jugé par mes pairs." (pp.674–75) / *"Gentlemen, I do not have the honor of belonging to your class; you see in me a peasant who revolted against the baseness of his fortune. Yet even were I less guilty, I see men who, without being stopped by the pity my youth deserves, will try to punish in me and discourage forever the class of young men who, born in an inferior class and, as it were, oppressed by poverty, have the good fortune of getting a good education, and have the audacity to mix with what the pride of the rich calls society. ¶ "That is my crime, Gentlemen, and it will be punished with all the more severity because, in fact, I am not being judged by my peers."*

Because he has revolted against the law of father and class, he is decapitated, a symbol of castration.[13] The women who look on and weep are perhaps the silent victims of that same system of castration.

The third scene, which takes place near the beginning of the novel, makes clearer the subservience of women as a group and connects the repression of Julien and women even more intimately to the threat of castration:

A peine entre-t-on dans la ville que l'on est étourdi par le fracas d'une machine bruyante et terrible en appparence. Vingt marteaux pesants, et retombant avec un bruit qui fait trembler le pavé, sont élevés par une roue que l'eau du torrent fait mouvoir. Chacun de ces marteaux fabrique, chaque jour, je ne sais combien de milliers de clous. Ce sont de jeunes filles fraîches et jolies qui présentent aux coups de ces marteaux énormes les petits morceaux de fer qui sont rapidement transformés en clous. . . . Si, en entrant à Verrières, le voyageur demande à qui appartient cette belle fabrique de clous qui assourdit les gens qui montent la grande rue, on lui répond avec un accent traînard: *Eh! elle est à M. le maire.* (pp. 219–20) / *Scarcely has one entered the town than one is deafened by the din of a noisy and terrible-looking machine. Twenty heavy hammers, pounding with a sound which makes the pavement tremble, are elevated by a wheel turned by the water from the river. Each of these hammers manufactures, each day, I could not tell how many thousands of nails. It is young women, fresh and pretty, who present to the blows of these enormous hammers the small bits of iron which are rapidly transformed into nails. . . . If, on entering Verrières, the traveler asks to whom belongs this lovely nail factory, which deafens those who go up the main street, he is answered in a drawling accent:* Eh! It belongs to the mayor.

Here, fresh, pretty young women put pieces of iron into the mayor's huge, deafening machine. This machine, which dominates by sheer strength and force, represents the machinery of the patriarchal, oppressive system, here that of Rênal as political leader and also that of Rênal as husband and father figure. [14] Curiously, in two places in the novel, Rênal actually says that women are machines; they have become, perhaps, in his eyes, personifications of their subjected, subservient role: "Il y a toujours quelque chose à raccommoder à ces machines-là! (p. 262). "Il y a toujours quelque chose de dérangé à ces machines compliquées" (p. 284) ("Something always needs fixing with those machines!" "There is always something out of order with those complicated machines"). Something always malfunctions in the machine of the woman's body according to him; she is always deficient, powerless, missing something, castrated.

Rênal's nail machine reminds one of another machine in the beginning of this text, Julien's father's huge saw that appears in the scene in which we view Julien for the first time: "A huit ou dix pieds d'élévation, au milieu du hangar, on voit une scie qui monte et descend" (p. 231) ("At an elevation of eight to ten feet, in the middle of the shed, one sees a saw which rises and falls"). This machine that cuts and goes up and down prefigures the guillotine at the end of the text. Here this cutting machine links up with the father, who punishes Julien for his rebellion (reading a book and refusing to obey orders) by delivering a glancing blow to his son's head (foreshadowing Julien's decapitation). This blow threatens Julien with dismemberment (symbolic castration) were he to fall into the moving parts of the saw: "Il allait tomber à douze ou quinze pieds plus bas, au milieu des leviers de la machine en action, qui l'eussent brisé" (p. 232) ("He was about to fall twelve or fifteen feet down into the middle of the machine's moving levers which would have crushed him"). The relation of this machine to the father's law, to authority, and to castration is evident here, and because of the link in images between this scene and the other scene depicting Rênal's nail machine, we again find Julien and the women in the same place, dominated and threatened by the "machinery" of a repressive and dangerous authority.

Since the nail machine belongs to the mayor, it represents perhaps the subjection of the group of women as an entire political class, a subservience parallel to Julien's class subjugation, and it exemplifies Luce Irigaray's linking of class and gender repression: "All the social regimes of 'History' are based upon the exploitation of one 'class' of producers, namely women." [15] In fact, women factory workers in nineteenth-century France were exploited because they were paid considerably less than their male counterparts, so much less that the factories sometimes replaced men with women so they could profit more. This practice caused some hostility toward female workers. [16]

The link between Julien, gender, and class stands out even more in a remarkable little scene later in the novel, when Julien carries on with the mayor's wife while the mayor is busy throwing rocks at a peasant girl, who, like Julien, takes an "improper" path: "Heureusement, M. de Rênal ne vit point cette nouvelle impertinence, elle ne fut remarquée que de madame Derville: son amie fondait en larmes. En ce moment M. de Rênal se mit à poursuivre à coups de pierres une petite paysanne qui avait pris un sentier abusif, et traversait un coin du verger" (p.270) ("Luckily, Monsieur de Rênal did not see this new impertinence; it was noticed only by Madame Derville: her friend burst into tears. At this moment Monsieur de Rênal began to throw rocks at a peasant girl, who had taken an unauthorized path and was crossing a corner of the orchard"). Here peasant merges with female; just as in Rênal's nail factory, the plight of the group of women merges with that of the *paysan,* Julien.

Furthermore, a curious connection establishes itself here between Fabrice and Julien, women, and "peasants." If, as we saw, women buy Julien's portrait before his trial, it is the "gens du peuple" (*La Chartreuse de Parme,* p.456) ("common people") who buy Fabrice's portrait because of his sermons. And if in Julien's trial, it is essentially a group of women of some economic means who weep for him, Fabrice is pursued by a group of peasant beggar women in *La Chartreuse de Parme* (p.215). The peasant's rise is figured by his success with beautiful women of the "propertied classes," the nobility's decline by Fabrice's nagging peasant women.

The representative of political power in *Le Rouge et le noir,* the mayor Rênal, changes nature (iron and the river) into a formed, useful thing (nails and power). In fact, one of his major accomplishments in the town of Verrières is to cut trees, which also relates to the authority of the church in its representative, Maslon: "Mais la volonté de M. le maire est despotique, et deux fois par an tous les arbres appartenant à la commune sont impitoyablement amputés. Les libéraux de l'endroit prétendent, mais ils exagèrent, que la main du jardinier officiel est devenue bien plus sévère depuis que M. le vicaire Maslon a pris l'habitude de s'emparer des produits de la tonte" (pp.223–24) ("But the mayor's will is despotic, and twice a year all the trees belonging to the municipality are pitilessly amputated. The liberals of the region claim, but they exaggerate, that the hand of the official gardener became much more severe when the vicar

Maslon made a practice of appropriating the clippings"). The mayor's and the church's authority amputates nature to make it conform to their preordained pattern; Julien's symbolic attempt to escape their system by escaping from his political class results in his decapitation (castration).

Similarly, in several descriptions, the main women characters in the text, Madame de Rênal and Mathilde, are victims of cutting of one sort or another. Both women cut off some of their hair and give it to Julien. Mathilde lops off such a huge piece that it is almost impossible to hide the mutilated section: "Si une aussi belle figure avait pu être gâtée par quelque chose, Mathilde y serait parvenue; tout un côté de ses beaux cheveux, d'un blond cendré, était coupé à un demi-pouce de la tête" (p. 561) ("If a face so beautiful could ever be spoiled by anything, Mathilde would have succeeded in spoiling hers; an entire side of her beautiful, ash-blond hair was cut off a half inch from her head").

In a more symbolic way, Mathilde harbors a death-cult worship for those who are decapitated, as evidenced in her annual mourning for her guillotined ancestor, Boniface de La Mole, and in her desire to hold Julien's severed head at the end of the novel. Death alone can distinguish a man in her eyes: "Je ne vois que la condamnation à mort qui distingue un homme, pensa Mathilde: c'est la seule chose qui ne s'achète pas" (p. 489) ("As I see it, only a death sentence distinguishes a man, thought Mathilde: It is the only thing that cannot be bought"). Clélia, too, lets herself love Fabrice during his imprisonment only when she fears he might die; and Lamiel becomes interested in d'Aubigné when he threatens to kill himself. For Mathilde, however, it would seem that only death by decapitation counts. Besides rebelling against authority in her love for Julien, she admires others who also reject the patriarchal system of their society and who put themselves, one might say, into the woman's place, the place of castration (precisely what Julien does). [17] Her rebellion represents a rejection of power but could also figure an acceptance and glorification of woman's plight.

Furthermore, the bodies of Julien's lovers (seen through his eyes), when examined in detail, sometimes appear as detached and independent body parts. Madame de Rênal's hand fascinates and attracts Julien:

Quoique bien ému lui-même, il fut frappé de la froideur glaciale de la main qu'il prenait; il la serrait avec une force convulsive; on fit un dernier effort pour la lui ôter, mais enfin cette main lui resta (p. 267).

Il voulut prendre une main blanche que depuis longtemps il voyait près de lui (p. 278). Elle est pourtant bien jolie, cette main! (p. 288) / *Although quite moved himself, he was struck by the glacial coldness of the hand he took; he squeezed it with a convulsive force; a last effort was made to take it away from him, but at last this hand stayed with him. . . . He tried to grasp a white hand which for a long time he saw near him. . . . It is after all very pretty, this hand!*

The use of the pronoun *on,* the indefinite article *une,* and the absence of Madame de Rênal's name in these sentences make the hand appear to be an independent entity.

Finally, in the church at Besançon, Madame de Rênal's head appears to be detached from her body (Julien also sees other isolated objects: shoulders, a necklace, her hair): "Julien, hors de lui, s'élança; la chute de madame de Rênal eût peut-être entraîné son amie, si Julien ne les eût soutenues. Il vit la tête de madame de Rênal pâle, absolument privée de sentiment, flottant sur son épaule. Il aida madame Derville à placer cette tête charmante sur l'appui d'une chaise de paille" (p. 400) ("Julien, beside himself, jumped forward; Madame de Rênal's fall would possibly have brought down her friend, too, if Julien had not supported them. He saw Madame de Rênal's head, pale, absolutely deprived of consciousness, rolling on her shoulder. He helped Madame Derville place that charming head on the back of a straw chair"). The head, hanging loose and "floating," is "placed" somewhere and reminds us of the decapitation of Julien at the end of the novel. (In fact, Madame de Rênal shares his fate when she dies three days after his death.) In the chapel scene we see a complicated prefiguration of Julien's decapitation that links it to women, the church, and seduction. Julien looks for and finds with some difficulty the statue of Saint Clément: "Il était couché sous l'autel, en costume de jeune soldat romain. Il avait au cou une large blessure, d'où le sang semblait couler. . . . A cette vue, la jeune fille voisine de Julien pleura à chaudes larmes, une de ses larmes tomba sur la main de Julien" (p. 319) ("He was lying under the altar, in the garb of a young Roman soldier. He had a large wound on his neck, from which blood seemed to flow. . . . At the sight of this, the young woman next to Julien wept bitterly; one of her tears fell on Julien's hand"). Here Julien, wearing soldier's spurs and cleric's cassock, looks at the soldier-saint who dies from a neck wound; thus the scene foreshadows Julien's decapitation. The young woman's tear falling on (for) Julien links the women, the saint, and Julien even more closely and prefigures the weeping women at Julien's death sentence. Thus like the saint, Julien dies in a sense because of the church, and like the women, he is seduced and powerless. These figures of the decapitation, powerlessness, and castration of women provide the closest link between the women and Julien.

If Julien's symbolic position in the text is ambiguous in the sense that he, a man, represents woman's place, his literal gender also creates an aporia in the text. Like Balzac's attractive male characters, he is almost feminine: he has a "figure de jeune fille" (p.239) ("the face of a young woman"); Madame de Rênal sees him as "une jeune fille déguisée" (p.241) ("a young woman in disguise"), as having "l'air timide d'une jeune fille" (p.242) ("the bashful look of a young woman"), and as having a certain "forme presque féminine de ses traits" (pp.243–44) ("an almost feminine form to his features"). Even the narrator compares him to "une jeune fille de seize ans" (p.298) ("a young woman sixteen years old"). His rather feminine body makes for a fascinating comparison with Lamiel's large and undisciplined body and her energetic and decidedly unfeminine way (in the code of the nineteenth century) of darting through life.[18] Fabrice, although less explicitly effeminate than Julien, plays a narrative role that traditionally belongs to a woman in the French novel: he retreats to his lonely, cloistered tower at the end of the novel, as the Princesse de Clèves and Armance retreat to their convents.

Yet, although one Julien is "feminine," another Julien, who identifies with Napoleon and his glory, is all "male." When Mathilde insults Croisenois, Julien reacts as follows: "Il faut que ce jeune homme aime furieusement l'argent, pour ne pas planter là cette fille, si riche qu'elle soit! pensait Julien. Et pour lui, indigné des outrages faits à la dignité masculine, il redoublait de froideur envers elle" (p.521) ("This young man must have a furious love for money not to drop the girl right now, no matter how rich she is! thought Julien. And as for himself, indignant at the outrages committed against masculine dignity, he doubled his cold attitude toward her"). Julien is double, undecidable, and it is perhaps this aporia more than anything that troubles the phallocentric authority in the text. He, a peasant, tries to cross social borders, to become a noble; he does battle with society: "C'était l'homme malheureux en guerre avec toute la société" (p.526) ("He was the unhappy man at war with all society"). This crossing of borders, the mixing up of the clear-cut polarities in society, is an act of political subterfuge, for which Julien is punished. But in the subtext of gender, it is not merely a class war but a sex war, for Julien puts himself simultaneously in the place of man and woman, undermining another of society's most important polarities. Julien, by blurring these borders, shows one possible way of undermining and deconstructing the repressive authority that hangs over him, but he is too much a part of that authority and submits to it in the end. The *iron* structure of society shackles him, as represented in the *iron* nails made by the women, the *iron* gate before Monsieur de Rênal's home that separates his house from the riffraff, and the *iron* cross that Julien sees on the door of the seminary. Julien's final "putting-in-place" is effected by the cold metal of the guillotine at the end.

Where do the women fit in, then, in this text? Their silent, intent scrutiny of Julien in the courtroom reveals to them their own plight because the women and Julien are metaphors for each other. Their interest in the outcome of his trial is an interest in their own ultimate fate. In this novel they do not escape; they, like Madame de Rênal, are condemned to death along with Julien. Their defeat can be seen on the last page of the text, where, instead of a group of women among the candles, we see, "Arrivés ainsi vers le point le plus élevé d'une des hautes montagnes du Jura, au milieu de la nuit, dans cette petite grotte magnifiquement illuminée d'un nombre infini de cierges, *vingt prêtres* célébrèrent le service des morts" (pp.698–99; emphasis added) ("Having arrived thus near the highest elevation of one of the high Jura mountains, in the middle of the night, in that small cave magnificently illuminated by an infinite number of candles, *twenty priests* performed the funeral services").

In the poetics of gender in this novel, Julien represents the woman's place, and his decapitation figures that of women in society. This metaphoric decapitation of the women in the text and the image of the silent, intent women in the courtroom remind one of a text by Hélène Cixous in which women are subjected to "an education that consists of trying to make a soldier of the feminine by force, the force history keeps reserved for woman, the 'capital' force that is effectively decapitation. Women have no choice other than to be decapitated, and in any case the moral is that if they don't actually lose their heads by the sword, *they only keep them on condition that they lose them*—lose them, that is, to complete silence, turned into *automatons.*"[19] They are the women subjected to the machine of castration in the factory scene, women viewed as machines or as automatons by Rênal, women seduced by power and materialism, by the machine of the church in the scene of the *chapelle ardente,* women silently watching the machine of society pronounce the death sentence on Julien, their own representative.[20] Thus in these three scenes which represent the three forces of subjugation in the text—the political and industrial, the church, and finally the law—Julien points in the direction of a possible deconstruction of this system of subjugation in his sexual and social undecidability, but for some reason he cannot continue in his struggle, and the machine wins out in the end. Julien's aporetic gender identity is dissolved, and he follows that conservative trajectory which moves away from aporia. Yet Julien's link to women, and the relation of gender and class that emerges in this novel, remain to haunt us and evoke a startling comparison with what has been called the emergence of the new feminine "underclass" and the feminization of poverty in our century.

BALZAC'S FAMILY FINANCES

Il [l'analyste]
ne comprend pas à quoi il a affaire quand il croit qu'interpréter, c'est montrer au sujet que ce qu'il désire, c'est tel objet sexuel. Il se trompe. – LACAN, *Séminaire II.* / He *{the analyst}* does not understand what he is dealing with when he believes that to interpret is to show to the subject that what he desires is this or that sexual object. He is wrong.

IN BALZAC'S *Le Père Goriot,* as Goriot raves on his deathbed and rails against his ungrateful daughters, he demands that they be brought before him because, being their father, he has the right to their respect: "La justice est pour moi, tout est pour moi, la nature, le code civil. Je proteste. La patrie périra si les pères sont foulés aux pieds. Cela est clair. La société, le monde roulent sur la paternité, tout croule si les enfants n'aiment pas leurs pères" ("Justice is on my side, everything is on my side, nature, the Civil Code. I protest. Our country will perish if fathers are trampled underfoot. That is clear. Society, the world depend on paternity, and everything collapses if children do not love their fathers").[21] Clearly in Goriot's world, the influence of the family is extremely important in the continuity of social and national institutions, and he believes the father should be powerful and have authority in the family structure.

These few words provide one of the most important links between gender identity and the institution of the family (and other social institutions) in the nineteenth century: the father's male gender identity relates to the power structures of the family and, in a larger context, to those of the state. In the remainder of this chapter, I will investigate the family structures that are linked to power and to gender identity in Balzac's world.

If for Freud, psychoanalytic gender identity is shaped by certain family structures, new French historical studies seem to confirm the family's importance in the *social* definition of gender identity in their observations that changes in the role of the home and the family in the nineteenth century influenced, and indeed more clearly polarized, gender identity. Of course, the nineteenth century was inaugurated with the drafting of the Civil Code, which "enshrined . . . the rigid differentiation of women from men" in many ways (but in particular in the structures of the family), and which worsened women's status "if not in absolute, then in relative terms." Goriot's views about the role of the father in the family coincide with the tenets of the code: the father could administer "the financial affairs of minor children . . . , could withhold consent to a child's marriage, and he retained the exclusive right to employ the ancient 'right of correction,' to imprison his children for six months." The wife was considered to be equivalent to a minor: she had no right to dispose of property without her husband's consent.[22] Thus even though some of the articles of the Civil Code did move toward a more egalitarian stance (for instance, the new inheritance laws prohibited primogeniture, and children of both sexes were awarded a portion of the estate), the general thrust of the laws concerning the family consolidated the power of the father and legalized the inferior status of the mother and children.

Of course, the everyday realities of family life in the nineteenth century were governed by class difference. The composition and function of a working-class family varied a great deal according to locality and type of work: the family life of a city laborer (man, woman, or child), who spent long hours at work as well as getting to work, differed enormously from that of a rural artisan or farmer, whose peasant life centered on the structure of the family.[23] It is outside the scope of this book to summarize the different types of lower-class family life since, until Emile Zola's works, the nineteenth-century novel was essentially (although not exclusively) interested in the "propertied classes" (in people belonging to a family of some economic means): in the upper classes, in the middle classes, in a character who was moving into those spheres, or in an employee (servant, actress, courtesan, teacher) in those spheres. Thus it is the picture of family life in those classes which interests me, a picture that is a bit clearer and more homogeneous than that of the working classes.

Not surprisingly, the father was generally responsible for the financial affairs of the family, and the mother was responsible for the care and education of her children at home: for boys until school age, for girls (preferably) until adulthood.[24] More significant, however, in the nineteenth century, the world of the home became increasingly separated from the world of production; the home became more and more the place of reproduction for the woman and of relaxation for the man. Thus the industrialization of France, which accelerated during the nineteenth century, more clearly separated not only home from work but also the gender role of the man, who "produced," and that of the woman, who lost what limited role in productivity she might have had and who was relegated to "reproductivity."[25] Although one generally assumes that industrialization works toward the emancipation of women as they become integrated into the work force, this was not the case for the "ladies of the leisure class," who became more imprisoned in their function. Even for working-class women, one study has shown that their choice of jobs and reasons for working were not motivated by a desire for independence or a quest for identity, but rather by their families' economic need.[26]

Since in the Balzacian universe the family plays an especially important structuring role (as opposed to the destructuring role it plays in Stendhal), I will next investigate gender identity in relation first to a Parisian family in *La Cousine Bette* and then to a provincial family in *Eugénie Grandet*. One common element will emerge from these discussions of the Civil Code and from analysis of the family structures in Balzac: the importance of economic factors in the family structure, which determine who controls possessions and who does not.

The title *La Cousine Bette* makes clear that the novel deals with the role of a woman in her family. Yet in the first paragraph that woman is nowhere to be found: "Vers le milieu du mois de juillet de l'année 1838, une de ces voitures nouvellement mises en circulation sur les places de Paris et nommées des *milords* cheminait, rue de l'Université, portant un gros homme de taille moyenne en uniforme de capitaine de la Garde nationale" ("Toward the middle of the month of July in the year 1838, one of those vehicles recently put into circulation around the squares of Paris and named *milords* made its way along the rue de l'Université, carrying a fat man of medium height in a captain's uniform of the National Guard").[27] Where is the woman, Bette, introduced by the title? Where is the family? Instead of a woman, we find a vehicle that transports a man, almost as though the woman of the title is but a vehicle for the identification of the "gros homme." Indeed, if we take the "vehicle" as a metaphoric replacement for the title's absent woman, its name suggests the title of a *man*, "milord." As a woman must take her name from a man, either her father or her husband, the woman of the title, Bette, must first be introduced, named, by a man.

Bette does, however, revolt against the lack of identity imposed by family structure; and, to understand her revolt, we must first examine the conventional family roles that women play in this novel. We will then come to the novel's surprising conclusions about this revolt and about the Balzacian family itself.

In this novel, Adeline's self-effacement, even though it is highly valorized, becomes an incarnation of the submissive. She has nothing of her own but gets all from her husband—fortune, title, and name (or identity): "Pour Adeline, le baron fut donc, dés l'origine, une espèce de Dieu qui ne pouvait faillir; elle lui devait tout: la fortune, elle eut voiture, hôtel, et tout le luxe du temps; le bonheur, elle était aimée publiquement; un titre, elle était baronne; enfin la célébrité, on l'appela la belle Mme Hulot, à Paris" (p. 76) ("To Adeline, the baron was, thus, from the very beginning, a kind of god who could not fail. She owed him everything: fortune (she had a carriage, a large house, and all the luxuries of the time); happiness (she was loved publicly); title (she was a baroness); renown (she was called the beautiful Madame Hulot in Paris)"). Even though Adeline gets everything from her husband, this "everything" amounts to very little, and eventually to nothing. She crystallizes a certain powerlessness of so many other Balzacian wives: Delphine and Anastasie in *Le Père Goriot;* Mme de Mortsauf in *Le Lys dans la vallée*. And she crystallizes the effect of the Civil Code on married women's property rights: "Married women . . . were totally interdicted from participating in the activities of jointly held property or from disposing of their own property without their husband's sanction."[28] So Adeline silently looks on as her husband spends all their money and ruins her entire family. But, most significantly, Adeline is deprived of her voice by being excluded from discourse. She never speaks of her suffering until she must do so to calm her daughter, Hortense, breaking, as she says, the "cachet sépul-cral . . . de ma lèvre" (p. 270) ("the sepulchral seal . . . of my lips"). Adeline's wifely role is to play the servant to the man who "created" her, who gave her fortune and identity: "Après s'être bien dit que son mari ne saurait jamais avoir de torts envers elle, elle se fit, dans son for intérieur, la servante humble, dévouée et aveugle de son créateur" (p. 76) ("After telling herself that her husband could never do her any wrong, she made herself, in her innermost being, the humble, devoted, and blind servant of her creator"). Adeline then passes this role on to her daughter, Hor-tense, who consequently "belongs" to her husband and interacts with him "comme un chien avec son maître" (p. 207) ("as a dog with its master"). This text, then, shows how the man, Hulot, creates the woman, Adeline, creates her identity, which is to be his slave, his possession, as Adeline says: "Je suis ta chose, fais de moi tout ce que tu voudras" (p. 355) ("I am but your thing, do with me as you wish").

Indeed, the legal status of a wife in nineteenth-century France was that of a servant who had to obey her husband, as the Civil Code mandates: "Le mari doit protection à sa femme, la femme obéissance à son mari' (Art. 213) ("The husband owes protection to his wife, the wife obedience to her husband"). Claire Goldberg Moses goes so far as to say that the Civil Code made women *worse* than slaves (like Mme de Rênal, whose condition Stendhal describes as worse than that of a harem woman): "The position of the nineteenth-century French woman was more rigid in some ways than that of a slave in classical times because, while a master could free a slave, a husband was formally forbidden by the code from abandoning any of his rights over his wife." [29] Balzac's *La Cousine Bette* hyperbolizes this nine-teenth-century image of the woman as obedient servant until the woman becomes a mere thing, a possession. Balzac thereby highlights the con-ventional identity of woman as selfless, angelic wife, but this identity is problematized because of its implausible excess.

The novel complicates the woman's conventional role as servant in two other ways. First, it reveals that being a wife is a *role* to be assumed and not an innate identity. Bette, for instance, tries to decide what role to play in relation to her protégé, Wenceslas Steinbock: "Elle aimait assez Stein-bock pour ne pas l'épouser, et l'aimait trop pour le céder à une autre femme; elle ne savait pas se résigner à n'en être que la mère, et se regardait comme une folle quand elle pensait à l'autre rôle" (pp. 118–19) ("She loved Steinbock enough not to marry him, and loved him too much to give him up to another woman; she could not resign herself to being only his mother, and considered herself crazy when she thought of the other role"). Mother or wife are the two principal family roles that women can assume in this novel and in a society in which "le mariage était, pour une femme, le seul moyen de s'intégrer dans la vie sociale" ("marriage was, for a woman, the only way to integrate herself into social life"). [30] (Bette's role as cousin has already put her in a marginal place.)

The woman's conventional identity becomes problematic in a second way when conflicts arise if a woman must play several roles at once. Adeline, the epitome of the subservient wife, is torn between the conflicting duties of mother and wife several times: "La baronne, muette et prise entre le sentiment maternel et le sentiment conjugal, offrait un visage bouleversé, couvert de larmes" (p. 290) ("The baroness, silent and torn between maternal and conjugal cares, showed distress on her face, which was covered with tears"). The conventional woman alternates between different, and sometimes mutually exclusive, roles, in a sense, between several discourses. Again, the revelation of the multiplicity of roles problematizes feminine identity as a unique given and uncovers its hidden "discursive" nature.

The conventional, family woman may have a conflict between several familial roles, but she never neglects one of them: she protects the family. Adeline's chief role is that of keeping the family structure together because, for her, the most horrible thing that could happen would be its destruction: "Sans regretter leur argent, les Hulot jeunes concevaient à la fois de la défiance et des inquiétudes à l'égard du baron. Ce sentiment assez visible affligeait profondément Adeline, elle pressentait la dissolution de la famille (p. 280) ("While not lamenting the loss of their money, the young members of the Hulot family developed toward the baron both suspicion and anxiety. Their feelings, which were quite visible, profoundly afflicted Adeline: she felt a premonition of the dissolution of the family"). Even though woman's identity in Balzac's fictional family is problematic and multiple, all of her identities serve to strengthen the institution of the family, and gender identity here serves to keep Adeline's family together.

After seeing the plight of the family women in this novel, the reader is not surprised that Bette goes through her life unmarried and resents her family. But the text does not glamorize Bette's role, and her universe is no more cheerful than the family woman's. It is, in fact, even more horrible.

Bette represents in almost every way the opposite of the conventional family woman. *She* has a voice; only she can make herself heard by the deaf maréchal Hulot: "La voix forte et claire de la Lorraine lui permettait de causer avec le vieillard. Elle fatiguait ses poumons, tant elle tenait à démontrer à son futur qu'il ne serait jamais sourd avec elle" (p.339) ("Her strong and clear Lorraine voice enabled her to chat with the old man. She wore out her lungs, so earnest was her attempt to show to her future husband that he would never be deaf with her"). Even as no one possesses Bette, since she has neither father nor husband, she, unlike the wives, has possessions. The Hulot family's possessions dwindle to nothing, but hers increase. Finally, all of her machinations have one goal: to ruin the Hulot family, not to preserve it. She, along with Valérie, represents the force of the dissolution of the family. Two different types of women would seem to oppose each other: family preservers and family destroyers.[31]

Bette has another, more curious, identity in the rhetoric of the text: she is sometimes considered to be less than human. Often given the name of a beast (a goat, a spider, a monkey), she bears a name that suggests the word *bête* (animal). Having an inexplicable savagery, being less civilized and more animal than the conventional woman, she is a monstrosity, as Balzac says, precisely because she has not been possessed: "La Virginité, comme toutes les monstruosités, a des richesses spéciales" (p.152) ("Virginity, like all monstrosities, has its own special riches").

Being less than human, she is described as being almost nothing or nothing at all: "'Il s'agit de ton mariage,' dit la cousine Bette à l'oreille de sa petite cousine Hortense sans paraître offensée de la façon dont la baronne s'y prenait pour les renvoyer, en la comptant pour presque rien" (p.57) ("'It concerns your marriage,' said Cousin Bette in her young cousin Hortense's ear, without appearing to be offended by the way the baroness went about sending them away, counting her for next to noth-ing"). Resigned to this role of absence, "résignée à ne rien être" (p.84) ("resigned to being a nothing, a nobody"), she leads an anonymous life: "C'était une de ces existences anonymes" (p.106) ("It was one of those anonymous existences"). Quite simply, Bette has no identity. She has not married, has not gotten an identity from a man, and, in the world of a novel that explores women's conventional family roles, she almost does not exist.

This same anonymity characterizes the second type of antifamily woman in this text, Valérie Marneff. Having started out as a wife, Valérie rejects traditional marriage and becomes a courtesan. As a result, she, like

Bette, becomes nothing at the end of her life: "La pauvre créature, qui, dit-on, était jolie, est bien punie par où elle a péché, car elle est aujourd'hui d'une ignoble laideur, si toutefois elle est quelque chose!" (p. 429) ("The poor creature, who, they say, was pretty, is now reaping what she has sown, because today she is vilely ugly; if, that is, she is anything at all!"). In the end, Valérie loses all identity, for she no longer even resembles herself: " 'Plus rien!' se dit Lisbeth épouvantée. 'Je ne reconnais ni ses yeux, ni sa bouche! Il ne reste pas un seul trait d'elle!' " (p. 432) (" 'Nothing left at all!' Lisbeth, appalled, said to herself. 'I recognize neither her eyes, nor her mouth! Not a single one of her features remains!' ").

These unconventional women pose a problem of interpretation in their lack of identity, as Hortense says of Bette: "Il y a quelque chose d'inexplicable en elle" (p. 133) ("There is something strangely inexplicable about her"); and of Valérie, Hulot says: "La femme . . . est un être inexplicable" (p. 235) ("Woman . . . is an inexplicable being"). It would seem that, in contrast with the family woman, who has multiple but well-determined identities, the unconventional woman has no identity. Too many identities or none at all: this seems to be woman's destiny.

One would hope that Bette's rebellion against the structures that deprive women of property and selfhood would be presented as a heroic and noble stance, but the opposite is true. Bette is a failed and vengeful villainess, and one is not unhappy when she dies at the end of the novel. But a closer look at her failure would reveal that it has nothing to do with a noble freedom fight for liberation from oppression. Bette rejects being possessed, and desires to possess, in particular to possess a person. Hence she is not merely the opposite of the conventional woman, she becomes the opposite of that woman by playing the role of the man as possessor of another. She tries to turn the family roles upside down when she becomes the husband who has a wife, a male wife, Wenceslas Steinbock, who plays the woman under her domination: "Il fut comme une femme qui pardonne les mauvais traitements d'une semaine à cause des caresses d'un fugitif raccommodement" (p. 116) ("He was like a wife who forgives a week's bad treatment upon receiving the caresses of a fleeting reconciliation"). Steinbock is her "dog" just as Hortense is later his: "Au dessert, elle (Bette) avait mis dans son sac des fruits et des sucreries pour son amoureux, et elle venait les lui donner, absolument comme une vieille fille rapporte une friandise à son chien" (p. 107) ("For dessert, she had put in her bag some fruits and sweets for her love, and she was on her way to give them to him, exactly as a spinster brings a treat to her dog"). Bette, like Hulot, gives her spouse everything he owns (p. 112), and, because of this gift, he belongs to her. As she says, "Vous m'appartenez" (p. 117) ("You belong to me").

At first, Steinbock gladly assumes the role of the slave-wife: "Vous serez tout pour moi, ma chère bienfaitrice, je serai votre esclave" (p. 112) ("You will be all to me, my dear benefactress, I will be your slave"). Bette, happy to have a slave of her own, goes so far as to incarcerate him when he tries to leave her. She desires to play the man who possesses in the symbolic inverted marriage: "le mariage de cette énergie femelle et de cette faiblesse masculine" (p. 110) ("the marriage of this female energy to this masculine weakness"). Bette, seen either as an inhuman beast or as an unfeminine man, incarnates Irigaray's precept that certain desiring females have an identity "between a sort of *animality . . .* and *the imitation of male models.*"[32]

Bette's attempt to invert the family hierarchy and to play the man's role does not work. Wenceslas gets away, falls in love with and marries Bette's cousin Hortense. But Bette, left alone and hungering for revenge, cannot relinquish her strategy of reversal and tries again to gain power, this time by going into league with the other antifamily woman, Valérie Marneff. The union of these two women serves their individual goals perfectly. Both play inverted roles because both desire to possess rather than to be possessed: Valérie wants to possess material things, and Bette wants to gain ultimate control over the Hulot family, which, in the past, had control over her. This assumption of inverted roles works so well that Valérie and Bette do become the possessors for a short time. They gain more and more money, more and more power, while their victims continue to believe them powerless.

The link of this desire for possessions to gender and power can be discovered when Valérie describes the statue of Samson and Delilah that she commissions Steinbock to make:

Faites Dalila coupant les cheveux à l'Hercule juif! . . . Mais vous qui serez, si vous voulez m'écouter, un grand artiste, j'espère que vous comprendrez le sujet. Il s'agit d'exprimer la puissance de la femme. Samson n'est rien là. C'est le cadavre de la force. Dalila, c'est la passion qui ruine tout. . . . Samson s'est réveillé sans

cheveux, comme beaucoup de dandies à faux toupets. Le héros est là
sur le bord du lit . . . les bras croisés, la tête rasée . . . Dalila est à
genoux. . . . Selon moi, la Juive a eu peur de Samson, terrible,
puissant, mais elle a dû aimer Samson devenu petit garçon. (pp.
259–61) / *Show Delilah cutting off the Jewish Hercules' hair! . . . But
you, who (if you listen to me) will be a great artist, I hope that you
understand the subject. It is about expressing the power of the woman.
Samson is for nothing in it. He is the corpse of force. Delilah is the passion
that destroys everything. . . . Samson has awakened without hair, like
many dandies with false toupees. There is the hero on the edge of the
bed . . . his arms crossed, his head shaved . . . Delilah is on her
knees. . . . In my opinion, the Jewess was afraid of Samson when he was
terrible, powerful; but she must have loved Samson when he became like a
little boy.*

This symbolic scene reveals the tie between possessions, gender, and
families: the phallus. Delilah takes away Samson's power and his man-
hood, making him a "petit garçon" ("little boy") in an image of symbolic
castration. She, on her knees and thus in the position of the servant or of
the one possessed, is actually now the more powerful one, for she has
stolen Samson's hair, the phallus, from him. In the same way, Bette and
Valérie use the power structure associated with the phallus and try to take
it over by reversing the male/female hierarchy. It would seem that here
Balzac, like Freud, could see a powerful woman only as being a man.

Actually, the machinery set in motion by the two women works too
well, and they end up killing (symbolically castrating) almost everyone
who has or desires the phallus, including themselves. The maréchal
Hulot dies, Crevel dies, Valérie dies, and Bette's death results from her
failed power play (she dies from lung troubles, which arise when her
machinations begin to fail). Bette and Valérie do not succeed because, in
trying to gain power by stealing possessions from the men, they merely
repeat the system's horror when they reverse it. Women who try to be men
thus remain trapped in a hierarchical system that castrates one-half of that
system. The tragic ending of this text shows that a mere reversal of the
hierarchy of the existing order does not cure its ills. Whether it be that of
the despoiled, castrated victim/wife, or of the "phallus-enviers," the
woman's identity in this text is impossible. This explains, to a certain
extent, why the world of this novel is so claustrophobic and oppressive:

the women face only two possible fates, both of which are unacceptable. The ultimate culprit is the economic system of the family, the cutthroat system of "possess or be possessed," or to put it another way, "possess the phallus and power" (be a man) or "be the phallus, be castrated and powerless" (be a woman).

The impossibility of escape from the closed system that equates phallus, possessions, and power appears in the proliferation of similes using family relations and in the incredible number of real family ties between the various characters in the novel. Since everyone is somehow related to everyone else, no one can escape from the family structure of possessor versus possessed. Chart 1 maps out the various relations between the main characters, and, as its complication makes clear, everyone has family ties to at least two other people (with the exception of Henri de Montès, the Brazilian).

This all-pervasive family structure invades nonfamily relations, when, in the rhetoric of the text, certain metaphors make family members of nonfamily characters; most often these metaphors represent Bette and Valérie. First Bette is called Valérie's aunt, then, more significantly, Bette and Valérie are sisters, as Valérie says: "Voulez-vous que nous soyons comme deux soeurs. . . . Voulez-vous surtout me jurer que vous ne me vendrez jamais, ni à mon mari, ni à M. Hulot?" (p. 145) ("Would you like us to be like two sisters? . . . Would you especially swear to me that you will never sell me out, not to my husband, not to Monsieur Hulot?"). Here, instead of Freud's male primal horde, the union of brothers against father, Balzac depicts the union of sisters against husbands and lovers. The sisters band together to steal the phallus, here represented by money, and swear never to go into league with the men by "selling out" the other. Whereas in Le Rouge et le noir, the groups of women remain silent, powerless onlookers, in La Cousine Bette, they have ominously acted to take over power.[33]

This proliferation of family ties becomes excessive when, on the one hand, one family relationship is doubled by another. Brothers become fathers and husbands become sons: "[Le maréchal] était venu fixer ses jours à Paris, près de son frère, auquel il portait toujours une affection de père" (p. 78) ("[The marshal] had come to Paris to settle himself near his brother, for whom he felt ever a fatherly affection"); "[Adeline] traitait enfin son Hector comme une mère traite un enfant gâté" (p. 77) ("[Adeline] ended up treating her Hector as a mother treats a spoiled child"). On

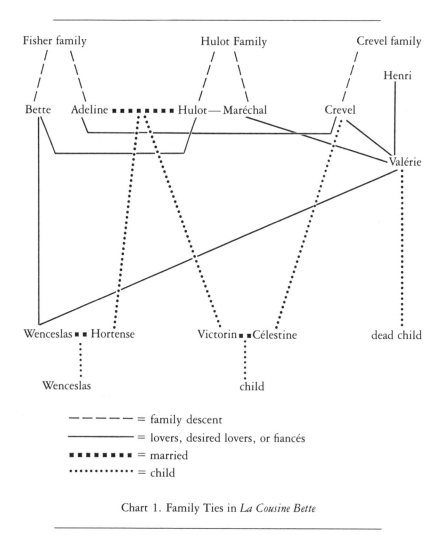

Chart 1. Family Ties in *La Cousine Bette*

the other hand, intermarriage complicates real, nonmetaphorical family ties when Bette becomes engaged to her cousin's husband's brother, the maréchal. And finally, fathers and sons become rivals for the same woman: Wenceslas and his father-in-law both become Valérie's lovers. As Bette says to Wenceslas: "Songez donc que vous seriez le rival de votre beau-père" (p.258) ("You should think about the fact that you would be your father-in-law's rival").

Although it would seem that Bette and Valérie try to destroy the family structure by corrupting normal family ties, by seducing the father so that he no longer lives with his wife, and by making the sons and fathers rivals for the same woman, in reality, by making the father and sons rivals, they merely repeat, and in a sense reinforce, the most primal family triangle: the Oedipus complex. In trying to destroy the family, they reinforce its most basic structure, and these Oedipal relations proliferate to an incredible extent. One's lover becomes one's cousin, first for Bette when Wenceslas marries her cousin Hortense, and then metaphorically when Valérie calls her lover, Henri, her cousin (p. 210). Bette and Valérie, called sisters, form a convoluted family structure in their odd marriage of male and female, ugliness and beauty: "Lisbeth et Valérie offraient le touchant spectacle d'une de ces amitiés si vives et si peu probables entre femmes, que les Parisiens, toujours trop spirituels, les calomnient aussitôt. Le contraste de la mâle et sèche nature de la Lorraine avec la jolie nature créole de Valérie servit la calomnie" (p. 195) ("Lisbeth and Valérie presented the touching spectacle of one of those friendships which, so strong and so improbable between women, cause Parisians, always too bitingly witty, to cast aspersions right away. The contrast between the hard, male nature of the Lorraine woman and the lovely Creole nature of Valérie gave weight to the aspersions"). As sisters/lovers, they again promulgate the incestuous family structures they try to destroy.

The other Oedipal role that both Valérie and Bette play is that of the mother who becomes a lover. Bette, who is really in love with Wenceslas, thinks of him as her son: "Je vous prends pour mon enfant" (p. 112) ("I take you as my child"). And Valérie, who is Wenceslas's mistress, pretends to love him as a son: "Je l'aime au grand jour comme si c'était mon enfant" (p. 400) ("I love him openly as if he were my child"). The parallel Oedipal relation also exists: the father's mistress is considered to be a daughter, as Crevel says of Joséphine: "Je voulais être à la fois son père, son bienfaiteur, et, lâchons le mot, son amant" (p. 63) ("I wanted to be, all at once, her father, her benefactor, and—let us speak plainly—her lover").

Relationships become even more complicated and, in fact, undecidable, since Valérie's baby has four possible fathers: Wenceslas, Henri, Crevel, and Hulot. These fathers resemble Freud's primal horde of brothers fighting for the woman, as Crevel says of Hulot and himself: "Nous sommes devenus comme deux frères. . . . Entre deux vieux papas, amis comme . . . comme nous l'étions, comment voulez-vous que nous n'ayons pas pensé à marier nos enfants? Trois mois après le mariage . . . l'infâme m'a soufflé ma petite Josépha" (p.65) ("We became like two brothers. . . . Between two old papas, between such friends as . . . as we were, how could we not have thought of marrying our children? Three months after the marriage . . . that scoundrel stole my little Josépha").

The Oedipal drama culminates in the murder of rivals and family members. A husband inadvertently kills his wife, who has been playing the role of his mother, when Adeline dies after learning of Hulot's ultimate infidelity. A man (the maréchal) tells his brother (Hulot) to commit suicide, which in the rhetoric of the text is like the father telling the son to kill himself. But ultimately this son/brother (Hulot) kills the father (the maréchal) because of the son's outrageous and dishonorable dealings in Africa.

In the end, the Oedipal family situation prevails, even flourishes, and the war between possessor and possessed wages on when the protagonists cannot escape from the family machine. The prisonhouse of family in this novel thus represents the prisonhouse of possession: one must either desire to have the phallus, which embodies power and being, or be reduced to nothingness.

Gender as defined in this text ultimately serves to strengthen certain institutional economic family structures because it plays a necessary part in the family economy. Being male here means being the one who possesses the "genderizer," the phallus, in the family. But if one were to ask the question of gender a bit differently by asking not what gender is but what woman is, the answer would be surprising. On the one hand, Bette and Valérie, relinquishing their identities as women by attempting to become men, end up with no identity. They do not represent "woman"; as Irigaray would say, they are "closed in upon the jealous possession of its [the phallic maternal] valued product . . . rivaling man in his esteem for productive excess."[34] Adeline, on the other hand, as hyperbolic wife, assumes so many roles and effaces her own self so completely that she has no identity either. The text makes explicit that Adeline, as subservient wife, is not a woman, has killed all self-interest: "Adeline avait dépouillé tout intérêt de femme, la douleur éteignait jusqu'au souvenir (p.287) ("Adeline had shed all her womanly self-interest; grief extinguished even its memory").

If Frederic Jameson is right in saying that "in Balzac's imagination disparate characters come together as separate manifestations of a single united force,"[35] then by taking an overview of the text, one can see "woman" not as the individual identities of the women characters but as a conglomeration of their various images. Both multiple and absent in an aporia, woman has no single, complete identity—the number one being, as Irigaray has shown, privileged by phallocentrism.

Just as woman, viewed from this perspective, has no unity, the "female" novel, *La Cousine Bette,* itself is not complete: it is only one part of a two-novel set; it goes hand in hand with its poor "male" cousin, *Le Cousin Pons* (or, as Balzac calls it, displacing the maleness of the title, Bette's "twin sister"). Neither "male" nor "female" novel is complete in itself; each must find its identity in an exchange of intertextual meaning. The male text (in which Pons is "married" to a man, his friend Schmucke), no more complete than the female *La Cousine Bette,* does not possess the necessary phallic unity either. If *La Cousine Bette* upholds phallic family order in its content, it undermines this order in its structural incompleteness, in its "feminization" by its twin, Pons.

This feminine incompleteness of art is made explicit in *Le Cousin Pons* when, at the end, Pons's art collection is called the novel's "heroine." Like the group of women in Bette who have multiple and empty identities, the art collection is "more than one" but never complete (more works can always be added). The collection, the relation of art works to one another, also perhaps reflects the group relation between the two novels, or even between group members of the family.

This relation between family members in *La Cousine Bette* is, as we have seen, based on possession (of the phallus). Likewise, the worth of the art collection in *Le Cousin Pons* is based on its market value; like the family women in *La Cousine Bette,* art is a commodity, a possession. The "consumable" family woman is linked to the work of art in the following striking simile in which the woman is a novel to be read and then discarded: "Le baron Hulot monta dans la voiture, en abandonnant Mlle Élodie sans lui dire adieu, comme on jette un roman lu" (p. 392) ("Baron Hulot climbed into the vehicle, abandoning Mademoiselle Elodie without saying good-bye to her, just as one discards a novel one has read"). Yet in *Le Cousin Pons,* the worth of art is not merely economic: it has, at the same time, an intrinsic, nonexchangeable value, because Pons cherishes his art works for their own sake, not just for their market value.

Could woman, too, have a value other than that assigned by the system of possessions? The possibility of woman as valued discourse in and of itself, as the inherent value of the novel or of the work of art, does not exist in *La Cousine Bette,* but appears only as a phantom, metaphoric possibility in the art collection/heroine of *Le Cousin Pons.* It is in the earlier novel, *Eugénie Grandet* (set significantly in the provinces, where the anonymous paper money was more suspect than in the city, and where gold was of value in and of itself),[36] that this woman becomes the subject of the novel and that family relations not based on possessions are possible.[37]

In the opening pages of *Eugénie Grandet,* the heroine seems unlikely to suggest an escape from this destructive familial economy and gender identity. Rather, she incarnates the submissiveness of Adeline in *La Cousine Bette* and the impuissance of the anonymous groups of women in *Le Rouge et le noir.* In this text, a typical Balzacian opening describes the characters' environment, centering on Eugénie's house as a symbol of her shadowy, self-effacing nature: "pâle, froide, silencieuse, située en haut de la ville, et abritée par les ruines des remparts" ("pale in color, cold, silent, located in the upper part of the town, and sheltered by the ruins of the ramparts").[38] This silence echoes the silent gaze of the women in *Le Rouge et le noir,* echoes Adeline's voiceless being, and symbolizes the silence of the women who live in the house: "[Nanon] pouvait entendre le moindre bruit par le silence profond qui régnait nuit et jour dans la maison" (p. 1044) ("[Nanon] could hear the slightest noise in the profound silence that reigned night and day in the house").

In this sepulchral home, an inane, mechanical routine makes up the day-to-day existence of Eugénie, an "ignorante fille sans cesse occupée à rapetasser des bas, à ravauder la garde-robe de son père, et dont la vie s'était écoulée sous ces crasseux lambris sans voir dans cette rue silencieuse plus d'un passant par heure" (p. 1058) ("uneducated girl ceaselessly occupied in patching up stockings, in mending her father's clothes, and whose life passed by under that dirty ceiling without seeing in her silent street more than one passerby an hour"). She is a perfect example of Monsieur de Rênal's machine woman because, for fifteen years, the lives of Eugénie and her mother consist of a robotlike coming and going from one workplace to another: "Depuis quinze ans, toutes les journées de la mère et de la fille s'étaient paisiblement écoulées à cette place, dans un travail constant, à compter du mois d'avril jusqu'au mois de novembre. Le premier de ce dernier mois elles pouvaient prendre leur station d'hiver à la cheminée" (p. 1041) ("For fifteen years, all the days of the mother and daughter had passed by peacefully in this place, occupied by constant work, from the month of April to the month of November. On the first of the latter month they could take up their winter station by the fire-place").[39] As Naomi Schor has shown, mother and daughter almost never leave their prisonhouse, which composes the entirety of their existence: "cette froide et obscure maison, qui pour elle composait tout l'univers" (p. 1176) ("this cold and gloomy house which constituted her whole universe").[40] Their chairs, placed either by the window or by the hearth, define their place in the world (p. 1107). A dog left in the kitchen attacks not only strangers attempting to enter but also the family attempting to get out. In contrast, in Balzac's universe, the male child of a provincial family—a Rastignac or a Lucien—often leaves the house and its limited world and makes his way to Paris. Thus, literally imprisoned in their house as Bette is symbolically imprisoned in the family system of posses-sion, mother and daughter in *Eugénie Grandet* are confined by the meta-phorical identity they must assume there; doing a "labeur d'ouvrière" (p. 1041) ("workwoman's toil"), they are but automatons, unpaid laborers ceaselessly repairing the master's clothes.

As the house rests in the shadows of the ruined ramparts, Eugénie's identity remains vague for the first thirty pages of the book; we see her only as she carries out her routine or as she receives her suitor's gifts. We never enter her thoughts or see what she looks like, and in fact, we do not even learn her name until the tenth page, even though a long and detailed description is given of her father, Félix Grandet.

This importance given to Grandet in the beginning of the text is certainly not gratuitous, for he, called "le père Grandet" (p. 1030) ("old man Grandet [literally 'father']") by several people in the town, represents the father, in an allegorical or Lacanian sense. Since his relation to Eugénie dominates this text, it is this relation which I will study in depth (as opposed to the mother-daughter bond analyzed by Schor[41]). Grandet is the law in the house, for he controls everything, above all the material possessions of the family. He alone passes out the necessities of life to his women, according to specified rules: "Ce jour-là (le premier novembre) seulement Grandet permettait qu'on allumât du feu dans la salle. . . . Depuis longtemps l'avare distribuait la chandelle à sa fille et à la Grande Nanon, de même qu'il distribuait dès le matin le pain et les denrées nécessaires à la consommation journalière" (p. 1041) ("It was only on that day [November first] that Grandet permitted a fire to be lighted in the main room. . . . For a long time the miser had doled out candles to his daughter and to Big Nanon, just as he doled out each morning whatever bread and money were necessary for that day's provisions"). One could not hope to find a more complete combination of the father, the law, and the possessor than that present in the character of Grandet.

Indeed, if in *La Cousine Bette,* possessing things means possessing the symbol of power, the phallus, in this text, Grandet epitomizes this possession in his avaricious hoarding of money. Grandet's unbounded desire for things colors his entire life, even his relation to his daughter, who, for him, represents his gold. He looks at her in the same way he looks at his money, with "un de ces regards de tigre affamé qu'il jetait sans doute à ses tas d'or" (p. 1084) ("one of those looks of a famished tiger that he doubtless cast upon his piles of gold"). In fact, she invites the metaphor in the sense that she, like gold and like her father's eyes, is yellow (p. 1066). In the house that represents her, her room faces the walled-off space where Grandet hides his fortune (p. 1070): she mirrors his money. And it would seem that Grandet relates to his daughter only because she, as his heiress, represents the future of his gold: "Cette figure annonçait une finesse dangereuse, une probité sans chaleur, l'égoïsme d'un homme habitué à concentrer ses sentiments dans la jouissance de l'avarice et sur le seul être qui lui fût réellement de quelque chose, sa fille Eugénie, sa seule héritière" (p. 1036) ("That face indicated a dangerous shrewdness, a probity without warmth, the egoism of a man accustomed to concentrating his emotions on the pleasures of avarice and on the only being who really meant something to him, his daughter, Eugénie, his only heiress"). (This is significantly the first time we encounter her name.) Eugénie *is* gold for her father, and the woman in this text is most definitely a commodity.

Grandet's relation to gold is often couched in terms of eating. Portrayed as a beast of prey in the images of a tiger and a boa, he stalks and devours money: "Grandet tenait du tigre et du boa: il savait se coucher, se blottir, envisager longtemps sa proie, sauter dessus; puis il ouvrait la gueule de sa bourse, y engloutissait une charge d'écus, et se couchait tranquillement, comme le serpent qui digère, impassible, froid, méthodique" (p. 1033) ("Grandet had a bit of the tiger and the boa in him: he knew to lie low, crouch, eye his prey for a long time, leap on it; then he would open the mouth of his purse, swallow a provision of coins, and lie down peacefully, like the serpent digesting, impassive, cold, methodical"). He reminds one of Balzac's other famous miser, Gobseck, who keeps both his treasures and his food locked in his secret rooms. The miserly Grandet thus incarnates a wild economic consumption and echoes the image in *La Cousine Bette* of Hulot, who reads and consumes a woman/book.

Of course, the devouring of money, in more general terms, symbolizes Grandet's unbounded avarice. He spends money only on absolute necessities or on lucrative financial ventures. This economization spreads to his entire style of living, for he never spends anything, be it money, energy, or movement: "Il n'allait jamais chez personne, ne voulait ni recevoir ni donner à dîner; il ne faisait jamais de bruit, et semblait économiser tout, même le mouvement" (p. 1035) ("He never visited anyone, wanted neither to accept nor to give invitations to dinner; he never made any noise, and seemed to economize everything, even his movement"). The most significant economization, however, takes place in his speech. For him, speaking is spending, and by making his financial opponents speak while he remains silent, Grandet forces them to relinquish their money: "[Il] avait appris l'art d'impatienter son adversaire commercial; et, en l'occupant à exprimer sa pensée, de lui faire constamment perdre de vue la sienne" (p. 1111) ("[He] had learned the art of making his commercial adversary lose patience; and, by making his adversary express Grandet's thoughts for him, he made his adversary constantly lose sight of his own"). If speaking means spending, then linguistic signifiers appropriately represent the universal signifier, money.

Grandet's deliberate stutter prevents him from "spending" his language too quickly and lets him possess his words for a short while longer: "Mon . . . on . . . on . . . on . . . sieur le pré . . . pré . . . pré . . . président, vououous di . . . di . . . di . . . disiiieeez que la faaaaiiillite . . ." (p. 1110) ("Ju . . . j . . . j . . . j . . . judge, Si . . . si . . . si . . . sir, youuouou we . . . we . . . we . . . were saying that the baaaannkruptcy . . ."). His wily use of stuttering reduces discourse to virtual emptiness of meaning, to a vehicle for making more money, for multiplying empty signifiers. In particular, he repeats one expression, "ta ta ta ta," many times, an expression meaning nothing in itself but functioning as a conversational filler which prevents him from "spending" more words. This trivial expression, however, will be very important in the evolution of Charles's function in the text.

In one instance, when Grandet actually caresses his gold, it becomes a fetish, which he enjoys touching and seeing: "Là, sans doute, . . . venait le vieux tonnelier choyer, caresser, couver, cuver, cercler son or" (p. 1070), "il demeurait des heures entières les yeux attachés sur les louis" (p. 1175) ("It was there, doubtless, . . . that the old cooper came to cuddle his gold, caress it, care for it, content himself with it, and cache it in casks . . . he stayed for hours on end, his eyes fixed on his coins").[42] For Freud, the cherishing of a fetish in part protects against the possibility of castration; for Grandet the possession of the gold/phallus doubly assures him of his paternal power.

The signifier, as fetish, becomes the object of desire and sheds its function as an element in a process of signification; it becomes a signified, in a sense. Money is no longer the means to possession but the object and representation of possession, itself a commodity (Grandet makes a great deal of money by selling his gold [pp. 1120–22]). Gold and the phallus, instead of being only signifiers, are elevated to the status of the ultimate signified, the object of desire. This is, as we recall, Lacan's understanding of what happens in the process of the differentiation between the sexes: the phallus, as signifier of universal difference, becomes concretized in the penis. The phallus turns into a thing that one does or does not have; it becomes, in a sense, reified as anatomical difference (and gold) and becomes, as for Grandet, a fetish circularly guaranteeing his own possession of it.

In an amazing way, Grandet's fetishization of money links up with a network of logocentric values. First, according to Balzac, Grandet is like all misers, who "ne croient point à une vie à venir, le présent est tout pour eux" (p. 1101) ("do not believe in an afterlife; the present is everything for them").[43] Grandet's privileging of the present makes sense, in Derrida's terms, for he also privileges the possession and presence of an object (money). Signifiers are normally once removed from the present moment because they refer to something else, but for Grandet, the signifier no longer signifies anything but itself. If phonocentrism relates to presence in the history of meaning,[44] then it is significant that Grandet never writes: "Il . . . n'écrivait point" (p. 1035) ("He . . . wrote not a bit"). Grandet seems to combine the concepts of possession, presence, the present, and the act of speaking in his paternal role as possessor.

We can now understand the image of Eugénie that appears at the beginning of this text as a faceless, soulless thing possessed by Grandet, as the object (literally) of the desire of the eligible bachelors in town: "Ce combat secret entre les Cruchot et les des Grassins, dont le prix était la main d'Eugénie Grandet, occupait passionnément les diverses sociétés de Saumur" (p. 1037). "La meute poursuivait toujours Eugénie et ses millions" (p. 1180) ("This secret struggle between the Cruchots and the des Grassins, of which the prize was Eugénie Grandet's hand in marriage, passionately occupied the attention of the various groups of Saumur society. . . . The pack of hounds continued to pursue Eugénie and her millions"). The woman is but a commodity to be exchanged in an economic deal: Eugénie has no identity or presence herself.

Like the family women in *La Cousine Bette,* Eugénie can be gold, can be the phallus, but she cannot herself possess the gold that symbolizes the father, power, and the phallus. Again, this situation echoes in the Civil Code: "Le père seul, durant le mariage, administre des biens personnels de ses enfants mineurs" (Art. 389) ("The father [alone] is, during marriage, administrator of the personal effects of his children being minors"). Even if it seems that Eugénie does have money because her father gives her valuable coins, he never really gives them to her: he always considers the money his. When he asks Eugénie to return the coins he had given her and finds that she gave them to Charles, he says: "Ce méchant mirliflor m'aurait dévalisé" (p. 1155) ("To think that that wicked, young fop has robbed me"). Charles has robbed *him,* not his daughter. Eugénie cannot possess the phallus as defined by Grandet, she is merely another coin box in which he can safely store his signified: "N'était-ce pas mettre son argent d'une caisse dans une autre?" (p. 1045) ("Was it not transferring his money from one strongbox to another?").

The Grandet women resemble the family women in *La Cousine Bette* in other ways. Eugénie obeys her father and lives in constant fear of him: "Elle eut dans le coeur de la terreur à l'aspect de son père, vit en lui le maître de son sort" (p. 1077) ("She felt in her heart terror at the sight of her father, saw in him the master of her fate"). He represents law and authority; he has the power to say no to all of her feeble desires, as when she gives voice to her desire to marry Charles and her father's response incarnates Lacan's "nom-du-père" ("name-of-the-father," which in French also gives rise to the word play between *nom* [*name*] and *non* [no], thus linking the name-of-the-father with a certain negativity: with death, the dead father, and the limitations of the law concerning desire):

"—J'aimerais mieux, voyez vooous, je . . . jeter ma fi . . . fi fille dans la Loire que de la dooonner à son cououousin: vous pou . . .

pou . . . ouvez aaannoncer ça." . . . ¶ Cette réponse causa des éblouissements à Eugénie. Les lointaines espérances qui pour elle commençaient à poindre dans son coeur fleurirent soudain, se réalisèrent et formèrent un faisceau de fleurs qu'elle vit coupées et gisant à terre (p. 1082). / *"I would prefer, youou see, to . . . to throw my dau . . . dau . . . daughter in the Loire than to giiiive her to her cououousin: you ca . . . ca . . . an prrroclaim that." . . . ¶ This answer made Eugénie dizzy. Those vague hopes, which for her were beginning to sprout in her heart, suddenly flowered, grew real, and formed a bunch of flowers which she saw cut down, lying on the ground.*

The image of castration seen in the cut flowers of her desire is particularly apt here.

Eugénie's mother presents a parallel but even more pathetic case than her daughter's. Like Eugénie she is the color of gold (p. 1152). Having no identity of her own, dispossessed of the fortune she gave Grandet, she assumes her role completely, like Adeline Fisher. She never acquires anything herself but always gives her things away: "Quoique ridicule en apparence, cette femme qui, par sa dot et ses successions, avait apporté au père Grandet plus de trois cent mille francs, s'était toujours sentie si profondément humiliée d'une dépendance et d'un ilotisme contre lequel la douceur de son âme lui interdisait de se révolter, qu'elle n'avait jamais demandé un sou" (p. 1046) ("Although ridiculous in appearance, this woman [who, by her dowry and her estate, had brought to old Grandet more than three-hundred thousand francs] had always felt so profoundly humiliated by her dependency on him and by her slavery, against which the meekness of her soul forbade her to revolt, that she had never asked for a cent"). She and Adeline Fisher could be twins: "Elle dormait, mangeait, buvait, marchait suivant les désirs de son mari" (p. 1134) ("She slept, ate, drank, walked according to her husband's desires"); she lives under an "entière servitude conjugale" (p. 1045) ("complete conjugal servitude"). The excessive wealth and avarice of Grandet, his extreme power as possessor, is counterbalanced by the servitude and suppression of his wife, totally dispossessed, powerless (lacking the phallus), and servile.

What is the difference between man and woman, then, at the beginning of this text? As in *La Cousine Bette,* possessions form the dividing line between them: only men can possess money and the phallus. In this text also, the exclusion of women from the economy becomes the exclusion of women from language; in one case, they cannot talk about money and must leave the room: "Madame Grandet, ce que nous avons à dire serait du latin pour vous, il est sept heures et demie, vous devriez aller vous serrer dans votre portefeuille. Bonne nuit, ma fille" (p. 1110) ("Madame Grandet, what we have to say to each other would be Greek to you; it is seven-thirty, you should go tuck yourself in your bed [literally, 'your wallet']. Good night, daughter"). Women are prohibited access to the power-giving signifier/phallus.

Women thus excluded from the economy of signifiers do not form fetishistic attachments to possessions but form a different relation to them, a relation that can be seen in a conversation between Eugénie and her father:

> "—Cela est clair: les peupliers ne doivent se planter que sur les terres maigres," dit Cruchot stupéfait par les calculs de Grandet. ¶ —0-u-i, monsieur," répondit ironiquement le tonnelier. ¶ Eugénie . . . regardait le sublime paysage de la Loire sans écouter les calculs de son père. (p. 1081) / *That is clear: poplars should be planted only on poor soil," said Cruchot, stupefied by the calculations made by Grandet.* ¶ *"Y-e-s, sir," the cooper answered ironically.* ¶ *Eugénie . . . was looking at the sublime Loire landscape, not listening to her father's calculations.*

Here Eugénie, barred from the economic discourse, ignores calculation and appreciates the natural beauty of the scenery, while her father speculates on that very nature. One gender values the object itself, whereas the other calculates by seeing only money in that object.

Furthermore, the gold that Grandet places in Eugénie's care differs from the gold he uses. On each of her birthdays, he gives her coins so beautiful that they are called pieces of art. These gold signifiers do not take their meaning simply from their potential substitutive value, but in and of themselves have meaning and beauty. Eugénie bears a different relation to possessions, which are themselves valued.[45] This relation could suggest a different relation to language, which would no longer be a transparent vehicle of representation (of wealth, power, and phallus) but becomes instead an opaque, valued, beautiful object in itself. Charles's relation to money appears to be parallel Eugénie's: the Parisian dandy, who contrasts so sharply with the provincials at the Grandet house, also enjoys the beauty of objects: "Charles emporta donc le plus joli costume de chasse, le plus joli fusil, le plus joli couteau, la plus jolie gaine de Paris"

(p. 1056) ("Charles thus took with him the loveliest hunting outfit, the loveliest gun, the loveliest knife, the loveliest sheath of Paris").[46]

The most telling instance of Eugénie's different relation to possessions can be seen in the way she disposes of "her" fortune. Grandet does business only with men, clearly excluding women from the marketplace, and in his dealings, he always finds the same privileged signified: gold and his own power. Eugénie, however, by giving the coins to Charles and receiving a golden box in return, bases her system on the exchange and circulation of differing signifiers between different subjects and sexes. In her, Irigaray's dream comes true: women normally unable to partake in the male "homosexual" economy in which "men make commerce *of* [women], but they do not enter into any exchanges *with* them,"[47] here cease to be mere possessions, mere commodities, and enter into transactions themselves. This exchange-based relation between Charles and Eugénie, not dominated by one proper and overpowering symbol, points perhaps to an economy that changes from the phallocentric one of Eugénie's father, in which all signifiers magnetically cling to the ultimate signified, money, to an economy in which signifiers circulate in exchange.

Not only do Eugénie and Charles enter into a different economic relation, they also seem to have a different gender identity. The exchange of coins and box between Eugénie and Charles represents a chiasmic exchange between traditional genders: Eugénie at first gives a home to Grandet's symbol of paternal phallic power, his gold; Charles possesses a box (a feminine image), which he got from his mother. Thus it is not, as Paul Perron and Roland Le Huenen see it, simply that Eugénie gives Charles his masculine identity, and vice versa; the text complicates this a bit more in the initial androgynous symbolism.[48] This reversal of normal gender identities reflects a deep-seated gender aporia in the text, for not only does Charles partake of a more "feminine" economy, he is like a woman: "Le dandy se laissa aller sur le fauteuil comme une jolie femme qui se pose sur son divan" (p. 1087) ("The dandy let himself down in the chair as would a pretty woman settling on her divan"); he is "mignon comme une femme" (p. 1071) ("delicate like a woman"), "moutonné comme une fille" (p. 1146) ("curly-haired like a girl"), similar to a "fille[s] à marier" (p. 1078) ("a daughter to be married"), has movements like "une petite-maîtresse" (p. 1088) ("an affected, stylish coquette"). He is another of those ambiguous nineteenth-century characters, neither totally male nor totally female.

Charles resembles women in ways other than the physical. The death of his father and the phallic power loss represented by his father's bank-ruptcy put him on an equal footing with the women. He becomes silent like them "il s'y tint muet" (p. 1109) ("he remained there in silence"), and he spends his time with the women in their prisonhouse: "Charles de-meurait entre la mère et la fille, éprouvant des délices inconnues à leur prêter les mains pour dévider du fil" (p. 1136) ("Charles stayed with the mother and the daughter, feeling unknown delights in letting them use his hands to wind yarn"). Just as Charles represents a feminine position in the text, Eugénie represents a masculine one. When she first sees Charles, her pleasure is like that a man takes in seeing a woman: "La vue de son cousin fit sourdre en son coeur les émotions de fine volupté que causent à un jeune homme les fantastiques figures de femmes dessinées par Westall" (pp. 1058–59) ("The sight of her cousin caused to well up in her heart those delicately pleasurable emotions that the fantastic figures of women drawn by Westall evoke in a young man").

Thus the feminine Charles and the masculine Eugénie enter into a relation that undermines a rigid genderized economy by exchanging gender properties and economic property. In their exchange of gifts, they reject Grandet's economic system and undermine the gender definitions of man and woman as having or not having the phallus. Symbolically, Eugénie gives away the gold, gives up her father's phallic power, in a sense, and rejects his fetishistic attachment to it. Likewise Charles gives up the signifier of his mother, her picture and box. Hence Eugénie's love for Charles does not seem to be merely, as Naomi Schor has described, a narcissistic love for melancholy, but a love for a man who would share her different gender identity and economy. Early in the novel, Charles does not represent melancholy but rather a momentary escape from it and from the system that produces it: "Elle saisissait sa félicité comme un nageur saisit la branche de saule pour se tirer du fleuve et se reposer sur la rive" (p. 1136) ("She latched on to her happiness as a swimmer latches on to a willow branch to draw himself out of the river and rest on the bank").

The introduction of the difference of Charles into Eugénie's life causes radical, even revolutionary, changes. His arrival falls on a very special night, Eugénie's birthday, and on this night "pour la première fois, il fut question du mariage d'Eugénie" (p. 1047) ("for the first time, the question of Eugénie's marriage arose"). The birthday is significant because it represents her birth to a new life, but even more significantly it represents her birth to life itself: before Charles's arrival, she was more dead than alive. She begins, in effect, "une vie nouvelle" (p. 1077) ("a new life") and becomes a woman (p. 1096). In her story, like that of Sleeping Beauty, the desire for a man wakes her from a dulled, sleeplike existence, an awakening generated by seeing: "Le seul aspect de son cousin avait éveillé chez elle les penchants naturels de la femme" (p. 1077) ("The mere sight of her cousin had awakened in her the natural inclinations of a woman").[49] Here what she sees is not that woman does not have the phallus (the scene that gives rise to the Freudian differentiation between the sexes) but that the "feminine" Charles does not possess the phallus either: he, too, is feminine.

It is as if the artificial economic polarization of the sexes exemplified in Grandet's system is so exaggerated and false that it can give rise neither to differentiation nor to desire. Before Charles arrives on the scene, Eugénie does not desire, is not yet a person. Only after she sees Charles, who, because he is both man and woman, has sexual difference in himself as she does, can Eugénie awaken. Real difference, not an artificial polarized construct, engenders desire, and when one thinks of Freud's question "What does woman want?" as we see here, it does not seem to be a fetishized phallus.

In one of the more comical and touching scenes in the text, another "masculine" woman, Nanon, accepts a dressing gown from the feminine Charles, thus also awakening to new desires: " 'J'aurais cette robe d'or? . . .' disait Nanon, qui s'endormit habillée de son devant d'autel, rêvant de fleurs, de tabis, de damas, pour la première fois de sa vie, comme Eugénie rêva d'amour" (p. 1073) (" 'Will I really get that golden robe? . . .'' said Nanon, who fell asleep dressed in her altar-frontal, dreaming of flowers, of rich silk, of damask for the first time in her life, as Eugénie dreamed of love"). Charles fulfills the desire even of Madame Grandet when he gives her a gold thimble before he leaves: "—Ma tante, voici le dé de ma mère, . . . dit Charles en présentant un joli dé d'or à Mme Grandet qui depuis dix ans en désirait un" (p. 1137) (" 'Aunt, here is my mother's thimble,' . . . said Charles, presenting a pretty golden thimble to Madame Grandet, who, for the past ten years, had wanted one").

Significantly, when Eugénie sees Charles, she finally sees herself; she looks into the mirror now, as if her recognition of the other instigated her recognition of herself and her first attempt at self-evaluation: "Elle se leva brusquement, se mit devant son miroir, et s'y regarda comme un auteur de bonne foi contemple son oeuvre pour se critiquer, et se dire des injures à lui-même" (p. 1075) ("She got up abruptly, stood in front of her mirror, and looked at herself in it, as an author in good faith contemplates his work to criticize and insult himself"). Now that she has desires, she has a body; we are finally given a description of her only after her meeting with Charles (pp. 1073–76). Now we enter her thoughts for the first time (pp. 1058–59); she is no longer a faceless, soulless thing to be acquired in marriage.

Charles's arrival also causes an upheaval in the family circle, as symbolized in the following quotation: "Au moment où Mme Grandet gagnait un lot de seize sous, le plus considérable qui eût jamais été ponté dans cette salle, et que la grande Nanon riait d'aise en voyant madame empochant cette riche somme, un coup de marteau retentit à la porte de la maison, et y fit un si grand tapage que les femmes sautèrent sur leurs chaises" (p. 1053) ("At the moment when Madame Grandet was winning a pot of sixteen sous, the largest that had ever been bet in that room, and as Big Nanon was laughing with pleasure to see her mistress pocketing that rich sum of money, the knocker sounded at the door of the house and made such a din that the women started in their chairs"). Charles jars the women in their places, prefiguring the changes that are about to take place in their identities and roles. Also, at the moment of his arrival, Madame Grandet's financial status changes, even though it is a small change. His arrival corresponds to a reversal of the former system of patriarchal possession, as she, by winning at their little social game, finally acquires some money of her own (only, of course, to give it to Grandet later).

Now Eugénie's physical position in the house changes. She prefers to look out of her window at the garden: "Eugénie se croisa bonnement les bras, s'assit à sa fenêtre, contempla la cour, le jardin étroit et les hautes terrasses qui le dominaient" (p. 1074) ("Eugénie simply crossed her arms, sat by the window, contemplated the courtyard, the narrow garden, and the high terraced walls that towered above it"). The garden becomes the symbol of her love and of a new freedom, for she meets Charles there, outside of the house that was her prison (p. 1075).

Eugénie's machinelike routine also changes. Having been like a robot, accomplishing tasks without thinking, she now rejects her slavish existence, at one point symbolically throwing down the sewing that represents her unpaid labor in the house so she can indulge in her affection for

Charles (p. 1085). Her attitude toward her prisonhouse has changed entirely: "Le lendemain du départ de Charles, la maison Grandet reprit sa physionomie pour tout le monde, excepté pour Eugénie qui la trouva tout à coup bien vide" (p. 1146) ("The day after Charles's departure, the Grandet house adopted its former aspect again for everyone, except for Eugénie, who suddenly found it very empty"). She develops a desire to leave the house, to escape its confines, even to escape the garden: "Elle pleurait souvent en se promenant dans ce jardin, maintenant trop étroit pour elle, ainsi que la cour, la maison, la ville: elle s'élançait par avance sur la vaste étendue des mers" (p. 1140) ("She often wept while walking in this garden, now too cramped for her, as were the yard, the house, the town; she struck out, in her imagination, onto the vast expanse of the seas"). But all she can do, until Charles returns, is to look longingly at the sky (p. 1147).

Her acquaintance with Charles makes her look at and criticize her father for the first time. Eugénie even defies his tyranny openly when, after Grandet has told Charles to use milk instead of the more expensive sugar, she silently insists that sugar be used (p. 1091). Furthermore, the three women in the house band together in their defiance of Grandet and begin to keep secrets from him: "A l'insu de son père, elle voulut que la chambre de Charles restât dans l'état où il l'avait laissée. Madame Grandet et Nanon furent volontiers complices de ce *statu quo*" (p. 1146) ("Without her father's knowledge, she wanted Charles's room kept in the same state in which he left it. Madame Grandet and Nanon were willing accomplices to this status quo"). A bond forms between them based on their mutual interest in Charles: "Cette vie domestique, jadis si monotone, s'était animée par l'immense intérêt du secret qui liait plus intimement ces trois femmes" (p. 1148) ("This domestic life, before so monotonous, had been enlivened by the immense importance of the secret which tied these three women together more intimately").

But this revolt destroys Madame Grandet, whose unique identity was to be Grandet's slave. In the very scene in which Eugénie confesses the loss of her gold to her father, her mother has an attack that will lead to her death. Madame Grandet must die when her identity as a slave is questioned by her daughter's revolt.

When Grandet discovers that Eugénie has given away his gold, he tries to bulwark the system by actually imprisoning his daughter: she must now stay in her room and eat only bread and water. Since her whole life had been spent in the prison of the Grandet house, this increased repression of her movement returns her to her former state and reinstates woman's identity as servant/slave.

Eugénie's father does win, for the new relation set up between Eugénie and Charles does not work. Charles leaves and uses Eugénie's money to make more money; he wants to become rich. Planning later to marry for money and not for love, he rejects Eugénie. Dealing in slaves literally, as Eugénie's father did figuratively (Grandet "owns" Eugénie and her mother), Charles becomes a "man" in Grandet's sense of the word: "Il ne soupirait plus, il s'était fait homme" (pp. 1138–39). "D'enfant que j'étais au départ, je suis devenu homme au retour (p. 1186) ("He no longer sighed; he had turned himself into a man." "If I was a child at my departure, I have become a man at my return"). Charles's becoming a man means his assumption of the phallocentric system of Grandet and rejection of the more ambiguous side of his identity; he turns from aporia to the second moment of the double trajectory.

Indeed, Charles grows to resemble Grandet more and more. He begins to sing a nonsensical little song strangely similar to Grandet's "ta ta ta ta" when he signs the "dear John" letter to Eugénie: " 'Tan, ta, ta. —Tan, ta, ti. —Tinn, ta, ta —Toûn! —Toûn, ta, ti. —Tinn, ta, ta, . . .' etc., avait chanté Charles Grandet" (p. 1188) (" 'Tan, ta, ta. Tan, ta, tee. Tin, ta, ta. Toon! Toon, ta, ti. Tin, ta, ta, . . .' etc., had sung Charles Grandet"). He now takes the same pleasure in the signifier/phallus as Grandet. This possible outcome apparently was in Charles's personality from the beginning, and it took only Eugénie's gift to set him on this road: "Les germes de l'économie politique à l'usage du Parisien, latents en son coeur, ne devaient pas tarder à fleurir" (p. 1126) ("The seeds of the political economy employed by the Parisian, dormant in his heart, would not be long in flowering").

In Charles's absence, Eugénie slowly becomes ensnared by her father's system, and he eventually trusts her so much that he leaves his affairs in her hands (p. 1173). She too begins to repeat a favorite expression of Grandet's: "*Nous verrons cela*" (p. 1192) ("*We'll see about that*"). She even tries to make herself look like him: "Elle prit le parti d'affecter à l'avenir l'impassible contenance qu'avait su prendre son père" (p. 1191) ("She decided to assume in the future that same impassive demeanor that her father knew how to don"). Thus the law of her father can remain intact even after his death, for Eugénie has "become" her father: "Malgré ses huit cent mille livres de rente, elle vit comme avait vécu la pauvre Eugénie Grandet, n'allume le feu de sa chambre qu'aux jours où jadis son père lui permettait d'allumer le foyer de la salle, et l'éteint conformément au programme en vigueur dans ses jeunes années" (p. 1198) ("Despite her eight hundred thousand francs in income, she lives as did the poor Eugénie Grandet, lights the fire in her room only on those days when her father permitted the fire to be lit in the hearth of the main room, and extinguishes it in conformity with the schedule in force during her younger years"). She seems to be a kind of blind Bette, who, by inheriting her father's money, inherits the phallic system with it and becomes a man.

Yet despite her inheritance of Grandet's fortune and ideology, she keeps the grain of a revolt. When she marries, she does not give herself completely to her husband because she refuses to have sexual relations with him. By partaking in marriage only as society defines it in this novel (as the exchange of women and money), she succumbs to the law, all the while showing marriage for what it is in her world: the exchange of commodities. Curiously, by her decision, her husband becomes her slave: " 'Je serai votre esclave!' lui dit-il" (p. 1194) (" 'I will be your slave!' he said to her"). In pointing out the laws that govern the exchange of women, she has shown that the "master" is in fact another slave of this economic family system.

She abides by this system in a way that points out its hidden rules but cannot escape from them. Residing in a limbo, in an aporia between acceptance of the system and its deconstruction, in the end she does not, appropriately, live happily ever after, nor does she die. She merely continues to exist indefinitely in her limbo when the text's ending continues the same old story: "Il est question d'un nouveau mariage pour elle" (p. 1199) ("It is a question of another marriage for her").

✳

These three texts show three different ways in which institutions affect gender identity in the nineteenth-century French novel. Whether it be the gender/class associations of *Le Rouge et le noir,* the familial divisions of power in *La Cousine Bette,* or an economical assignation of gender in *Eugénie Grandet,* institutions heavily influence the definition of gender identity. Of course, the study of gender and institutions is not limited to the literary sphere: the effects of certain changes in various institutions on gender identity have been the subject of recent historical and social analyses. Elizabeth Janeway, for instance, has shown how the definition of a gender role can change because of a change in the politico-economic system; more specifically, the imperative that women be chaste originated as a response to a change in the rules of inheritance: "Chastity became important only when society began to worry about legitimate male descent. That concern appears to be linked to the ownership of individual property."[50] Only chastity of the woman could guarantee legitimate inheritance, hence the role and identity of woman was shaped by changes in the economic and political institution.

Janeway claims that gender identity and institutions work together to uphold certain structures: "Female sexuality, I think, has always been used by society as a sort of glue to hold structures together."[51] Clearly, Adeline's self-sacrifice counteracts her husband's wild spending and enables the family to survive; Eugénie's submission to and imprisonment by her father allow his economic/familial system to thrive; and Julien's adherence to the patriarchal order at the end of *Le Rouge et le noir* covers over the aporia of gender and class. In fact, in texts written by the major thinkers of the aristocracy of Restoration France (as well as in Goriot's thinking), the assignation of certain gender roles was believed to be tightly linked to the smooth functioning of the state's power. As Moses writes, "The subjugation of wives to husbands and the confinement of wives to the domestic sphere were deemed to be as necessary to the restoration of the primacy of royalty and church as Rousseau had earlier considered patriarchy necessary to the Republic."[52] When Jules Simon claimed in his 1860 text, *L'Ouvrière,* that "la femme devenue ouvrière n'est plus une femme" ("the woman who has become a laborer is no longer a woman"),[53] he expressed in these few words the intricate and complicated linking of gender roles and institutions.

The preceding analyses of these literary texts, however, show us that the reverse is also true. Problems of gender identity can have certain effects on the institutions in place: Julien's aporetic gender and class threaten traditional class and gender divisions; Bette's inversion of gender roles upends certain repressive familial and economic structures; and Eugénie's subversion of roles by her androgynous economy threatens her father's phallic power. Thus, even as changes in the institutions—be they social, economic, familial, or other—can transform prescribed gender roles; so the departure from the conventions of gender identity can threaten certain institutions and bring to light conflicts inherent in gender identity.

It is perhaps in the historical example of a young person who lived in nineteenth-century France that this institutional definition of gender and the problems posed by any disruption of gender identity become clearest. In the margins of what otherwise would be a standard birth certificate of a French female child in 1838, one finds the following bizarre and disturbing note:

> By the judgment of the civil court of Saint-Jean d'Angély dated 21 June 1860, it has been ordained that the record opposite should be rectified in this sense:
>
>   1) that the child registered here will be designated as being of the masculine sex;
>
>   2) and that the first name Abel shall be substituted for Adélaide Herculine.[54]

This laconic official document outlines the tragic circumstances of Herculine Barbin, a biological hermaphrodite who lived from 1838 to 1868 and who wrote an account of her strange experience of life. Having grown up as a girl, at age twenty-one she was deemed by societal institutions (the medical profession and the state) to be a man, after which she changed her name to Abel. Raised as a woman, trained to function in society as a woman, she had no place as a man, so she ended her life by suicide, destroyed by and destroying a gender identity that could never take hold.[55]

If Lacan claims, as we saw in the Introduction, that the newborn child is immediately inserted into the general discourse by the choice of a name, the newborn Herculine Barbin shows that the individual entering into this general discourse is situated there by gender as well as by name. Gender identity in society is an either/or proposition, and its structure is that of a dichotomous opposition.

In the nineteenth-century narratives this dichotomous, hierarchical opposition of genders sometimes malfunctions, as in the cases of Julien, Bette, and Eugénie and in the autobiographical narrative of Herculine Barbin. Barbin was, in fact, both male and female (although more male than female), both in her own perception of herself (she uses both grammatical genders to qualify herself) and in the perception of the doctors, who, although they call her a man, remain ambivalent in their reports. In her memoirs, she calls herself an exile because, being both sexes at once, she ends up with no gender identity and thus has no place in society's polarized system of categorization. She implies that her problematic gender has made her cross a certain limit that must not be crossed: "Il y a . . . une limite qu'il serait dangereux à l'homme de franchir. Ses facultés s'y opposent, son bonheur en dépend"⁵⁶ ("There is a limit beyond which it would be dangerous for a man to go. His mental powers do not allow it, his happiness depends on his stopping short," English version, p. 106). She lived in the margins of society's gender classifications, just as her masculine identity inhabits the margins of the official register. Male and female have become confused. The two polarized terms, no longer separated, reveal their dichotomous structures as well as their conventional, "discursive" nature, for in Herculine Barbin's case, gender shows itself to be a performative power of language, a decree or fiat which the state uses to assign and even to change gender. "Gender glue" no longer holds; male and female blur together to show that, in the symbolic cases of Julien, Bette, and Eugénie, and in the literal case of Herculine Barbin, the separation of the genders is linguistic and always inhabited by difference. What may be even more fearsome is that this linguistic nature of gender makes unmistakably clear that of institutions and of identity.

Of course, gender identity does not remain in this aporetic state in these early "realist" novels and thus displays the same double trajectory as Freud's texts. Even though they do show the aporia of gender in Julien's, Eugénie's, and Bette's identities, these texts also eliminate that aporia when the individuals who do not conform to the pattern prescribed by society either die or are forced to conform, and thus conventional gender classifications remain intact in the end.

This return of gender identity to convention appears in one image repeated in all of these texts: that of a machine, which relates somehow to the feminine position. There are the nail machine, the guillotine, and Rênal's "machine woman" in *Le Rouge et le noir;* the all-encompassing family "machine" in Bette's world; and finally Eugénie's machinelike routine. Is it any surprise, then, that Napoleon said that "les femmes ne sont en réalité que des machines à faire des enfants" ("women are really only machines for making babies")?⁵⁷ It is this mechanization of gender rhetoric and its relation to femininity that will be investigated in the next chapter on gender, rhetoric, and cliché.

TWO

Gender

AND RHETORIC:

BALZAC'S CLICHÉS

Un voyageur
anglais raconte l'intimité où il vivait avec un tigre; il l'avait élevé et le
caressait, mais toujours sur sa table tenait un pistolet armé. ¶ Julien ne
s'abandonnait à l'excès de son bonheur que dans les instants où Mathilde ne
pouvait en lire l'expression dans ses yeux. Il s'acquittait avec exactitude du
devoir de lui dire de temps à autre quelque mot dur.—STENDHAL, *Le
Rouge et le noir.* / *An English traveler tells of the intimacy in which he lived with a
tiger; he had raised it and would caress it, but he always kept a loaded pistol on his
table. ¶ Julien abandoned himself to the excess of his happiness only at those
moments when Mathilde could not read the expression in his eyes. He fulfilled with
exactitude the duty of saying something harsh to her from time to time.*

A S MIDDLE-CLASS women in the nineteenth century were increasingly relegated to the domestic sphere and as their role in society
was limited to reproduction, their perceived relationship to nature grew
stronger. As Bonnie Smith has shown, the women in the north of France
represented this stronger bond to nature in a certain domestic rhetoric:
"Women also expressed their closeness to the natural world in domestic
symbolism. They decorated their homes in floral motifs and repeated it in
their clothing. Anniversaries, weddings, birthdays as indicative of natural cycles were occasions—from the female perspective—for floral symbols of nature. They chose flowers for embroidery or as a pattern to
decorate cakes or refashion food. . . . A women's group in the Nord
selected the daisy as its emblem."[1] Although their relationship to nature

was ambivalent and complicated, natural images dominated their domestic rhetoric.

The goal of this chapter will be to follow "feminine" metaphors in Balzac's texts, that is, certain figures of discourse used to name and identify woman. I will often call these metaphors "clichés" because of their widespread predominance, and here the link between machines and rhetoric in the concept of the cliché is suggestive. As Margery Sabin explains, the word *cliché* originated in the beginning of the nineteenth century:

> The clatter of new typesetting machines had generated the onomatopoetic verb *clicher* for the copying process, and the noun *cliché* for the metal plate from which reproductions of print or design could be made in unending quantity. *Cliché* was a neutral technical term for this achievement of modern technology, like the English *stereotype* for the same device. Only towards the middle of the century did both English *stereotype* and French *cliché* begin to be transferred for purposes of derision to other kinds of (figuratively) mechanical moulds, especially of verbal expression. [2]

As we study the "mechanical molds" that are applied to women in several Balzac texts, we will see that, if women are linked to machines, as they were in the works studied in Chapter 1, women are also linked to rhetoric and to "mechanized" clichés, as in Freud's theory.

In analyzing rhetoric and femininity in the works of Balzac, we are avowedly examining the metaphors and images of an author generally considered to be misogynist and to promulgate certain Romantic clichés that describe woman as child, mother, muse, a sensitive and fragile creature (albeit with a disquieting underside in the Bettes and in the Valéries). Naomi Schor even claims, in an interesting correlate to Bonnie Smith's findings, that Balzac strives toward "total naturalization" of woman's passivity in his works. [3] Certainly all three of the Balzac texts studied in this chapter continue to propagate this Romantic ideology: the image of purity in the natural flower-woman, Mme de Mortsauf; the dangerous feminine animality of "Une Passion dans le désert"; the unending clichés of feminine ignorance and passivity in *Sarrasine*. Yet we will see also that Balzac's metaphors do not function quite so simply and that behind the apparently mechanized clichés of femininity, a redoubtable difference lurks.

In *Le Lys dans la vallée,* Félix introduces the story of his relationship with Blanche de Mortsauf as "cette histoire . . . véritable épopée domestique, aussi grande aux yeux du sage que le sont les tragédies aux yeux de la foule, et dont le récit vous attachera autant pour la part que j'y ai prise, que par sa *similitude avec un grand nombre de destinées féminines*" ("this tale . . . a veritable domestic epic, as great in the eyes of the wise man as are tragedies in the eyes of the crowd, and whose story will interest you as much for the part I played in it as for its *similarity to a great number of feminine destinies*").[4] This story, says he, represents a certain universal feminine destiny: woman in this text, as in so many nineteenth-century texts, is a "cliché." Woman can be either an angel or a demon, either a pure mother or a lascivious fallen woman. Two of the most well-known studies treating the dual cliché of angel and demon are Nina Auerbach's *Woman and the Demon,* which shows how demonic and monstrous images of woman, such as the mermaid or the giantess, reflect a certain fear of the hidden powers lying dormant beneath the drugged facade of the weak, Victorian angel-woman;[5] and Sandra Gilbert and Susan Gubar's *The Madwoman in the Attic: The Woman Writer and the Nineteenth-Century Literary Imagination,* which discusses two images of woman as angel and monster in nineteenth-century fiction. The image of the pure mother is incarnated in the character of Blanche de Mortsauf (or "Henriette," as Félix calls her), who inspires platonic love, whereas the fallen woman, Arabelle, Félix's physical lover, inspires carnal desire. These two types contrast with and mutually exclude each other in this text: "Eh bien, lady Arabelle contente les instincts, les organes, les appétits, les vices et les vertus de la matière subtile dont nous sommes faits; elle était la maîtresse du corps. Mme de Mortsauf était l'épouse de l'âme" (p. 1146) ("Well, Lady Arabelle satisfies the instincts, the organs, the appetites, the vices, and the virtues of the subtle matter of which we are made: she was the mistress of the body. Madame de Mortsauf was the wife of the soul").

If most literary studies dealing with these contradictory images of woman have ably illustrated their overwhelming, hackneyed presence in many texts, very few studies unravel the detailed causes and effects of this polarity in the dynamics of particular texts. Some analyses have gone further, linking the two images to the good and bad mother, but again stop short of a full analysis in the text. One philosophical study has investigated the full implications of this polarity: Sarah Kofman's analysis of Kant and Rousseau, *Le Respect des femmes.*[6] A dialogue set up between

Kofman's and Balzac's texts may reveal the mechanism at work in this polarity in *Le Lys dans la vallée*.[7]

The demon woman, Arabelle (or Lady Dudley as she is sometimes called), belongs to an infamous family which turns up elsewhere in *La Comédie humaine*, most notably in one of Balzac's most sexually explicit stories, "La Fille aux yeux d'or." An energetic and forceful woman, she can ride a horse well, an activity that deprives her of an essential element of her female nature: "J'ai remarqué depuis que la plupart des femmes qui montent bien à cheval ont peu de tendresse. Comme aux amazones, il leur manque une mamelle, et leurs coeurs sont endurcis en un certain endroit, je ne sais lequel" (p. 1190) ("I have since noticed that most women who ride a horse well have little tenderness. Like the Amazons, they lack a breast, and their hearts are hardened in a certain place, I am not sure where"). She "unnaturally" cuts off her feminine nature and makes herself masculine and active. The "natural" then coincides with traditional femininity: the weak, natural woman does not sacrifice her femininity (her breast) for active Amazonian pursuits, as Kofman says: "It is, indeed, nature which, fearing for the survival of the species, would have rooted, in the nature of woman, fear in the face of bodily attacks and timidity in the face of physical dangers" (Kofman, p. 38).[8]

Arabelle scandalously exhibits her active body as well as her desire in public: "Mme de Mortsauf aurait dérobé son bonheur à tous les regards, lady Arabelle voulait montrer le sien à tout Paris" (p. 1188) ("Mme de Mortsauf would have hidden her happiness from everyone's gaze; Lady Arabelle wanted to show hers to all of Paris"). This "unnatural" woman does not shut herself off from society in the silence of the home, as does Eugénie Grandet, but leaves her home and family to follow Félix, even to the borders of Mme de Mortsauf's property. She parades herself in the world, like Rousseau's "comédiennes" (the most unnatural women, according to him): "Actresses, indeed, are bereft of all modesty. They seek out the gaze of men, show themselves in public, which already dishonors them. They are prostitutes" (Kofman, p. 128).[9] Showing oneself in public, leaving the sanctity of the home, makes one a fallen woman.

The visibility of the unnatural woman's body gives rise to the question of woman's pleasure, and indeed, Lady Arabelle is related to pleasure: "à elle les désirs et les plaisirs de la passion fugitive" (p. 1159) ("to her go the desires and pleasures of fleeting passion"). But in another cliché, woman's pleasure in this text turns into a fearful, bottomless sexual avidity: "Elle était toujours insatiable comme une terre sablonneuse" (p. 1189) ("She was always as insatiable as sandy soil"). [10]

Why does this happen? Both this story and Kofman's analyses come up with similar answers, answers which are now familiar to us. Arabelle belongs to no one: "Ces femmes sont trop maîtresses d'elles pour vous bien appartenir" (p. 1187) ("These women are too much their own mistresses to be able to belong to you very well"). And in her self-sovereignty she threatens to dominate the man, to make him a slave (as does Bette), in a reversal of the "natural" state of affairs. This slavery takes two basic forms manifested both in Balzac and, as Kofman shows, in Kant and Rousseau. First, the masculine woman physically restricts the man's body (just the opposite of the "natural" situation in which the woman, like Eugénie, is confined). She chains man to her world, and he remains locked up in the home, as Henriette warns him in a letter, and as he later recognizes:

Celle-ci vous intéressera par ses malheurs, elle paraîtra la plus douce et la moins exigeante des femmes; mais quand elle se sera rendue nécessaire, elle vous dominera lentement et vous fera faire ses volontés; vous voudrez être diplomate, aller, venir, étudier les hommes, les intérêts, les pays? non, vous resterez à Paris ou à sa terre, elle vous coudra malicieusement à sa jupe. (p. 1095) ¶ Aussi employa-t-elle ses coquetteries à me garder chez elle. (p. 1185) / *The latter will interest you by her misfortunes; she will seem to be the gentlest and the least demanding of women. But when she has made herself necessary, she will slowly dominate you and will make you do as she wishes. Would you like to be a diplomat, to come, to go, to study men, interests, nations? No, you must stay in Paris or on her lands; she will maliciously tie you to her apron strings. ¶ So she used her coquetry to keep me at her house.*

Thus by revealing her body, by seducing man, she gains the ascendancy and traps him, imprisons him, and then threatens him with suffocation in the home:

Woman holds him from then on in her chains, tries to shut him up in the darkness of her enclosure. Instead of being a mother, of *giving him life* [giving him light], of leaving him out in broad daylight, she wants to keep him in her den, to make him go back again into her belly, *to smother him* with lack of air and mobility. (Kofman, p. 119) It is he [the masculine sex] who must be protected from an excessive expenditure, from the sexual avidity of women, from their absolute phallic and castrative power. (Kofman, p. 15) For such is the avidity of women! They abandon the man only when he is no longer alive. (Kofman, p. 77)[11]

The powerful woman strips others of their identity when she reverses the roles of male and female, when, like Bette, she becomes the aggressor: "La marquise [Arabelle] est la femme forte qui franchit les distances et agit avec la puissance de l'homme" (p. 1173) ("The marquise is the strong woman who covers distances and acts with the power of man"). Man, once imprisoned, is thereby feminized: "To be a woman: such is, perhaps, the fear, the most profound desire, of Rousseau" (Kofman, pp. 146–47).[12] Arabelle represents the danger of feminine sexuality, which can create an aporia by blurring the clear-cut distinction between the sexes. One must avoid this contamination of the sexes at all costs because it represents the death of identity and of proper place: "And this loss of the virtues proper to her sex is more fearful than Saint-Preux seems to say, because it makes one run the risk not only of the extinction of the entire human species, but also makes man run the risk of losing his proper characteristics. Woman, become man, could well want to take his *place*" (Kofman, p. 113; emphasis added).[13]

The threat of death posed by the unnatural woman represents, however, a more symbolic death. By unveiling herself, by showing her lack of a phallus, woman unveils the possibility of castration. For this reason, woman must be kept at a distance, must be veiled: "For to put women on a throne, to make them goddesses or queens, is also to keep oneself from discovering that they have no phallus" (Kofman, p. 16).[14]

Arabelle plays not only the role of the unnatural woman but also of the bad mother. Even though she has children, she abandons them for her own pleasure, and thus, as Mme de Mortsauf shows, she represents the unthinkable: "Comment, il se rencontre des femmes qui sacrifient leurs enfants à un homme? La fortune, le monde, je le conçois, l'éternité, oui, peut-être! Mais les enfants! se priver de ses enfants!" (p. 1158) ("What! There are women who sacrifice their children for a man? Fortune, the world; I understand that. Eternity? Yes, perhaps! But one's children! To deprive oneself of one's children!"). Indeed, a fearsome horde of bad mothers lurks on the underside of this text. Félix's real mother ignores him, favors his siblings over him, and actually seems to be trying to torture him. As does the fallen woman, the bad mother threatens the child with emasculation in his excessive fear of her, even though Félix manages to avoid this fate: "Suivant les caractères, l'habitude de trembler relâche les fibres, engendre la crainte, et la crainte oblige à toujours céder. De là vient une faiblesse qui abâtardit l'homme et lui communique je ne sais quoi d'esclave" (p. 971) ("For certain characters, habitual, frightened quivering relaxes one's fibers, engenders fear; and fear always compels one to give in. From that comes a weakness which degenerates man and infects him with a certain slavelike quality"). These images of bad mothers converge in Félix's description of Mme de Mortsauf's mother and form an archetypal image, a horrible "race" (p. 1044). In conclusion, then, Arabelle, as a model, combines the image of the bad mother who neglects or tortures her children with the image of the fallen woman who thinks of her own pleasure and gains ultimate control. Both of these images threaten the lives of those who deal with them.

Mme de Mortsauf exactly opposes Arabelle. Called many times in the novel an angel, "l'ange de Clochegourde," she embodies the Victorian image of the woman as the angel in the house. Mme de Mortsauf is, if not the angel of the house, the angel of the castle, in the sense that, except for the initial ball scene that permits her to meet Félix, she never leaves the premises. Her home, as Nicole Mozet shows, contains naught but silence and opacity: she and her husband do not communicate in the "la froide atmosphère de son ménage" (p. 1132) ("the cold atmosphere of her home").[15] Again we see a woman like Eugénie Grandet, whose entire identity derives from her home (or her garden) and her image as its silent angel.

The angel, of course, is totally pure: "Elle était pure comme un enfant, et sa pensée ne se jetait dans aucun écart" (p. 1020) ("She was pure as a child, and her thoughts never strayed from the right path"). This purity is symbolized in her family's motto: "*Voyez tous, nul ne touche!*" (p. 991) ("*For all to see, none to touch!*"), and in her name, which implies a purity saved by death. The angel metaphor used to describe her sometimes even seems to literalize itself since her body lacks substance; unlike the stronger Arabelle, Mme de Mortsauf has no visible muscles: "Ses muscles n'y dessinaient point de cordes et partout les lignes s'arrondissaient en flexuosités désespérantes pour le regard comme pour le pinceau" (p. 996) ("Her muscles did not show any cords, and everywhere her lines were rounded in flexuosities frustrating to the eye and to the paint-brush").

The lack of body symbolizes the lack of physical relations between Mme de Mortsauf and Félix. She raises an uncrossable barrier between her body and his, which separates chaste kisses from sensual ones, as it separates one side of her hand from the other and as it separates her from her own desire: "Puis j'étais jeune! assez jeune pour concentrer ma nature dans le baiser qu'elle me permettait si rarement de mettre sur sa main dont elle ne voulut jamais me donner que le dessus et jamais la paume, limite où pour elle commençaient peut-être les voluptés sensuelles (p. 1049) ("Besides, I was young; young enough to concentrate my nature in the kiss she so rarely let me place on her hand, giving me only the back, never the palm, the limit for her where perhaps began sensual pleasures").[16] Realizing that death would punish her for any physical pleasure, she says that if she gave in to desire, she would die like a Greenlander transplanted from the icy tundra to Italy.

This pleasureless, bodiless woman epitomizes the good mother: Mme de Mortsauf lives for her children. Even her husband resembles a child more than a man (pp. 1030–31). As she says, her identity *is* her motherhood: "—Moi! reprit-elle, de quel *moi* parlez-vous? Je sens bien des moi en moi! Ces deux enfants, ajouta-t-elle en montrant Madeleine et Jacques, sont des *moi*" (p. 1136) (" 'Myself!' she went on, 'of which *self* are you speaking? I feel many *selves* in me! These two children,' she added pointing to Madeleine and Jacques, 'are some of my *selves*' "). By the end of the seventeenth century, this identity was indeed universal when the new emphasis on boyhood contributed to a new domestic role for adult women: an intensified role as mother.[17] That she rarely even looks at anyone but her children shows that she centers her desire on them (p. 997).

Thus she can relate to Félix only as a mother to a child, and she in fact notices him in the first place only because she takes him for a child: "Trompée par ma chétive apparence, une femme me prit pour un enfant prêt à s'endormir en attendant le bon plaisir de sa mère, et se posa près de moi par un mouvement d'oiseau qui s'abat sur son nid" (p. 984) ("Deceived by my weakling looks, a woman took me for a child about to fall asleep while awaiting his mother's wishes, and she sat down next to me with the movement of a bird as it lands on its nest"). Félix becomes her third offspring, and, as she orders, he must remain that for her: "Si votre politique est d'être homme avec le Roi, sachez, monsieur, qu'ici la vôtre est de rester enfant" (pp. 1112–13) ("If your policy is to be a man to the King, then you must know, Sir, that here it is to remain a child"). As a result, Félix has no choice but to relate to her as a child to a mother; at one point, he even calls her "maman" (p. 1060).

In this love affair between a symbolic mother and son, in which physical desire must be repressed, we see a symbolic Oedipal relation in which the son must thwart his desire for the mother and the mother must remain at a respectable physical distance.[18] Any intimacy merely introduces a larger distance: "Près d'Henriette, il se respirait un parfum du ciel, il semblait qu'un désir reprochable devait à jamais vous éloigner d'elle" (p. 1129) ("Near Henriette, you would breathe in a celestial fragrance, and it seemed that any reproachable desire must forever distance you from her"). The distance imposed by respect for women, for mothers, then, seems to have at its base the interdiction against desire for the good mother.

It is, then, not simply Mme de Mortsauf's virtue that prevents her from giving herself to Félix but also the prohibition against incest; she, like so many other heroines, equates desire for him with the death of her children: "Mais, mon ami, ces deux petites créatures si faibles qui sont en avant de nous, Madeleine et Jacques, ne resteraient-ils pas avec leur père? Eh bien, croyez-vous, je vous le demande, croyez-vous qu'il vécussent trois mois sous la domination insensée de cet homme?" (pp. 1136–37) ("But, my friend, these two small, feeble creatures who go before us, Madeleine and Jacques, would they not remain with their father? If so, do you believe, I ask you, do you believe that they could live three months under the senseless domination of that man?").[19] Were the incestuous deed committed, the children would die at the hands of the father, so Mme de Mortsauf must refuse Félix's love. When Félix discovers that she does indeed desire him, his punishment looms large in a daydream of an Oedipal nature in which either a part of his body must be cut off or he must die: "Je tâchai de me détacher moi-même de cette force par laquelle je vivais; supplice comparable à celui par lequel les Tartares punissaient l'adultère en prenant un membre du coupable dans une pièce de bois, et lui laissant un couteau pour se le couper, s'il ne voulait pas mourir de faim" (p. 1204) ("I tried to detach myself from that force by which I lived, a torture comparable to that which the Tartars used to punish adultery by wedging a member of the guilty person's body into a wooden beam, and leaving him a knife with which to amputate it, if he did not want to die of hunger").

Monsieur de Mortsauf, repeatedly exercising an arbitrary and all-powerful tyranny in the Mortsauf household, does play the role of the Oedipal father in the text. Félix naturally feels a rivalry with him and determines to steal his "treasure," but he fears this Oedipal father at the same time: "Deux sentiments me dominèrent, la haine et la peur" (p. 999) ("Two emotions dominated me: hate and fear"). In a rather incredible image, it is the count's phallic eye, yellow like Grandet's, that settles on one in an uncanny way: "Son oeil clair, jaune et dur tombait sur vous comme un rayon du soleil en hiver, lumineux sans chaleur, inquiet sans pensée, défiant sans objet" (p. 1002) ("The gaze of his clear, yellowish, hard eye would fall upon you like a sunbeam in winter, luminous without heat, uneasy without thought, suspicious without cause"). All the elements of the Oedipal triangle fall into place and prohibit a relationship between the angel and Félix.

Their first meeting reveals another aspect of their Oedipal ties. Mme de Mortsauf, thinking that Félix is a child, sits down next to him at the ball, and he, upon seeing her, becomes totally enamored of her shoulders:

> Mes yeux furent tout à coup frappés par de blanches épaules rebondies sur lesquelles j'aurais voulu pouvoir me rouler, des épaules légèrement rosées qui semblaient rougir comme si elles se trouvaient nues pour la première fois, de pudiques épaules qui avaient une âme. . . . Ces épaules étaient partagées par une raie. . . . Je me plongeai dans ce dos comme un enfant qui se jette dans le sein de sa mère, et je baisai toutes ces épaules en y roulant ma tête. (p. 984) / *My eyes were suddenly struck by white, well-rounded shoulders in which I would have liked to bury myself; slightly pink shoulders which seemed to blush as if they found themselves bare for the first time; chaste shoulders which had a soul. . . . These shoulders were separated by a furrow. . . . I buried myself in that back as a child who throws himself onto his mother's breast, and I kissed those shoulders all over while rolling my head around there.*

The concentration on the shoulders in this scene transforms this body part into a fetish object, which then generates a platonic love. Kofman links this fetishizing tendency to respect for women since respect keeps woman at a distance and prevents her unveiling, keeps one from seeing her body: "To respect them is to hold them always in respect, at a distance, in order not to be tempted to lift their veil" (Kofman, p. 53). [20] The prohibition against incest and the distance one must keep from the mother give rise to this fear of raising the veil and possessing the woman: "an act guilty because of the prohibition against incest, but above all dangerous, doubly dangerous" (Kofman, pp. 53–54). [21] Kept at a distance, woman is elevated to the status of a fetish, and she remains veiled, a cover-up that hides the absent phallus and the possibility of castration: "The raising of the veil threatens to overwhelm man, to crush him, to paralyze him, *and* to take from the woman, the mother, all her phallic dignity, to emasculate her. To place women/mothers high above, to respect them, is to avoid seeing that they do not have a penis, 'that they have nothing to hide.' The economy created by respect would be that of the fear of castration, and it would be linked with a fetishist act" (Kofman, p. 54). [22]

Hence the fear of castration gives rise to the fetishization of Mme de Mortsauf, for Félix would be taking his own "good mother" if he loved her. He loves not her but her shoulders, her phallus, which guarantee that castrative loss does not take place. Just like Rousseau in Kofman's analysis, Félix manages to keep the shoulder/veil between the woman and himself:

> Desire in Rousseau must assume a fetishist, indeed a perverse, position, which lets him satisfy himself by transferring his desire onto a symbolic substitute for the desired person, while leaving Rousseau himself and the woman he loves intact. He devours her with his eyes or by means of an intermediary mirror (a supplementary mediation); he does not possess her . . . he manages to introduce a veil between him and her, a barrier which to the very last maintains the saving distance and separation. (Kofman, pp. 64–65) [23]

Félix similarly peers through the veil of Mme de Mortsauf's clothing in the primal shoulder scene: "Je me haussai tout palpitant pour voir le corsage et fus complètement fasciné par une gorge chastement couverte d'une gaze" (p. 984) ("Thrilled, I raised myself up to see her breast; and I was completely fascinated by a bosom chastely covered by gauze"). [24]

To increase the ineluctable distance between Félix and Mme de Mortsauf, he gives her another name. He never calls her Blanche (her real name, reserved only for her husband's use) but calls her the name that her "good mother" called her, "Henriette." As Félix does not pronounce her literal name, for this would expose her too much, would lift the veil, so too Rousseau, as Kofman notes, must call women by a name that distances them: "Furthermore, although generally Rousseau deplores the use of signs which are substituted for the things themselves, when it comes to women it is the opposite; it is necessary, in their case, that what represents be substituted for the thing represented, the sign for the thing itself" (Kofman, p.96).[25]

This text, then, seems to present in almost too simple terms the two prototypes of women, angelic and fallen. Mme de Mortsauf, the pure mother, keeps a respectable distance from Félix, does not desire, and becomes a reassuring fetish. This lack of relation between Henriette and Félix is paradoxically "natural": "The respectful distance is, as a matter of fact, a way of preserving the true natural relations, the most sacred relations, the only sacred ones, thanks to which each sex is maintained in the place that nature would have assigned her" (Kofman, p.71).[26] Arabelle, the fallen woman, is unnatural because she rejects the fetishizing distance between man and woman/mother, and she unnaturally cuts off this feminine natural state. In her exposure of her desire and body, she threatens by showing the possibility of castration inherent in the desire to return to the mother. But if we look a bit closer at the rhetoric of the text to analyze what happens to Mme de Mortsauf at the end, we will find that this distinction between the two women may not be as clear-cut as it seems.

In the construction of the images of angel and demon, nature plays a very important part: it takes these images beyond the basic distinction between the "natural," desireless mother and the "unnatural," desiring fallen woman. Indeed, an extensive rhetoric of nature develops in this text (one of Balzac's rare, more Romantic ones in its description of nature) in the standard Romantic symbolism that equates mankind and nature: "En ce moment les champs étaient dépouillés, les feuilles des peupliers tombaient, et celles qui restaient avaient la couleur de la rouille. . . . Toujours en harmonie avec mes pensées, la vallée où se mouraient les rayons jaunes d'un soleil tiède me présentait encore une vivante image de mon âme" (p. 1083) ("At that time, the fields were bare, the poplar leaves were falling, and those leaves that remained were the color of rust. . . . Still in

[86]

harmony with my thoughts, the valley, where the yellow rays of a warm sun were dying, presented me again with a living image of my soul").

This nature represents the mother first in the image of the garden, where, as a young boy, Félix would escape his "bad," biological mother to gaze whimsically at his special star:

> Je bénissais mon abandon, et me trouvais heureux de pouvoir rester dans le jardin à jouer avec des cailloux, à observer des insectes, à regarder le bleu du firmament. . . . Un soir, tranquillement blotti sous un figuier, je regardais une étoile avec cette passion curieuse qui saisit les enfants. . . . A l'âge de douze ans, au collège, je la contemplais encore en éprouvant d'indicibles délices. (pp. 971–72) / *I blessed the abandon to which I was left, and was happy to be able to stay in the garden to play with pebbles, to observe insects, to gaze at the blue of the firmament. . . . One evening, while I was peacefully nestled under a fig tree, I studied a star with that passionate curiosity which absorbs children. . . . At the age of twelve, at school, I still would contemplate it while experiencing inexpressible delights.*

The garden and the star actually take on the role of the good mother for Félix (Mme de Vandenesse, Mme de Mortsauf's aunt, the other good mother, often walks with him in the gardens of her estate), a role later to be assumed by Mme de Mortsauf, as she says: "—Bien, je veux être l'étoile et le sanctuaire, dit-elle en faisant allusion aux rêves de mon enfance" (p. 1081) ("'Good. I want to be the star and the sanctuary,' she said, alluding to my childhood dreams"). The pure mother is then pure nature.

The Romantic rhetoric of the text, however, proceeds to obscure this relation of nature to woman's purity: "La Nature s'était parée comme une femme allant à la rencontre du bien-aimé, mon âme avait pour la première fois entendu sa voix, mes yeux l'avaient admirée aussi féconde, aussi variée que mon imagination me la représentait dans mes rêves de collège" (p. 992) ("Nature had adorned herself as would a woman going to meet her love; my soul had heard her voice for the first time, my eyes had admired her, as fertile, as varied as my imagination had represented her in my schoolboy dreams"). In this metaphor, nature/woman desires (she goes to meet her loved one) and thereby contradicts the image of the angelic woman set up by the text. This sensuality of nature and thus of the natural woman appears consistently throughout the descriptions of nature in the text, as seen in the co-presence of purity and sensuality in the following quotation in which a water image connotes both baptismal purification and sensual fecundation: "Les sentiments courent toujours vifs dans ces ruisseaux creusés qui retiennent les eaux, les purifient, rafraîchissent incessamment le coeur, et fertilisent la vie par les abondants trésors d'une foi cachée, source divine où se multiplie l'unique pensée d'un unique amour" (p. 1139) ("Intense emotion, a living spring, always flows in those channels which hold back the water, purify it, incessantly refresh the heart, and fertilize life with the abundant treasures of a hidden faith, a divine spring where the unique thought of a unique love multiplies"). Mme de Mortsauf understands this because, recognizing nature's ability to give rise to sensuality, she fears remaining in the symbolic garden: "Elle pouvait bien se trouver avec moi sur cette tiède terrasse embaumée, quand son mari serait couché; mais elle redoutait peut-être de rester sous ces ombrages à travers lesquels passaient des lueurs voluptueuses" (p. 1165) ("She could well have been with me on that warm, fragrant terrace, after her husband had gone to bed; but she feared, perhaps, remaining under those trees, through which passed voluptuous glimmers"). Indeed, nature explicitly calls one to love: "Un soir je la trouvai religieusement pensive devant un coucher de soleil qui rougissait si voluptueusement les cimes en laissant voir la vallée comme un lit, qu'il était impossible de ne pas écouter la voix de cet éternel Cantique des Cantiques par lequel la nature convie ses créatures à l'amour" (p. 1019) ("One evening I found her piously pensive before the setting sun, which reddened the mountain peaks so voluptuously, the valley appearing like a bed below, that it was impossible not to heed the voice of that eternal Song of Songs, by which nature invites her creatures to love").[27]

One specific image clearly shows this contradiction in nature—the image that most often represents Mme de Mortsauf, that of the flower. This image is a literary commonplace, an emblem that has represented woman since the beginnings of art, and specifically in nineteenth-century domestic symbolism. Mme de Mortsauf is the "lys dans la vallée," another fetishistic name given to her by Félix: "—Henriette, idole dont le culte l'emporte sur celui de Dieu, lys, fleur de ma vie" (p. 1112) ("Henriette, my idol, whom I worship more than God, lily, flower of my life"). She combines the flower and the star in one being: "Cette fleur sidérale m'éclaira la vie" (p. 1013) ("This sidereal flower illuminated my life").

Again, even though purity is the basic element in the metaphor equating flower with woman, a troubling difference, a troubling sensuality, disrupts the symmetry of the image: "Rappelez-vous le parfum chaste et sauvage de cette bruyère . . . cette fleur dont vous avez tant loué le noir et le rose, vous devinerez comment cette femme pouvait être élégante loin du monde, naturelle dans ses expressions, recherchée dans les choses qui devenaient siennes, à la fois rose et noire" (p.997) ("Remember the chaste and wild fragrance of that heather . . . that flower whose black and pink color you praised so much, and you will divine how this woman could be elegant while living away from society, natural in her expressions, selective in those things which became hers, at once pink and black"). That both pink, symbolizing purity and innocence, and black, symbolizing a darker side to the metaphor, reside in the image of the flower is telling, for the flower image in this text implies not only purity but also sensuality and sex.[28] On the one hand, the lily has connotations of Christ and of resurrection: "moi qui désirais demeurer belle et grande dans votre souvenir, y vivre comme un lys éternel" (p.1201) ("I, who wanted to abide in your memory beautiful, great; to live there like an eternal lily"). On the other hand, the flower is a machine of reproduction, a body that gives rise to desire in the flowery rhetoric of the following quotation:

Du sein de ce prolixe torrent d'amour qui déborde, s'élance un magnifique double pavot rouge accompagné de ses glands prêts à s'ouvrir, déployant les flammèches de son incendie au-dessus des jasmins étoilés et dominant la pluie incessante du pollen, beau nuage qui papillote dans l'air en reflétant le jour dans ses mille parcelles luisantes! Quelle femme enivrée par la senteur . . . ne comprendra ce luxe d'idées soumises, cette blanche tendresse troublée par des mouvements indomptés, et ce rouge désir de l'amour qui demande un bonheur refusé dans les luttes cent fois recommencées de la passion contenue, infatigable, éternelle? (p.1057) / *From the heart of this prolix torrent of love which overflows, springs forth a magnificent, red double poppy with its buds about to open, spreading the sparks of its fire above star-shaped jasmines and dominating the incessant rain of pollen, a beautiful cloud which flickers in the air, reflecting the light in thousands of glowing particles! What woman, intoxicated by the scent . . . would not understand this luxury of subjugated ideas, this white tenderness troubled by untamed impulses, and this red desire of a love which demands a happiness denied it in the struggles, begun again and again a hundred times, of restrained, indefatigable, eternal passion?*

Félix even uses these inebriating flowers to seduce Mme de Mortsauf, going out every day and working for several hours to compose elaborate bouquets for her. These floral gifts of love reveal, as he says, his wishes, his desires, and she understands them very well: "Figurez-vous une source de fleurs sortant des deux vases par un bouillonnement, retombant en vagues frangées, et du sein de laquelle s'élançaient mes voeux en roses blanches, en lys à la coupe d'argent? . . . L'amour a son blason, et la comtesse le déchiffra secrètement. . . . Elle était à la fois honteuse et ravie" (pp. 1053–54) ("Can you picture a fresh spring of flowers bubbling out of two vases, falling back in fringed waves, and from the heart of which sprung forth my wishes in white roses, in lilies with silver cups? . . . Love has its blazonry, and the countess deciphered it secretly. . . . She was at the same time ashamed and delighted"). Both pleased and ashamed, Mme de Mortsauf struggles with two contradictory emotions which correspond to the two contradictory, aporetic aspects of the flower image.

How, then, can the image of the pure mother coincide with this contradictory image of the pure/sensual flower? What does this text tell us about the polarized distinction between angel and demon, between mother and fallen woman? Obviously, Mme de Mortsauf, locked into the image of the saintly, bodiless, undesiring mother, is not simply that: she is split and in fact incorporates both of the contradictory images of woman in herself. Mme de Mortsauf has desires, and this is scandalous. She tries desperately to hide them, but the veil rises (for the reader if not for the narrator): "Mais encore ces deux événements furent-ils enveloppés d'un voile qui ne se leva qu'au jour des aveux suprêmes" (p. 1133) ("Yet still these two events were enveloped in a veil, which was not raised until the day of the supreme avowals"). Indeed, one must wonder at Félix's incredible blindness when he fails to see that Mme de Mortsauf is constantly struggling against her desires, almost as if he chooses symbolic blindness over the threat of the castrative blindness that would result from recognizing the mother's desire.[29] We, unlike Félix, do notice several instances in which the woman's desire reveals itself. When Félix sometimes notices some odd behavior on the part of Mme de Mortsauf but cannot interpret it, the reader sees the irony of Félix's blind, literal reporting of the events, sees that he believes Mme de Mortsauf's motherly rhetoric:

Pendant le reste de ce mois, quand j'accourais par les jardins, je voyais parfois sa figure collée aux vitres; et quand j'entrais au salon, je la trouvais à son métier. Si je n'arrivais pas à l'heure convenue sans que jamais nous l'eussions indiquée, parfois sa forme blanche errait sur la terrasse; et quand je l'y surprenais, elle me disait: "Je suis venue au devant de vous. Ne faut-il pas avoir un peu de coquetterie pour le dernier enfant?" (p. 1058) / *All the rest of that month, when I hastened in from the gardens, I would sometimes see her face glued to the window, and when I would enter the drawing room, I would find her at her frame. If I did not arrive at the agreed-upon time (not that we ever fixed a specific time), sometimes her white form would be roaming on the terrace; and when I would surprise her out there, she would say to me: "I came out to meet you. Mustn't one reserve some special attentions for one's last child?"*

In another instance, although Félix has ample opportunity, he again does not interpret this veiled desire. When he plays peacefully with her children during the count's illness, he notices that she is watching them through the window. Suddenly, when he hears a horrible sigh, he runs in to her:

J'y vis la comtesse assise dans l'embrasure de la fenêtre, un mouchoir sur la figure; elle reconnut mon pas, et me fit un geste impérieux pour m'ordonner de la laisser seule. Je vins, le coeur pénétré de crainte, et voulus lui ôter son mouchoir de force, elle avait le visage baigné de larmes. . . . Je l'emmenai sur la terrasse et lui demandai compte de son émotion; mais elle affecta la gaieté la plus folle et la justifia par la bonne nouvelle que lui avait donnée Origet. (p. 1134) / *I saw the countess seated there in the recess of the window, her handkerchief to her face; she recognized my step and with an imperious gesture ordered me to leave her alone. I came in, my heart filled with fear, and tried to force off the handkerchief; her face was bathed in tears. . . . I led her out onto the terrace and asked her to explain why she was disturbed, but she affected the wildest mirth and accounted for it by saying it was because of the good news Origet had given her.*

Even though she finally gives a more satisfying explanation, saying that she feared for herself, the real truth of her desire (that Félix should take the place of the count, the father) is not revealed in any literal form. And Félix does not comprehend her tears because the mother's desire is, in the ideology of this text, impossible, too scandalous to be real.

Mme de Mortsauf covers up her desire because she knows desire is criminal, because she can satisfy her longing for Félix only if the father, the count, were to die: "Il y a crime à se forger un avenir en s'appuyant sur la mort, crime à se figurer dans l'avenir une maternité sans alarmes, de beaux enfants jouant le soir avec un père adoré de toute sa famille" (p. 1170) ("It is a crime to found one's future on death, a crime to imagine in the future a motherhood free from anxiety, to imagine lovely children playing in the evening with a father adored by the whole family"). The Oedipal nature of the mother's desire is the horrible crime, and it is this that splits the image of the woman into two, one-half pure, one-half desiring: "The prohibition against incest introduces a split between tenderness and sensuality, between the two faces of the mother, the virgin and the whore" (Kofman, p. 97).[30]

Fittingly, when Mme de Mortsauf openly admits her desires at the end of the book, she dies. The absolute horror felt when the mother reveals desire turns into the horror one feels at the hideous image of a dying woman who tries to seduce, an image richly elaborated in the text of an emaciated face tinged with the green of magnolia flowers, of white lips smiling the smile of death (p. 1200). Now that her desire shows through, she loses her identity, becoming like Bette and Valérie "le quelque chose sans nom de Bossuet" (p. 1200) ("that something without a name of Bossuet"): she can no longer be "Henriette."

Félix, who should feel incredible joy at her admissions, feels only disgust and shame at this declaration of love made by a near cadaver. In fact, the mother can reveal her desire in full only when she is a cadaver, in a letter written to Félix which she forbade him to read until after her death. In this letter we discover that, from the very first, from the time Félix kissed her shoulders at the ball, she desired. The mother, despite the "feminine" rhetoric, always desired in this text: "Vous souvenez-vous encore aujourd'hui de vos baisers? ils ont dominé ma vie, ils ont sillonné mon âme; l'ardeur de votre sang a réveillé l'ardeur du mien; votre jeunesse a pénétré ma jeunesse, vos désirs sont entrés dans mon coeur" (p. 1215) ("Do you still remember your kisses? They dominated my life, they dug furrows in my soul; the ardor of your blood aroused the ardor of mine. Your youth penetrated my youth, your desire entered my heart"). The natural woman appears to be entrapped in a double bind in which death is the only outcome. Either she starves a vital part of her being, her desires, and lives the life of a dead person, as Mme de Mortsauf tries to do; or she shows her desires and literally dies of hunger and thirst (p. 1192)— an anorexia that must be compared to Grandet's and Gobseck's phallic gluttony. In this text, to name a woman a flower is to kill her in one way or another. When Henriette is called a flower, a mother, a lily, when she is "natural," these names cut off her desire, "castrate" her, and eliminate all the ways in which she differs from the cliché. Zola seems also to have tapped the resources of this metaphor when, in *La Faute de l'abbé Mouret*, Albine, who must renounce her love for the abbé Mouret, commits suicide by locking herself in a room filled with flowers whose odor suffocates her. When woman becomes flower, in the fetishistic distance of the metaphor, one can avoid woman's desire and difference, can avoid seeing her nonphallic nature, can protect the integrity of the phallus, and can remain on the conventional route of the double trajectory. The metaphor of woman as flower in the text acts like Derrida's heliotrope: always returning to the same, to the repetitive cliché.

In a sense, then, the very existence of the rhetorical bad mother and her separation from the natural woman kill Henriette. Significantly, in this text, it is Henriette's (bad) mother who sets in motion the events leading to her death when she tells her daughter about Arabelle, the other bad mother, thus opening up the possibility of Henriette's own desires (p. 220). And it is the rhetorical machine of naming, of separating mother from desire, that kills Henriette, when her bad mother, symbolizing the (bad) mother in herself, is actually called by Félix a mill-like machine that mutilates her: "Ma solitude avait été comme un paradis, comparée au contact de la meule sous laquelle son âme fut sans cesse meurtrie, jusqu'au jour où sa véritable mère, sa bonne tante l'avait sauvée en l'arrachant à ce supplice dont elle me raconta les renaissantes douleurs" (p. 1028) ("My solitude had been like a paradise, compared to the contact of that mill-stone under which her soul was ceaselessly bruised, until the day when her true mother, her good aunt, had saved her by tearing her away from that torture, whose recurrent woes she described to me").

But woman's difference creeps out in metaphoric difference; the pure lily flower turns into sensual desire. Feminine rhetoric does not completely return to the same, "natural" purity, but it reveals difference in the metaphoric elements that cannot make sense, in the desiring, aporetic flower/mother.[31]

Inasmuch as *Le Lys dans la vallée* problematizes this role of the good natural mother who commands civilized respect, Balzac's "Une Passion dans le désert" problematizes the other image of the desiring woman, who, according to Kofman, "could not be a moral person worthy of respect . . . a sexual object sufficiently abased so as not to evoke the mother" (Kofman, p. 55).[32] And what better image of this denigrated, carnal woman, lowered to a noncivilized status, than that of a beast (like Bette), the wild, fearsome panther of one of Balzac's most extraordinary texts? The events of this story take place during Napoleon's campaign in Egypt, when a nameless soldier falls into the hands of the enemy, the desert nomads known as the Maugrabins. When the nomads, fleeing with their captive, stop to rest, the soldier escapes with a horse and manages to reach a small oasis. There he finds a cavern in a hill and takes shelter for the night, only to wake up face to face with a female panther. Noting the blood on her paws and muzzle and concluding that she has recently eaten, he decides to try to prevent her from devouring him by taming her, a taming that is actually a kind of scandalous physical seduction: "Par un mouvement aussi doux, aussi amoureux que s'il avait voulu carresser la plus jolie femme, il lui passa la main sur tout le corps, de la tête à la queue, en irritant avec ses ongles les flexibles vertèbres qui partageaient le dos jaune de la panthère" ("With a movement as gentle, as loving as if he were caressing the prettiest of women, he passed his hand over her entire body, from her head to her tail, while scratching with his nails the flexible vertebrae which divided the yellow back of the panther").[33] Having appeased the panther momentarily, he tries to escape from her the next night but falls into quicksand. The panther arrives on the scene to save his life, and so he decides to remain with her until someone might come to rescue him. Having become, as the Frenchman says, her first love (p. 1228), he lives with her contentedly until one day, when she turns on him because of some unknown wrong and bites his leg, he stabs and kills her.

At first glance, this story is shocking because of the innuendos of relations between man and panther, innuendos which the text carefully prevents from becoming assertions of fact. But the scandal fades when one understands that the story was based on certain events which occurred in

Paris in 1829, the year before the story's writing. At that time, Henri Martin, an animal trainer, had a show in Paris, where such large tamed animals as lions were not often seen. So popular was his act that melodramas were written around it so that he could appear in the last scene; he was even the subject of a racy poem later written by Auguste Marseille Barthélemy, who suggested that Martin was able to tame the animals so well because he seduced them.[34] Thus the affair between the panther and the soldier alludes in a somewhat humorous way to a risqué popular event of that time.

What is interesting therefore is not so much the scandalous love of the soldier for a panther but, on the contrary, and here I agree with Patrick Berthier, is what mitigates the tale's scandalous nature: the use of the panther as a metaphor for a woman.[35] The text slowly generates this figure, first simply suggesting the similarity between the panther's body and that of a very large woman: her thigh and stomach fur "étincelait de blancheur" ("sparkled with whiteness") (the snow-white ideal of feminine beauty of the time), and her spots "formaient de jolis bracelets autour des pattes" (p. 1224) ("formed pretty bracelets around her paws"). Eventually the text explicitly compares the panther with a woman: "C'était joli comme une femme" (p. 1231) ("She was pretty as a woman"). This link between women and the feline in Balzac (and throughout nineteenth-century literature) poses an interesting problem in Le Père Goriot, in which Vautrin is said to resemble a lion. This imagery could feed into an analysis of his aporetic gender identity and of the fact that he is the male character in Balzac who most clearly crosses over society's boundaries: from arch-criminal he becomes the chief of police.

This comparison between woman and panther grows more and more explicit, in a sense more and more literal, until one has difficulty determining whether the panther merely symbolizes woman or is a real one. She resembles a "petite maîtresse" (p. 1225) with her gentle and coquettish movements. Qualified as a "courtisane impérieuse" (p. 1226) ("imperious courtesan") and a "femme artificieuse" (p. 1227) ("a crafty woman"), she seems to "[faire] un petit bout de toilette" (p. 1225) ("tidy herself up a bit") as she cleans off the blood of the night's kill. She becomes more and more human, more and more feminine, until the soldier claims: "Elle a une âme" (p. 1231) ("She has a soul").

In other respects, the panther seems to reincarnate a specific woman, the soldier's first mistress: "Il songea involontairement à sa première maîtresse, qu'il avait surnommée *Mignonne* par antiphrase, parce qu'elle était d'une si atroce jalousie, que pendant tout le temps que dura leur passion, il eut à craindre le couteau dont elle l'avait toujours menacé. . . . 'L'âme de Virginie aura passé dans ce corps-là, c'est sûr!' " (pp. 1228–31) ("He involuntarily thought of his first mistress whom he had ironically nicknamed *Mignonne* because she was so atrociously jealous that, all during the time of their passion, he had to fear the knife with which she had always threatened him. . . . 'Virginie's soul must have passed into this body, that is certain!' "). The threat of death which the panther constantly poses so reminds him of his first mistress that he names the panther after her, literally identifying the two, and the panther justifies this identification when she becomes jealous of a passing eagle that attracts the soldier's eye. Thus, in effect, the soldier's relationship with the panther must be read as if it were a relationship with a mistress, and the panther's identity represents the threatening sexuality of the fallen woman we saw in Arabelle.

Recent scholarship has shown the equation of woman with certain images of beasts and monsters to be quite extensive in literature.[36] This Balzac story, however, allows one to go beyond the simple ascertainment of the existence of the metaphor, for an analysis of the panther's identity and of the soldier's relationship with her leads to an understanding of the causes behind its formulation. Furthermore, the text hints at certain inconsistencies and dangers in the construction of this metaphor and, in so doing, exposes the pitfalls of a certain method of interpretation.

The major link between the panther and the woman in this metaphor is the danger they pose to the soldier. Mignonne, his mistress, threatens to stab or cut him, whereas the panther seems threatening because she might turn on him and devour him. This fear of being devoured by a wild beast appears in the story before the soldier encounters the panther: the thought of spending the night in the desert "lui donna la peur d'être dévoré pendant son sommeil" (p. 1223) ("made him fear being devoured during his sleep"). The only beasts he can imagine are those that consume humans: "Était-ce un lion, un tigre, ou un crocodile?" (p. 1223) ("Was it a lion, a tiger, or a crocodile?").

Certain images of the desert introduce the themes of wildness, savagery, cutting, and devouring (and the text equates the panther with her surroundings for she resembles the sands of the desert: "dorée comme eux, blanche comme eux, solitaire et brûlante comme eux" [p. 1231] ["golden like them, white like them, solitary and burning like them"]). The soldier, having escaped from the near-savage Maugrabins, quits the last outpost of humanity to embark upon the desert. Leaving behind the laws and customs of civilization, he enters into (or returns to) a primal, savage, and ungoverned place, the heart of darkness of our own nature. Thus the journey to the habitat of the panther connotes a journey to the wild, repressed state of uncivilized humanity.

The equation of this wild state with an image of the woman appears in two symbols used to characterize the desert, symbols that have traditionally been used to represent woman and whose significance psychoanalysis has elucidated. The first is the image of the cave in which the soldier meets the panther for the first time and in which he is trapped and fears she will attack him if he moves. The cave or cavern has long been used to represent woman, often representing the womb in particular, and usually suggests a fearful aspect of the mother's body.[37]

In the second image, the sands of the desert resemble a black and limitless ocean: "Il voyait un océan sans bornes. Les sables noirâtres du désert s'étendaient à perte de vue dans toutes les directions. . . . L'horizon finissait, comme en mer" (pp. 1221–22) ("He saw a boundless ocean. The blackish desert sands spread farther than the eye could see in all directions. . . . The horizon ended as at sea"). Significantly, Balzac changes the color of the sands from gold to black, reinforcing their sinister and frightening aspect, yet also creating certain inconsistencies in his text when he changed only a few of the descriptions of the color of the sand (this could, in fact, be seen to link up with certain paradoxes in the panther's nature). The panther-woman, associated metonymically with an ocean, a mer, suggests again perhaps the mother, the mère. As Karen Horney observes in commenting on another literary passage: "Here once more it is water (representing, like the other 'elements,' the primal element 'woman') that swallows up the man who succumbs to a woman's enchantment."[38] The sands of the desert do actually swallow up the soldier when he falls into the quicksand. These two images, then, associate the desert home of the panther with a primal image of the dangerous mère or mother.

In a slightly different image, the desert resembles a cutting edge: "[Les sables] étincelaient comme une lame d'acier frappée par une vive lumière" (p. 1221) ("[The sands] sparkled like a steel blade struck by a bright light"). "L'horizon finissait . . . par une ligne de lumière aussi déliée que le tranchant d'un sabre" (p. 1222) ("The horizon ended . . . with a line of light as sharp as the cutting edge of a saber"). The fatal panther, the engulfing ocean, the cutting blade, and the imprisoning cave all congeal to form the image of a monstrous mother uncannily close to Melanie Klein's descriptions of children's images of their parents:

> We get to look upon the child's fear of being devoured, or cut up, or torn to pieces, or its terror of being surrounded and pursued by menacing figures, as a regular component of its mental life; and we know that the man-eating wolf, the fire-spewing dragon, and all the evil monsters out of myths and fairy-stories flourish and exert their unconscious influence in the phantasy of each individual child, and it feels itself persecuted and threatened by those evil shapes. But I think we can know more than this. I have no doubt from my own analytic observations that the real objects behind those imaginary, terrifying figures are the child's own parents, and that those dreadful shapes in some way or other reflect the features of its father and mother, however distorted and phantastic the resemblance may be.[39]

The panther-woman would thus appear to be an incarnation of the frightening mother of earliest childhood (as were the bad mother figures in Le Lys dans la vallée), and indeed, some of the examples given by Klein echo the elements of this story in a remarkable way: "Thus, the boy Gerald . . . repeatedly made me act the part of a boy who crept by night into the cage of a mother-lioness, attacked her, stole her cubs and killed and ate them. Then he himself was the lioness who discovered me and killed me in the cruellest manner. . . . At a later period, for instance, the boy himself enacted the part of the miscreant who penetrated into the lion's cage, and he made me be the cruel lioness."[40] One is tempted to see in this strange short story certain reflections of our earliest and most fearsome fantasies. The evolution of the relation between the panther and the soldier, however, warns away from this equation of the woman with the devouring mother and points to a fallacy in its nature.

At first, a struggle for supremacy forms the relationship between the panther and the soldier, for he feels himself to be her prisoner and is called her slave. She has power over him, that of saving his life or killing him, and all he can do is try to escape. She represents the enemy, whom he must master in order to reverse their roles, and, according to the soldier, this struggle determines who will be killed and who will not.

When he attempts to tame her, he covers up his murderous intentions with a semblance of goodwill, but the violence beneath the surface manifests itself when he actually caresses her with his knife: "Et, s'apercevant de ses succès, il lui chatouilla le crâne avec la pointe de son poignard, en épiant l'heure de la tuer" (p. 1226) ("And, seeing his success, he tickled her skull with the point of his dagger, watching for the right moment to kill her"). This action, perfectly comprehensible when viewed in the light of his relation with a wild beast, takes on a different meaning when the panther represents woman. His seduction of her harbors an ulterior motive of control and domination represented by the knife, a symbol of phallic power. In the end the soldier seems to seize the power, to become her master: "Elle joua comme un jeune chien joue avec son maître (p. 1229) ("She played as a young dog plays with its master"). She appears to have been tamed into the civilized woman, for, as the narrator says, by being tamed, a wild animal can be given "tous les vices dus à notre état de civilisation" (p. 1219) ("all the vices that come from our state of civilization").

The narrative frame of this text, as of many other Balzac short stories, mirrors the events of the main tale by presenting a parallel power struggle between a real woman (not a beast) and the male narrator. In the frame, whose events take place after those of the main story, a woman and the narrator leave the menagerie of M. Martin (the name of the real lion tamer of the time), who has tamed his wild animals so thoroughly that the woman is amazed. The narrator, on the contrary, does not find it particularly amazing and claims that he could tell her a story to prove his point, to make the taming seem "tame." She becomes so curious, and makes him so many promises, that he finally sends her the text of the main story, which he obtained from the soldier himself.

This frame parallels the main text, obviously in the theme of the taming of wild beasts but, more subtly, in the relationship of superiority and inferiority between the man and the woman, which resembles that between the soldier and the panther. In the main text, before the soldier tames the panther, he occupies the inferior position of powerlessness, whereas the panther appears to have physical power and control. After her taming, however, their roles are reversed, and she assumes the subordinate, "tamed" position, which ends in her death. In the frame, the narrator has the power of superior knowledge from the outset, and the woman occupies the powerless, ignorant position.

A second story in the frame shows another identical situation, for the way in which the narrator gets the story from the soldier also manifests this power struggle:

> "Mais, repris-je, en voyant M. Martin pour la première fois, j'avoue qu'il m'est échappé, comme à vous, une exclamation de surprise. . . . Après avoir regardé fort attentivement le propriétaire de la ménagerie . . . , mon compagnon plissa les lèvres de manière à formuler un dédain moqueur par cette espèce de moue significative que se permettent les hommes supérieurs pour se faire distinguer des dupes. Aussi, quand je me récriai sur le courage de M. Martin, sourit-il, et me dit-il d'un air capable en hochant la tête: 'Connu! . . .' " ¶ Après quelques instants pendant lesquels nous fîmes connaissance, nous allâmes dîner chez le premier restaurateur dont la boutique s'offrit à nos regards. Au dessert, une bouteille de vin de Champagne rendit aux souvenirs de ce curieux soldat toute leur clarté. (pp. 1219–20) / *"But," I resumed, "when I saw M. Martin for the first time, I admit that I let out an exclamation of surprise, as you did. . . . After having carefully studied the proprietor of the menagerie . . . , my companion pursed his lips in such a way as to express a mocking disdain with that significant pout which superior men use to distinguish themselves from the dupes. And so, when I exclaimed at the courage of M. Martin, he smiled and said to me with an able air while shaking his head: 'Known! . . .' " ¶ After we spent a few moments making each other's acquaintance, we went to dine at the first restaurant that came into sight. During dessert, a bottle of champagne restored to the memories of this odd soldier all of their clarity.*

Here the soldier has the superior knowledge ("Connu!"), and uses it to differentiate himself from the inferior "dupe," the narrator, who himself uses the same knowledge to master the woman. Thus all three sets of relationships are founded on a struggle for the superior position.

In the frame, significantly, the soldier tells the story only after he gets something in return: a good dinner with champagne. In the same way the narrator sends the story to his female companion only after "elle me fit tant d'agaceries, tant de promesses" (p. 1220) ("she flirted so teasingly, made me so many promises"). *He* gets something (promises of sexual favors?) in return. Those with the knowledge use it to seduce the other and to obtain the fulfillment of a desire; they dominate by means of seduction, just as the soldier seduces the panther so he can dominate her. At first, both the narrator and the soldier begin in the powerless position, but they establish themselves in the superior one with their superior knowledge.

The woman of the frame becomes interested in the story because she cannot understand how M. Martin has been able to tame the animals so well, and she expresses her amazement in a curious way: "Par quels moyens, dit-elle en continuant, peut-il avoir apprivoisé ses animaux au point d'être assez certain de leur affection pour. . . ." (p. 1219) (" 'By what means,' she continued, 'can he have tamed his animals to such a point that he is sure enough of their affection to. . . .' "). Her unfinished sentence raises the question: what *is* he able to do with these animals? In effect, both the main story and the frame show that taming by means of sexual seduction gives power, that of life and death, over those seduced and thus, through the metaphor of the panther as woman, over woman herself. Through the story of the taming of the panther, who is murdered because she is not fully tamed, the narrator gains control of his female companion, tames her, and this event then understandably shocks the woman: as she says, "Ce spectacle est effrayant" (p. 1219) ("This show is frightful"). In light of this "taming," Leo Bersani's interpretation of *Le Lys dans la vallée* becomes particularly significant: "Balzac's work investigates the taming, civilizing possibilities of various kinds of order."[41] This would, in *Le Lys dans la vallée* and "Une Passion dans le désert," be the taming power of certain metaphors.

It must be stressed, however, that the threat of death does not always taint the soldier's relations with the panther, for they get along quite well most of the time. He kills the panther in the end because he makes a mistake, an interpretive mistake: "Elles ont fini comme finissent toutes les grandes passions, par un malentendu!" (p. 1231) ("They ended as do all great passions, by a misunderstanding!"). This misunderstanding not only affects the panther, but the soldier too is "cut," he has one leg amputated, and thus this power struggle castrates both the woman and the man. Since the main story is told for the most part from the soldier's perspective, an analysis of his point of view can expose his error because it is he who understands the relationship in terms of the will to power.

The soldier cuts things from the very beginning: first the cords that shackle him, then a tree which he thinks of as a friend, a tree that protected him from the desert sun and helped save his life (here the tree is a prefiguration of the panther): "Il réussit à l'abattre. Quand, vers le soir, ce roi du désert tomba, le bruit de sa chute retentit au loin, et ce fut comme un gémissement poussé par la solitude" (p. 1223) ("He succeeded in cutting it down. When, toward evening, this desert king was downed, the sound of its fall resounded in the distance, and it was like a moan from the solitude"). The soldier cuts the panther (and runs his poor horse into the ground before that), but even before he does so, he envisions several ways of taking her life: by stabbing her with the knife that caresses her and, finally, by decapitating her: "Il mit la main deux fois sur son cimeterre dans le dessein de trancher la tête à son ennemi" (p. 1224) ("He put his hand twice on his scimitar with the aim of cutting off the head of his enemy"). Until the very end of the text, the panther does nothing to threaten the soldier: on the contrary, when he first sees her she is sleeping; she later purrs and rubs against his legs like a house cat, and he calls her a "créature inoffensive" (p. 1228) ("an inoffensive creature"). Even at the end she bites him only "faiblement" (p. 1232) ("lightly") as the soldier himself admits. She does not, by any of her actions, introduce the will to power and the threat of castration; it is the soldier who does so. The text is therefore ironic in the sense that the reader sees more than the main character, sees that the soldier makes an interpretive mistake by reading his relationship to the panther-woman in terms of power and castration. Melanie Klein analyzes the genesis of the image of the devouring mother in the same way. The child creates a maternal image that really simply reflects certain of the child's own fantasies: "It *is* clear why in a child of about *one year* old the anxiety caused by the beginning of the Oedipus conflict takes the form of a dread of being devoured and destroyed. The child himself desires to destroy the libidinal object by biting, devouring and cutting it, which leads to anxiety, since awakening of the Oedipus tendencies is followed by introjection of the object, which then becomes one from which punishment is to be expected."[42]

The panther cannot fit into this structured relationship set up by the soldier. Her real nature is completely undecidable and aporetic, for the text does not permit one to know for certain whether or not she is dangerous. She is sometimes submissive and friendly, sometimes forceful and threatening: "Elle fit entendre un de ces *rourou* par lesquels nos chats expriment leur plaisir; mais ce murmure partait d'un gosier si puissant et si profond, qu'il retentit dans la grotte comme les derniers ronflements des orgues dans une église" (p.1226) ("She made one of those purring sounds with which our cats express their pleasure; but this murmur came from a throat so strong and so deep, that it resounded in the cave like the last booming sounds of a church organ"). She is undecidable, both a threat, the fiend who could always destroy the soldier, and his only friend, the source of all his affections. She confuses categories in another way, for not only does she resemble a woman, she has also, in psychoanalytic terms, masculine characteristics, seen in her phallic attributes: her claws, her teeth, her forked tongue, her whiskers, and most of all her tail, "cette arme puissante, ronde comme un gourdin . . . haute de près de trois pieds" (p.1227) ("that powerful weapon, round like a club . . . almost three feet long"). She manifests several opposing elements at once, both masculine and feminine, powerful and submissive, animal and human; her nature is undecidable in the terms used by the soldier.[43]

By associating with this heterogeneous creature, the soldier cannot maintain his position as master. In the main text one cannot tell just who has the power, the soldier or the panther, who is the master and who the slave, who the host and who the guest, in the familiar ambiguity of the French word *hôte*. The soldier leads a paradoxical life: "Il eut l'âme agitée par des contrastes . . . C'était une vie pleine d'oppositions" (p.1229) ("His soul was stirred up by contrasts . . . It was a life full of oppositions"), a life that collapses traditional polarities in upon one another: "Dans le désert, voyez-vous, il y a tout, et il n'y a rien" (p.1232) ("In the desert, you see, there is everything and there is nothing"). His life with the panther, for a short while, is not based on the polarized powerful-powerless relation but on a relation in which both are heterogeneous. No domination exists, no hierarchial structure in which a privileged term rules over a subordinate one, as seen in the soldier's description of the desert: "C'est Dieu sans les hommes" (p.1232) ("It is God without mankind").

This is perhaps what the soldier must repress. To tame the panther is to eliminate her more aggressive, powerful aspect. When it reemerges, however, when she bites him, he murders her. If in *Le Lys dans la vallée*, the mother's phallus is protected by rhetorical veiling, in this text the woman is "castrated," is violently deprived of any aggressive elements. In reasserting his superior position by killing her, the soldier symbolically suppresses her masculine aspect as well as his own feminine one, his own heterogeneity. What he cannot accept is that the traditionally feminine or powerless pole also constitutes himself; for instance, that he actually *likes* being the powerless one, the prisoner of his political enemy, the Maugrabins: "Il se repentait déjà d'avoir quitté les Maugrabins dont la vie errante commençait à lui sourire" (p. 1221) ("He already repented having left the Maugrabins whose wandering life was beginning to appeal to him"). Mignonne's phallic attributes manifest, as Janet Beizer states, the "refusal to accept female sexuality," but, even more important, they also make manifest the soldier's refusal to see that his way of distinguishing between the sexes, his polarizing structure, does not work and that he too is feminine in his own terms.[44] Thus, by cutting the panther, he ironically cuts himself (he is "amputé de la jambe droite" [p. 1219] ["his right leg is amputated"]) (although how he loses his leg is left unexplained): he cuts off his feminine side relegating it to the "other," to the panther, to the woman to be dominated. His understanding of castration (or powerlessness) as the identity of the woman ironically castrates *him*.

The soldier's power play brings to light the fallacy of his interpretation. To read his relation to the panther in terms of the will to power is to read it in terms of his other relations, to see only repetitions of the same structures and to be blind to difference. For instance, his relation to the panther is the same as that between the Maugrabins and himself. His purpose in Egypt is to conquer them, to dominate them and to assert France's power, but this situation reverses itself, and the soldier becomes instead the Maugrabins' prisoner. When he meets the panther he transfers the same conditions to their relation, reversing their original positions, transferring the structure of one situation onto the other. Similarly, he sees his relation to the panther only in terms of his other relation to Mignonne, his first mistress.

The soldier's mistake thus implicates a reading that privileges similarity at the expense of difference. For example, the text hints at a simple parallel between historical events and those of the text when the narrator suggests that a second title for the story could be "Les Français en Egypte" (p. 1220) ("The French in Egypt"). Implying that the entire story allegorizes the adventures of Napoleon's army in Egypt, this title makes the panther represent the suppressed, native people of the land, the Maugrabins. The soldier's trespassing in her home and his domination of her then would reflect the French army's role.

But the end of the panther's story does not parallel the historical events. The soldier kills the panther after he tames her, thus reasserting his power, but Napoleon's army had to leave Egypt unvictorious. The panther's story, in differing from the historical "text," prevents a simple equation of the two and undermines a neat historical reading. Any attempt to make such a historical interpretation would have to take a step back from the level of simple analogy to observe how the text differs from history, what mechanisms might underlie this difference, and at this level, how the interrelationship between the text and history might be interpreted. [45] A psychoanalytic interpretation is similarly implicated if it sees only the resemblance of the panther to the image of the devouring mother, and not her difference from this predetermined image.

To be sure, the text lures the reader into this interpretation: it gives the second title, thus setting up the comparison between text and history: it provides the frame that mirrors the main text so well; and it very obviously uses the conventional image of the bestial woman. In fact, one cannot imagine reading in a way that would not base itself on a recognition of similarity. The text, then, does not simply negate this reading but rather points out its dangers and warns against equating different images, discourses, or structures too completely, for, like the sands of the desert, such mirroring can become a mirage of identity and a machine of metaphor. When the soldier first glances around him in the desert, he thinks he sees his native Provence in the hypnotizing light of the desert sand: "Enfin, son imagination méridionale lui fit bientôt entrevoir les cailloux de sa chère Provence dans les jeux de la chaleur qui ondoyait au-dessus de la nappe étendue dans le désert. Craignant tous les dangers de ce cruel mirage, il descendit le revers opposé à celui par lequel il était monté, la veille, sur la colline" (p. 1222) ("Then his southern imagination soon caused him to see the stones of his dear Provence in the play of the heat waves which undulated above the vast expanse of the desert. Fearing all the dangers of this cruel mirage, he went down the back side of the hill opposite the side he had climbed the day before"). This mirage causes one to make an interpretive mistake by which one sees a familiar image and cannot see the real scene. The danger is of falling into the quicksand hidden by the mirage, the quicksand of the consequences of a reading that sees only a comfortable symmetry and is blind to the text's fearful difference.

In the mirage, the soldier sees his own past, his own obsessions, in a sense, he sees himself, and the desert's mirage thus acts as a mirror in which one does not see what is really there but sees only oneself: "Il ne savait pas si c'était une mer de glaces ou des lacs unis comme un miroir" (p. 1221) ("He did not know whether it was a sea of mirrors or some lakes smooth like a mirror"). Thus the soldier's failure stems from his inability to see how the panther-woman differs from his own preconceived notions of what she should be. He persists in reading her in a way that cuts off her difference, and, in a sense, cuts off the metaphorical elements that do not return to the same, to the conventional, to his own image. Even though the rhetoric of the text does create the image of this woman-beast, almost as if rhetoric were a machine from which escape were impossible, in this very metaphor her difference escapes.

Thus paradoxically, *Le Lys dans la vallée* and "Une Passion dans le désert" both propagate standard clichés of femininity yet at the same time undermine these clichés from within. Similarly, our final text, Balzac's *Sarrasine,* which seems at first to be a text on male gender identity and on the dangers it faces, turns out to make an important statement about the clichéd notion of gender identity. Indeed, so many of the critical texts written on *Sarrasine* study the horrors of the decrepit old castrated man, the fearful contagion of his castration, and the significance of castration for literature and criticism that one must ask how a text that seems to make of castration the foundation of its truth could say anything unusual about gender identity. In fact, the critics' preoccupation with castration makes them overlook a different, metaphorical, "feminine" story: this text defines the ideal woman and the essence of what it means to be a woman. The singer, La Zambinella, epitomizes ideal feminine beauty for the main character, Sarrasine: "Sarrasine poussa des cris de plaisir. Il admirait en ce moment la beauté idéale de laquelle il avait jusqu'alors cherché çà et là les perfections dans la nature. . . . La Zambinella lui montrait réunies, bien vivantes et délicates, ces exquises proportions de la nature féminine si ardemment désirées" ("Sarrasine let out cries of pleasure. He admired at that moment the ideal beauty whose perfections he had until then sought, some here, some there, in nature. . . . La Zambinella showed to him, all together, very alive and delicate, those exquisite proportions of feminine nature so ardently desired").[46] The ideal woman in this text is La Zambinella, a castrated man. Or, in another instance, she herself castrates: the mother of Marianina and Filippo is the kind of passionate, dangerous, but desirable woman who threatens man with symbolic castration and death and in whose hands he has no power to protect himself, here to protect himself from losing his fingers: "Pour ces sortes de femmes, un homme doit savoir, comme M. de Jaucourt, ne pas crier quand, en se cachant au fond d'un cabinet, la femme de chambre lui brise deux doigts dans la jointure d'une porte. Aimer ces puissantes sirènes, n'est-ce pas jouer sa vie?" (p. 1045) ("With women of this sort, a man must be able, like M. de Jaucourt, to keep from crying out when, while he is hiding in the back of a closet, the maid breaks two of his fingers in the edge of a door. To love these powerful sirens, is it not to stake one's life?") In any case, it is precisely this relation of the woman to danger and to castration that makes her desirable: "Et voilà pourquoi peut-être les aimons-nous si passionnément!" (pp. 1045–46) ("And that is why, perhaps, we love them so passionately!")

Readers of this text, including Roland Barthes, who concentrate on the horrors of discovering the truth of castration and on Sarrasine's blindness, have themselves been blind to this metaphorical aspect of the text.[47] In centering the text on the man's fear, they ignore this secondary metaphor of femininity, which, for us in the twentieth century, echoes the fundamental Freudian concept: a woman, in both men's and women's eyes, is a castrated man. As Freud says in his essay "Female Sexuality": "One thing that is left over in men from the influence of the Oedipus complex is a certain amount of disparagement in their attitude towards women, whom they regard as being castrated. . . . [The female] acknowledges the fact of her castration, and with it, too, the superiority of the male and her own inferiority" (Freud, "Female Sexuality," in *SE*, 21:229). This Balzac text uncannily prefigures and gives life to the Freudian precept that a certain "ideal woman" is a castrated man. Only Barbara Johnson, it seems, notes that La Zambinella represents ideal femininity for Sarrasine; but since the subject of her analysis is a critical concept in Barthes's text, ideal femininity is mentioned as a tangential issue.[48] What I wish to pursue, then, is the analysis of this cliché of femininity, which so closely parallels Freud's definition of female gender identity, to map out its function in this text. Thus, although my reading of Sarrasine often overlaps with those of Barthes and Johnson, it also slightly displaces their interpretations in analyzing not so much the male problem of castration as the rhetoric of ideal femininity.

Whether one views the concept of woman's castration as Freud's literal "fact" of woman's castration or as a metaphor for the symbolic subordinate place of woman in society, we again confront the structure of a hierarchy to which both men and women are submitted, the structure of a preexisting metaphorical definition of gender identity that mechanizes it by fitting it into a polarized opposition. Significantly, in the Balzac text, the castrato is actually linked to a machine image (as are the women in *Le Rouge et le noir*), almost as if this image itself were set into motion by the machinery of a preexisting structure: "Il semblait être sorti de dessous terre, poussé par quelque mécanisme de théâtre. . . . Un sentiment de profonde horreur pour l'homme saisissait le coeur quand une fatale attention vous dévoilait les marques imprimées par la décrépitude à cette casuelle machine" (pp. 1050–51) ("He seemed to have come through the floor, pushed up by some type of stage mechanism. . . . A feeling of profound horror for man seized the heart when a fatal attention unveiled the marks imprinted by decrepitude on that fragile machine"). Furthermore, certain mechanical clichés of feminine identity continually define the ideal woman in this text, inasmuch as La Zambinella's feminine attributes are very stereotyped and superficial notions of nineteenth-century femininity: "Il lui trouva de l'esprit, de la finesse; mais elle était d'une ignorance surprenante, et se montra faible et superstitieuse. La délicatesse de ses organes se reproduisait dans son entendement" (p. 1066) ("He found her witty, subtle, but surprisingly ignorant, and she seemed weak and superstitious. The delicacy of her organs was reproduced in her understanding"). "C'était la femme avec ses peurs soudaines, ses caprices sans raison, ses troubles instinctifs, ses audaces sans cause, ses bravades et sa délicieuse finesse de sentiment" (p. 1070) ("This was woman, with her sudden fears, her unreasoning caprices, her instinctive worries, her groundless audacities, her bravado, and her delicious subtlety of feeling"). This Balzac text sets the machine of gender identity in motion and yet, at the same time, gives an extremely negative view of its tragic effects on the people who invent and use it.

Let us first examine what a Freudian analysis of this castrated woman might be. She could represent a fantasmatic image of the phallic mother: the woman who originally has the phallus but who subsequently loses it. The image of the phallic mother originates in a fetish, as Sarah Kofman calls it: "So childhood prejudices are built up into infantile 'sexual theories' that endow girls with a little penis, fetishist fashion."[49] It is this image of phallic completeness that seduces Sarrasine. All the other women whom he meets in his life are "incomplete," missing something important, the privileged signifier of wholeness and the "all": the phallus. Only La Zambinella seems to possess it, to possess totality:

Il admirait en ce moment la beauté idéale de laquelle il avait jusqu'alors cherché çà et là les perfections dans la nature, en demandant à un modèle, souvent ignoble, les rondeurs d'une jambe accomplie; à tel autre, les contours du sein; à celui-là, ses blanches épaules; prenant enfin le cou d'une jeune fille, et les mains de cette femme, et les genoux polis de cet enfant, sans rencontrer jamais sous le ciel froid de Paris les riches et suaves créations de la Grèce antique. La Zambinella lui montrait réunies, bien vivantes et délicates, ces exquises proportions de la nature féminine si ardemment désireé. (p. 1060) / *He admired at that moment the ideal beauty whose perfections he had until then sought, some here, some there, in nature; taking from one model, often ignoble, the rounded lines of a consummate leg; from another, the contours of a breast; from that one, her white shoulders; taking then the neck of a girl, the hands of that woman, and the smooth knees of that child, without ever encountering under the cold sky of Paris the rich and harmonious creations of ancient Greece. La Zambinella showed to him, all together, very alive and delicate, those exquisite proportions of feminine nature so ardently desired.*

This image of a phallic mother exists, according to Freud, before the gender differentiation between the sexes, and it is consequently destroyed when the child discovers that the mother does not have a phallus. Thus one could view the entire story of Sarrasine as a repetition of this primal scene of recognition that the phallic mother is not phallic; she does not have a penis.

But we must not forget that La Zambinella is not a woman, she is a man (although again, one must question just what it means to be a man). The woman is missing in this text, which presents a mistaken understanding of just what she is. Just as women could not appear on the stage of the theater in this story, the "real" woman never takes center stage in this text (and the other women play only secondary roles). For instance, no mention is made of Sarrasine's mother, whereas a long description of his father and surrogate father, Bouchardon, are given (Bouchardon is described as having a "bonté paternelle" [p. 1059] ["fatherly kindness"]). This entire story is that of a mistake for Sarrasine: he has confused a man for a woman, never to see the "real" woman at all.

This metaphor of the ideal phallic woman is of course shown to be just that: a metaphor, a fictional construction. Just like Pygmalion, Sarrasine creates the fiction of La Zambinella in the statue he creates of her and also in his own image of her as the ideal woman, when, in fact, she is not a woman. In desperation, Sarrasine tries to destroy the statue, thus symbolically trying to destroy this imaginary ideal woman, but he misses the mark and the statue remains to spread this ideal to others later, specifically to the narrator and to his female companion.

The fiction is created precisely because Sarrasine is looking for the ideal feminine, for the truth, the essence of the feminine. In a sense, it is this search for woman's identity that is at fault. This quest for the truth of woman parallels the quest for truth introduced when the narrator's female companion, who appears in the frame of the story, wants to know the true identity of a very old man who suddenly appears at a party. No one knows who he is because his family keeps the truth shrouded in mystery: he lives behind a hidden door and is for all "un secret . . . bien gardé" (p. 1049) ("a well-guarded secret"). But most important, the old man's gender identity is hidden behind a veil, or here a sail (in French, *voile* means sail or veil depending on the gender of the noun): "Il portait une culotte de soie noire, qui flottait autour de ses cuisses décharnées en décrivant des plis comme une voile abattue" (p. 1051) ("He wore black silk knee breeches, which floated around his fleshless thighs, falling in folds like a limp sail").

If we did not know that this man is in fact the castrato, La Zambinella, grown old, the rhetoric of the text would point it out to us because La Zambinella also lived hidden under veils: "Pendant une huitaine de jours, [Sarrasine] vécut toute une vie, occupé le matin à pétrir la glaise à l'aide de laquelle il réusissait à copier la Zambinella, malgré les voiles, les jupes, les corsets et les noeuds de rubans qui la lui dérobaient" (p. 1062). "Sa poitrine, dont une dentelle dissimulait les trésors par un luxe de coquetterie, étincelait de blancheur" (p. 1066) ("In about a week, [Sarrasine] lived an entire life, busy in the morning modeling clay with which he succeeded in copying La Zambinella, despite the veils, the skirts, the waists, and the bows which hid her from him." "Her breast, whose treasures were hidden by lace in a wealth of coquetry, gleamed in whiteness"). This veiling of one's sexual identity is explicitly linked to feminine sexual identity in another place in the text: "Qui n'aurait épousé Marianina, jeune fille de seize ans, dont la beauté réalisait les fabuleuses conceptions des poètes orientaux? Comme la fille du sultan dans le conte de *La Lampe merveilleuse,* elle aurait dû rester voilée" (p. 1045) ("Who wouldn't have married Marianina, a young woman of sixteen, whose beauty realized the fabulous conceptions of Oriental poets? Like the daughter of the sultan in the tale of *The Magic Lamp*, she should have remained veiled"). Here, as in *Le Lys dans la vallée*, woman should remain veiled; one should not see her fearful, castrated identity.[50]

But this text goes on to dramatize the dangerous desire to pierce this veil, to rend it so as to see the truth hidden on the other side, to see the truth of woman, to verify the image of the ideal woman as the castrated half of man's plenitude. This attempt to see, to unveil, and to arrive at the truth is violent in this text: "Sarrasine voulait s'élancer sur le théâtre et s'emparer de cette femme. Sa force . . . tendait à se projeter avec une violence douloureuse" (p. 1061) ("Sarrasine wanted to rush onto the stage to seize hold of that woman. His force . . . tended to burst forth with a woeful violence"). Sarrasine decides to kidnap ("enlever") La Zambinella, violently to "lift" ("enlever") her veils to get at the truth, and he knows that this attempt is dangerous even to him, as he says: "Etre aimé d'elle, ou mourir" (p. 1061) ("To be loved by her or to die").

All those in this text who attempt to lift the veil and to discover the truth of woman are caught up in Sarrasine's problem: this is Barthes's castration epidemic.[51] Indeed, deciphering the enigma posed by the old man (or the enigma of the sphinx) is a fatal enterprise, for Sarrasine dies from it; anyone who even looks at the old man suffers a profound horror for man. Thus it seems that the belief in the truth of the ideal castrated woman behind the veil and the violent attempt to seize that truth reveal one's own castration: the attempt itself castrates. Oedipus is blinded by the truth he learns.

On one level, the cause of this dangerous epidemic of castration is the mysterious, unidentifiable nature of the castrato's sex: according to Barbara Johnson, "Zambinella is actually fragmented, unnatural, and sexually undecidable."[52] He calls into question the limits between masculine and feminine, thereby undermining the status of those with whom he comes into contact. This transportation across borders is symbolized by the cold associated with the castrato, which first appears in the important opening scene. There the narrator finds himself on the border between two opposing states: "Ma jambe était en effet glacée par un de ces vents coulis qui vous gèlent une moitié du corps tandis que l'autre éprouve la chaleur moite des salons" (p. 1044) ("My leg was, in fact, chilled by one of those drafts which freezes one part of your body while the other feels the moist warmth of drawing rooms"). Each time the castrato approaches other characters in the story, they are contaminated by this cold, which also symbolizes gender aporia. Furthermore, the search for the phallus behind the veil is intimately linked with the feebleness of barriers separating things, as we see in the following example of the woman's desire to know the castrato, a desire symbolized by her desire to look at a (phallic) snake when she is dangerously and precariously close to it: "Elle était sous le charme de cette craintive curiosité qui pousse les femmes . . . à regarder des boas, en s'effrayant de n'en être séparées que par de faibles barrières" (p. 1051) ("She was under the spell of that timid curiosity which pushes women . . . to look at boas, frightened all the while at being separated from them only by weak barriers"). Finally, the old man, representing castration, appears only at borderline times, at midnight during the ball and at equinoxes and solstices.

But on a second level, the contagion spreads because this problem of castration and female gender identity is a metaphor deconstructed by this text, a deconstruction which leaves open and unanswered the essential question: what is a woman, then, if this text reveals only her fiction? By leaving out the possibility of a solid, grounded definition of female gender identity, all gender identity is put into question and borders between the genders become undecidable.

This questioning of limits relates also to the problem of textual and artistic frames. The narration of the past story is framed and repeated by the present story, in the sense that Sarrasine's text becomes that of the narrator and his companion, and, by contagion, it becomes our story, too. Which is the inside, which the outside of the narrative frame? Of the book itself? What is the limit between reality and fiction? When the narrator enters the boudoir with his companion and sees the portrait of La Zambinella painted when he was a young man, attention is drawn to the frame of the picture as if it itself were a work of art, were *the* work of art: "une toile magnifiquement encadrée") (p. 1054) ("a painting magnificently framed"). The frame of the picture, as in this text the narrative frame, echoes the text's subject because it reveals the undecidable space between opposing elements, between fiction and reality, story and frame. In speaking of the old man's clothes, his "veils," his "frame," the narrator claims: "Le cadre était digne du portrait" (p. 1052) ("The frame was worthy of the portrait"). The clothes or veils act as frames to separate reality from fiction, and when these veils are lifted, borders become undecidable.[53] When the veil is raised and the frame put into question, what is revealed is not the phallus or the lack of the phallus but rather the putting into question of the limits between being castrated and not. This text does not bowdlerize castration, which would simply repeat Sarrasine's blind gesture of denying La Zambinella's nature, but through the play of the signifier across the borders between opposites, and through the revelation of the fiction of woman, castration is put into question.

When the borders between opposing elements disappear, those opposites combine to form uncanny composite entities, the old man being the figure of these collapsed polarities. He hovers between life and death, as the young woman expresses when she claims: "Si je le regarde encore, je croirai que la mort elle-même est venue me chercher. Mais vit-il?" (p. 1053) ("If I look at him again, I will think that death itself has come seeking me. But is he alive?"). The borders between dream and reality are also blurred. As the narrator reflects upon his undecidable state between outer and inner, between the party and the garden, between death and life, his daydream becomes reality: "Par un des plus rares caprices de la nature, la pensée en demi-deuil qui se roulait dans ma cervelle en était sortie, elle se trouvait devant moi, personnifiée, vivante . . . elle avait tout à la fois cent ans et vingt-deux ans, elle était vivante et morte" (p. 1050) ("By one of the rarest caprices of nature, the thought in half-mourning which I turned over and over in my brain had emerged from it, stood before me, personified, living . . . it was at once one hundred years old, and twenty-two; it was alive and dead"). This "elle," this "pensée," is, of course, the narrator's vision of the old man standing next to his beautiful female companion. Here man and woman create a strange ambiguous "chimère hideuse à moitié, divinement femelle par le corsage" (p. 1053) ("chimera, half hideous, with a divinely female upper body"). But since the old man himself is aporetic (in this passage he is described as a male with a "coquetterie féminine" [p. 1052] ["feminine coquetry"]), the two "levels"—that of the blurring of borders and that of the problem of woman's identity—unite in the strange marriage of the feminine Marianina and the already undecidable La Zambinella: "Il [le vieillard] tira la plus belle des bagues dont ses doigts de squelette étaient chargés, et la plaça dans le sein de Marianina. La jeune folle se mit à rire, reprit la bague, la glissa par-dessus son gant à l'un de ses doigts. . . . 'Qu'est-ce que cela veut dire? me demanda ma jeune partenaire. Est-ce son mari?' " (p. 1055) ("He [the old man] removed the most beautiful of the rings which covered his skeletal fingers, and placed it in Marianina's bosom. In her folly,[54] the young woman began to laugh, took up the ring, slipped it over her glove onto one of her fingers. . . . 'What does that mean?' my young partner asked me. 'Is he her husband?' "). Thus we do not even have a stable undecidability between woman and man in the image of the ambiguous old man, but this ambiguity is itself dislocated in the uncertain marriage (or "hymen" in Derrida's sense) between the undecidable and the woman (a significant marriage indeed).

How does this undecidability relate to the search for the truth of ideal femininity? In a Freudian explanation of truth, what is discovered is the "truth" of feminine sexuality, that the little girl and the mother have been castrated. This would be the "truth" that woman must veil, as Derrida says of Lacan's texts: "What is veiled/unveiled in this case is a hole, a non-being [*non-étant*]; the truth of being [*l'étre*], as non-being. Truth is 'woman' as veiled/unveiled castration."[55] But if this is so, the narrative technique of undecidability and the absence of the woman displace this truth. As Barbara Johnson has noted, the text does not give a literal answer to the enigma of La Zambinella's sex. Rather than telling us that La Zambinella is literally castrated, the text asks questions and leaves out the truth. The truth of woman's gender is never revealed, for when one looks for woman and lifts the veils, the wrong person is uncovered (we find a "man," not a woman). One gets only more veils, more enigmas, and never reaches the truth of woman.

We could say that what is revealed in this text is a certain fiction (Sarrasine's invention of the woman's castration), or the process of the production of fiction. This fiction does not necessarily hide or distort the truth, but instead points out the assumptions one must make in looking for the truth: it is a deconstruction of the system of truth itself. After all, this text reveals the fiction of woman, not her truth, for there is no real woman as the subject of the text. We have only what is always already an imaginary, cultural construct of her identity. Castration in this text, in relation to the real woman, is not a literal castration, for that is the fiction of woman. Rather, castration is the pointing out of this fiction and its pitfalls and a dislocation of the drive for the truth. What this text does, then, is to subvert the meaning of castration as the truth of woman.

The curious Parisians are always trying to find out how the Lanty family made its fortune; the origin of this fortune is, on a simple level, the castration that makes possible La Zambinella's voice. But in a surprising symbolic scene, this original castration, which gives rise to the voice, is not La Zambinella's literal castration but rather another lopsided, undecidable union: "Elle porta la main sur le phénomène avec cette hardiesse que les femmes puisent dans la violence de leurs désirs; mais une sueur froide sortit de ses pores, car aussitôt qu'elle eut touché le vieillard, elle entendit *un cri* semblable à celui d'une crécelle. *Cette aigre voix,* si c'était une voix, s'échappa d'un gosier presque desséché" (p. 1053; emphasis added) ("She placed her hand on the phenomenon with the boldness which women tap from the violence of their desires. But a cold sweat came out of her pores, for as soon as she had touched the old man, she heard a grating *cry. This shrill voice,* if it indeed were a voice, escaped from a throat almost completely dried out"). Castration, as the origin of the voice, is not the affirmation of woman's loss, but rather the marriage of the undecidable old man with the narrator's young female companion, their touching. When one looks for truth, for origins, what is revealed is castration but not castration as the absence of a penis. What is revealed is castration as what Derrida calls "essential dislocation and irreducible parcelling," the dislocation of the drive for truth and the irreducible parceling of both sexes in aporia.[56]

Thus this text, by showing the tragedy of a certain definition of woman and of the belief in this image as truth, warns us away from this understanding of her as castrated and points the way to another understanding of woman and castration as the undecidable slipping between polarities, woman as that which shows the undecidable difference between the sexes, and not woman as missing what is proper to man. If the word *metaphor* connotes *transposition* in its etymological sense, then the metaphor of ideal femininity in this text reveals the transposition of the gender identities of both sexes.

Significantly in this text the one who dies is not the character who undermines gender identity but the one who paranoiacally asserts the castrative definition of the ideal woman in his desire for totality, for the total woman, in his desire for a woman who is just like a man but missing only one thing. This is, in a sense, the desire to abolish the difference, the *distance between* man and woman, to create a narcissistic mirror image of the woman: "Il n'existait pas de distance entre lui et la Zambinella" (p. 1061) ("There existed no distance between him and La Zambinella"). It is the image of a woman who springs from the man's head that is Sarrasine's fiction, as in the image of Minerva used to describe the narrator's daydream: "Elle avait jailli comme Minerve de la tête de Jupiter, grande et forte" (p. 1050) ("It had burst forth, like Minerva from Jupiter's head, tall and strong"). What is overlooked is the real woman, who plays no part in the theater or in the literal text but who appears as the deconstruction of the rhetoric of ideal femininity.

*

In studying the rhetorical structures used to name and define femininity in these texts, we see that these structures manifest two tendencies. The metaphors are divisive: they divide woman into two, into pure floral mother and desiring natural beast; they divide woman from herself and cut off an aspect of her nature in a symbolic castration. They also seem to divide woman from man, to separate them into opposites that must not overlap: the soldier cannot manifest his femininity and cannot tolerate the androgynous nature of the panther. This attempt at differentiation is an assignation of proper elements to each of the genders.

At the basis of this assignation of proper roles is the assignation of the rights to desire. Mme de Mortsauf is denied those rights, the panther-woman must be tamed into the submissive, civilized woman, into the ideal of femininity of La Zambinella. If for Freud, only males as possessors of the phallus can possess desire, if libido is always masculine, so these metaphors assign the proper rights of desire to him and relegate woman to the space of absence. We find here a hierarchy of terms in which male property and presence take priority over female lack and absence.

But it is in this similarity to Freud that the rhetorical strategies of differentiation reveal themselves to be, paradoxically, strategies that propagate sameness. It is the sameness revealed by the attempt on the part of the soldier to see the panther in his own terms and not in terms of her (and his) difference. It is the sameness revealed in the definition that sees ideal femininity in terms of masculinity merely missing one thing. It is a way of defining the feminine by reference to the proper male term, and thus the literal male comes first, he is proper and has property (the phallus); the female absence *figures* his proper meaning and plenitude, is a mirroring metaphor for him. We can now understand the linking of femininity to rhetoric and poetry in Freud.

But if these texts employ the rhetorical strategies that Derrida might call heliotropes, always returning to the same, the specific metaphors in the text do not always return to similarity. Mme de Mortsauf shows herself to be different, the flower desires; Mignonne is undecidable, both the same and different; and La Zambinella is not a woman, is different from woman. The clichéd, mechanized metaphor "explodes" itself when certain meanings do not fit into the machine. This explosion is perhaps allegorized in Zola's *La Bête humaine* when the metaphor of the passive, mechanical woman, embodied in Séverine, figuratively explodes into her "other," into the desiring woman, when Séverine awakens to desire for Jacques (she is, of course, killed at the end of the novel). The other woman, however, the desiring, galloping Flore (who literally explodes the passive locomotive/woman, La Lison) finally kills herself by running headlong into the machine (the locomotive). In another way, Flaubert's text, *L'Education sentimentale*, explodes these rhetorical strategies when Rosanette, the courtesan/fallen woman, becomes a mother; and when Mme Arnoux, the pure mother figure, implicitly offers herself to Frédéric in the closing pages of the novel. We find, then, through realist texts and beyond, the double trajectory of gender identity when mechanical clichés tame gender into preset, polarized categories and when unruly differences sabotage that machine.

THREE

Gender

AND REPRESENTATION

FLAUBERT'S ANDROGYNOUS REPRESENTATIONS

J'ai des épaules
de portefaix et une irritabilité nerveuse de petite-maîtresse. –Letter to Mlle
Leroyer de Chantepie, May 18, 1857, GUSTAVE FLAUBERT, *Correspondance*. / *I have the shoulders of a porter and the jittery irritability of a* petite-maîtresse.

IN FLAUBERT, the push toward realism in the nineteenth century finds its apogee, and it is in Flaubert's works that an investigation of the relation between representation and gender should be launched. If one views realism as the attempt to map language onto reality in a one-to-one correspondence, then the representation of gender realities would, in the most elementary way, be the simple facts of biological gender as they appear in the text, in, for instance, the gender of the personal pronouns. This notion of the origin of gender in the real would parallel the conservative route of the double trajectory in Freud's works, when gender simply comes back to biology, to the reference to a natural phenomenon in reality. But for those who know Flaubert's works, it comes as no surprise that gender does not function quite so simply as all that. For example, there does not seem to be much disagreement that *Bouvard et Pécuchet* turns traditional gender identity into a textual game. On the one hand, a certain rhetoric of gender identity appears in the "male/female" couple, Bouvard and Pécuchet: Charles Bernheimer writes, "Angular Pécuchet, still virgin at forty-seven, afraid of draughts and spices, deferential toward religion, prudish, plays the female role, while rotund Bouvard, bon vivant, liberal, pipe-smoking, ribald, atheistic, has the male lead."[1] But, on the other hand, the categories of masculinity and femininity are undermined not only because both characters are male, and hence are the same literal gender, but also because they are actually more alike than different in many ways. Furthermore, as Claudine Gothot-Mersch has shown, Flaubert reverses the male/female polarity first set up between Bouvard and Pécuchet in one projected scenario when Bouvard becomes more feminine than Pécuchet. Thus rather than finding the simple, conservative route of biological gender in Flaubert's realism, we find again the double trajectory of the presence of clichéd gender categories alongside the undermining of those very clichés.[2]

If critics seem to be in agreement about the aporetic nature of gender identity in *Bouvard et Pécuchet,* the gender of Emma Bovary has instead seemed to prompt conflicting interpretations. From one perspective, she appears to epitomize the powerless plight of the nineteenth-century heroine for whom energetic action is denied. Madame Bovary herself claims (even though this is in part ironic) that her husband, Charles, is an "obstacle à toute félicité, la cause de toute misère, et comme l'ardillon pointu de cette courroie complexe qui la bouclait de tous côtés" ("obstacle to all felicity, the cause of all misery, and like the sharp tongue on that complex belt which buckled her in on all sides").[3] She must rely on others to help her escape from her provincial prison, but these others, like Rodolphe, are not reliable. Indeed, Madame Bovary herself expresses this impuissance when she thinks of her as yet unborn child and hopes for a boy because a male can act in the world. As Jonathan Culler suggests: "We could see Emma not as a person with a given character but as the product of a role and position defined by the title of the novel and by its other occupants."[4] It is indeed significant that a book with the title *Madame Bovary* should begin with a description of her husband; clearly she is understandable only through him.

From another perspective, something about Emma does not match this "feminine" identity. Charles Baudelaire, in his 1857 essay, first ascertained her unusual nature (and many others since then have wrangled over androgyny and Flaubert):

Il ne restait plus à l'auteur, pour accomplir le tour de force dans son entier, que de se dépouiller (autant que possible) de son sexe et de se faire femme. Il en est résulté une merveille; c'est que, malgré tout son zèle de comédien, il n'a pas pu ne pas infuser un sang viril dans les veines de sa créature, et que madame Bovary, pour ce qu'il y a en elle de plus énergique et de plus ambitieux, et aussi de plus rêveur, madame Bovary est restée un homme. / *It only remained for the author, in order to accomplish the* tour de force *in its entirety, to shed (as much as possible) his sex and to turn himself into a woman. The result was a marvel: despite all his theatrical zeal, he could not keep from infusing a virile blood into the veins of his creature; and Madame Bovary, in what is the most energetic and ambitious, and also the most like a dreamer about her, Madame Bovary remained a man.*[5]

Certainly, as everyone knows, Madame Bovary dresses as a man several times: "Elle portait, comme un homme, passé entre deux boutons de son corsage, un lorgnon d'écaille" (p.579) ("She wore, like a man, slipped between two buttons on her blouse, a tortoiseshell eyeglass"). "Puis, cent pas plus loin, elle s'arrêta de nouveau; et, à travers son voile, qui de son chapeau d'homme descendait obliquement sur ses hanches, on distinguait son visage" (p.628) ("Then, one hundred paces further on, she stopped again; and, through her veil, which from her man's hat descended slanting over her hips, one could make out her face"). The masculine apparel, the lorgnon, and the hat, juxtaposed specifically with very feminine body parts, her breast and her hips, create the androgyny of a being with a woman's body and masculine behavior, customs, and clothing.

This is precisely Baudelaire's observation: "Ce bizarre androgyne a gardé toutes les séductions d'une âme virile dans un charmant corps féminin" (p.652) ("This bizarre androgyn kept all the seductions of a virile soul in a charming feminine body"). For Baudelaire, her virile qualities are her energy, her ambition, her imagination, her sexuality, and her domination; in other words, her *desire* is a masculine desire, or rather, as we have seen time and again, to desire is to be male in a realist ideology.[6] Both of the scenes in which she wears male clothing are accompanied by scenes in which her desire is at issue: first, when she and Charles meet, her lorgnon is described, second, when she and Rodolphe go riding together and make love, she wears the hat. Certain critics have gone so far as to suggest that what Emma desires is not simply to dress like a man but to be a man, to have the phallus. Naomi Schor sees Emma as a failed writer, failed because she lacks the phallus.[7] Jonathan Culler, in a more general way, suggests, "What is envied is a social role and condition."[8] Here her desire to have a lover, to have a man, reveals her desire to be a man, and desire remains forever masculine.

This masculine passion in a feminine body curiously parallels a reverse androgyny that Baudelaire seems to have hit upon but does not articulate. For Baudelaire, Emma is "comme *la Pallas armée,* sortie du cerveau de Zeus" ("like *the armed Pallas-Athena,* sprung from the brain of Zeus").[9] Did Baudelaire recall that Emma gave her father a certain pencil sketch that becomes highly significant in the light of Baudelaire's comments: "Il y avait, pour décorer l'appartement, accrochée à un clou, au milieu du mur dont la peinture verte s'écaillait sous le salpêtre, une tête de *Minerve* au crayon noir, encadrée de dorure, et qui portait au bas, écrit en lettres gothiques: 'A mon cher papa' " (p.579; emphasis added) ("As a decoration for the apartment, hanging on a nail in the middle of the wall, whose green paint was scaling off due to the saltpeter, was a head of *Minerva* drawn in black, framed in gold, and which bore underneath, written in Gothic letters: 'To my dear Papa' ")? Minerva/Pallas Athena leaps full grown from her father's head, as motherless Emma seems to do, and indeed, as the female Emma is born from the male Gustave Flaubert. In counterpoint to Emma's desire to be a man, do we not here see the man's desire to give birth to a clone of the opposite sex, to transform himself thus into a woman? This certainly agrees with Sartre's thesis that Flaubert wants to be a female, a "fille adorée par une mère" ("daughter adored by a mother").[10] The strange androgyny Baudelaire sees in this text tells the complicated story of a man's (Flaubert's) desire to be a woman and who therefore gives birth to a woman (writes Emma into existence); this woman then desires to be a man (desires the phallus), has (male) desires, and desires to give birth to a male child but gets only a daughter.

This androgynous mix-up of feminine birthing metaphors and masculine phallo-pens must lead us away from purely historical and thematic questions to look at gender in relation to the real literary problem of this text: the problem of meaning. Naomi Schor rightly sees that the opposition between Emma and Homais incarnates the opposition between male and female: "a fundamental opposition half-expressed, half-concealed by their names, which should be read "Femm(a) vs. Hom(ais)—*Femme* (Woman) vs. *Homme* (Man)."[11] Rather than pursuing Schor's dichotomy between those who possess the phallo-pen and those who do not, or her dichotomy between decoders and nondecoders, I will investigate a dichotomy that does not so neglect the textual assignation of gender and more adequately parallels the characters' explicit genders in the text. [12] This thematic and representational opposition between male and female forms along the axis of two different relationships to language, the first of which is that between signifiers and signifieds. To introduce this opposition in the simplest of forms, let us rehearse the observation made so many times before: Emma believes that behind signifiers, behind words, lie deep, significant meanings which one can grasp if one tries hard enough: "Et Emma cherchait à savoir ce que l'on entendait au juste dans la vie par les mots de *félicité,* de *passion* et *d'ivresse,* qui lui avaient paru si beaux dans les livres" (p.586) ("And Emma tried to figure out just what was meant in life by the words *felicity, passion,* and *ecstasy,* which had seemed to her so beautiful in books"). For her, a rich system of meaning lies under the surface of words if one can just penetrate to it. In literature, she looks not at the plastic beauty of the surface image but for the symbolic (and Romantic) sentiment behind the landscape (p.586). For her, things and "reality" have meaning only if they pass through language, only if they belong to a signifying discourse; for example, she does not really think about her impending motherhood until Charles talks about it, until a story has been made up about it.

Continuing to explore this gender difference on this very elementary level, we see that the men in the novel have a different relation to language, Charles's being the most obvious. Again, let us rehearse a familiar argument (albeit one that has not yet been linked to gender): the very first word he utters in the novel is "un nom inintelligible" (p.575) ("an unintelligible name"), a sound, a signifier cut off from meaning. When he does manage at last to articulate a discernible word, it comes out as the infamous "Charbovari." This ridiculous signifier introduces his identity by means of a silly sound, which is senselessly but humorously repeated over and over again. The signifier, the sound, takes on a life of its own, repeats and propagates itself, turns itself into a veritable symphony divorced from its proper meaning. If Emma ignores the plasticity of the signifier, Charles simply cannot get beyond it. His mode is the parrotlike production and repetition of sound without sense.

Repetition is indeed an important aspect of Charles's discourse (as it is of Félicité's and of her parrot's discourse in "Un Coeur simple"), for when Charles does manage to speak intelligibly, he uses clichés, which, like stale metaphors, have lost contact with any lively meaning (p.588).

Charles never understands the meaning of his coursework but succeeds by rote repetition, by his memorization of the answers to the questions (pp. 577–78). Words for him are opaque surfaces, unopenable doors to dark chambers, where, instead of meaning, obscurity resides:

> Le programme des cours, qu'il lut sur l'affiche, lui fit un effet d'étourdissement; cours d'anatomie, cours de pathologie, cours de physiologie, cours de pharmacie, cours de chimie, et de botanique, et de clinique, et de thérapeutique, sans compter l'hygiène ni la matière médicale, tous noms dont il ignorait les étymologies et qui étaient comme autant de portes de sanctuaires pleins d'augustes ténèbres. (p. 577) / *The list of courses, which he read on the posted announcement, made him dizzy: anatomy courses, pathology courses, physiology courses, pharmacy courses, chemistry courses, and botany, and clinical medicine, and therapeutics, not counting hygiene and materia medica:*[13] *all names whose etymologies he did not know and which were like so many doors to sanctuaries filled with august obscurities.*

Thus Charles never quite understands things: words and events remain for him impenetrable entities. He does not understand his first wife's jealous allusions (p. 580). When Charles and Emma go to the theater, Charles does not even understand the simplest part of a play, the plot (p. 650). This incomprehension becomes his tragedy because the events of his life slip by him in an abstruse series which he calls fate, "la fatalité" (p. 637).[14]

But if his inability to comprehend is in part his tragedy, it also makes up his joy in the novel, for he loves the contingent, meaningless details of his existence; in a sense, he loves signifiers. What he appreciates in Emma is not her personality, her heart, or her mind, but her *things:*

> Il aimait à se voir arriver dans la cour, à sentir contre son épaule la barrière qui tournait, et le coq qui chantait sur le mur, les garçons qui venaient à sa rencontre. Il aimait la grange et les écuries, il aimait le père Rouault, qui lui tapait dans la main en l'appelant son sauveur; il aimait les petits sabots de mademoiselle Emma sur les dalles lavées de la cuisine; ses talons hauts la grandissaient un peu, et, quand elle marchait devant lui, les semelles de bois, se relevant vite, claquaient avec un bruit sec contre le cuir de la bottine. (p. 580) / *He liked to see himself arrive in the courtyard, to feel against his*

shoulder the gate as it turned, and he liked the rooster which crowed on the wall, the boys who came out to meet him. He liked the barn and the stables, he liked old Rouault, who slapped his hand while calling him his savior; he liked Mademoiselle Emma's little wooden clogs on the scrubbed tiles of the kitchen floor; her high heels made her a bit taller, and when she walked in front of him, her wooden soles, springing quickly back up, would click with a crisp sound against the leather of her boots.

The heart of what Barthes called Flaubert's realism, the gratuitous physical details,[15] is in fact what Charles loves; these details make up his happiness. Paradoxically, then, meaningless contingency turns into his continuity, his happiness: "Un repas en tête-à-tête, une promenade le soir sur la grande route, un geste de sa main sur ses bandeaux, la vue de son chapeau de paille accroché à l'espagnolette d'une fenêtre, et bien d'autres choses où Charles n'avait jamais soupçonné de plaisir, composaient maintenant *la continuité de son bonheur*" (p.585; emphasis added) ("A meal with just the two of them, a walk in the evening on the main road, a gesture of her hand on her hair, the sight of her straw hat hung on the window latch, and many other things, which Charles never suspected could give pleasure, now formed *the continuity of his happiness.*")

If Charles loves the physical, concrete presence of details associated with Emma, she, on the contrary, loves a man better in his absence: "Elle était amoureuse de Léon, et elle recherchait la solitude, afin de pouvoir plus à l'aise se délecter en son image" (p.610) ("She was in love with Léon, and she sought solitude to revel more readily in his image"). As for Charles, the less he understands her contingent details, the happier he is: "Moins Charles comprenait ces élégances, plus il en subissait la séduction" (p.595) ("The less Charles understood these refined things, the more he succumbed to their seduction"). The more opaque and meaningless the signifier, the more it ironically means to (for) him. In an early episode of the novel, one metonymic detail actually seems to give birth to the entire story of Emma. In this scene, Charles visits the Rouault farm for the first time, and, as he arrives, he sees the outlying areas of the yard, then the buildings, then some *blue* equipment, whereupon he immediately sees another *blue* thing, Emma's dress, and then Emma herself, almost as if there were a necessity in the very contingency of repeated "blueness":

Il y avait sous le hangar deux grandes charrettes et quatre charrues, avec leurs fouets, leurs colliers, leurs équipages complets, dont les toisons de laine *bleue* se salissaient à la poussière fine qui tombait des greniers. La cour allait en montant, plantée d'arbres symétriquement espacés, et le bruit gai d'un troupeau d'oies retentissait près de la mare. ¶ Une jeune femme, en robe de mérinos *bleu* garnie de trois volants, vint sur le seuil de la maison pour recevoir M. Bovary. (p.579; emphasis added) / *In the shed were two large carts and four plows, with their whips, their collars, their complete harnesses, whose fleeces of* blue *wool were being dirtied by the fine dust which fell from the granaries. The courtyard sloped up, planted with symmetrically spaced trees, and the merry sounds from a flock of geese came noisily up from the pond.* ¶ *A young woman, in a dress of* blue *merino wool trimmed with three flounces, came to the doorstep of the house to receive M. Bovary.*

In this scene, the contingent detail, the color *blue* related to the *charrettes (carts)* and *charrues (plows),* seems to prepare and make necessary Charles's meeting with Emma in her *blue* dress. Thus for Charles, meaning is generated backward, in the sense that contingent details (signifiers) generate the story of his life. This is, in fact, Jean Ricardou's interpretation of one aspect of narrative generation in Flaubert: the letters of Charles's name, the literal signifiers, generate the letters in the words of the description that follows his name, a description that, in a second moment, makes sense. [16] In a way, Charles puts the cart before the horse in our normal ideas of what meaning should be: that is, that meaning is expressed in a secondary signifier and not generated by it; or perhaps we should say, in the French idiom, and in continuing the tradition of wordplay on Charles's name, that he puts the *charretes (carts)* and *charrues (plows) devant les boeufs (before the oxen):* Char-bovari. [17]

Most of the other male characters in the novel relate to signifiers in this same general way, with personal variations on the theme. Homais, for example, makes his appearance for the first time in the very ornate physical signifiers of his storefront, in the gold letters of his name:

Mais ce qui attire le plus les yeux, c'est, en face de l'auberge du *Lion d'Or,* la pharmacie de M. Homais! . . . . Sa maison, du haut en bas, est placardée d'inscriptions écrites en anglaise, en ronde, en moulée: "Eaux de Vichy, de Seltz et de Barèges, robs dépuratifs, médecine Raspail, racahout des Arabes, pastilles Darcet, pâte Regnault, bandages, bains, chocolats de santé, etc." Et l'enseigne, qui tient toute la largeur de la boutique, porte en lettres d'or: *Homais, pharmacien.* Puis, au fond de la boutique, derrière les grandes balances scellées sur le comptoir, le mot *laboratoire* se déroule au-dessus d'une porte vitrée qui, à moitié de sa hauteur, répète encore une fois *Homais,* en lettres d'or, sur un fond noir. (p. 598) / *But what catches the eye the most is, facing the inn of the* Lion d'Or, *the pharmacy of M. Homais!* . . . *His house, from top to bottom, is covered with inscriptions written in longhand, in round, in lower case: "Vichy, Seltzer, and Barrège waters, depurative gum drops, Raspail patent medicine, Arabian racahout, Darcet lozenges, Regnault ointment, trusses, baths, laxative chocolate, etc." And the store's sign, which takes up the entire width of the storefront, bears in gold letters:* Homais, Pharmacist. *Then, in the back of the store, behind the large scales sealed to the counter, the word* Laboratory *spreads its letters out on a scroll above a glass door which, halfway up its height, repeats one more time* Homais *in gold letters on a black background.*[18]

What draws one's eyes, what stands out, is the inscription of the advertising, the words *pharmacy, laboratory,* and, again, the repetition of a name. Our first glimpse of Homais is of a physical signifier and not of person with a deep inner meaning.

Like Bovary, Homais memorizes signifiers, rotely repeats language, but his source is the newspaper (p. 607). Repetition is his mode, for when he becomes exasperated, he lapses into a recitation of memorized quotations (p. 658), and he makes his entrance into the Bovary house every evening repeating the same phrase time after time (p. 607).

Homais loves words, signifiers, especially scientific words, listing them at great and tedious, albeit humorous, length: "Et cette chaleur, cependant, qui à cause de la vapeur d'eau dégagée par la rivière et la présence considérable de bestiaux dans les prairies, lesquels exhalent, comme vous savez, beaucoup d'ammoniaque, c'est-à-dire azote, hydrogène et oxygène (non, azote et hydrogène seulement), et qui pompant à elle l'humus. . . ." (p. 601) ("And this heat, nevertheless, which, because of the water vapors emitted by the river and the considerable presence of livestock in the fields, livestock which exhale, as you know, a lot of ammonia, that is to say nitrogen, hydrogen, and oxygen [no, nitrogen and hydrogen only], and which, sucking up the humus. . . ."). Sometimes Homais's signifiers, like Charles's name repeated in symphonic proportions, turn into alliterative poetry: "les gisements géoliguiques, les actions atmosphériques, la qualité des terrains, des minéraux, des eaux, la densité des différents corps et leur capillarité" (p.619) ("geological strata, atmospheric activity, the quality of the soil, the minerals, the waters, the density of different bodies and their capillarity"). The alliterations and rhymes are impossible to translate in entirety.

This material relation to language emerges most clearly when Homais reveals his opinions on literature, opinions which exactly oppose Emma's. She loves the ideas, the meanings hidden behind the words, whereas Homais loves Racine for another reason: "De cette tragédie, par exemple, il *blâmait les idées,* mais il admirait le style; il maudissait la conception, mais il *applaudissait à tous les détails,* et s'exaspérait contre les personnages, en *s'enthousiasmant de leurs discours*" (p.604; emphasis added) ("In this tragedy, for example, he *criticized the ideas,* but he admired the style; he detested the conception, but he *applauded all the details,* and he was exasperated by the characters, while *being excited about their speeches*"). Like Charles, he loves the signifiers, here the discourse itself, not the meaning. As has already been noted, he loves newspaper writing (whose relation to meaning would seem to be simpler than that of literature to meaning), and, in a comical sense, it seems he believes one of Shakespeare's lines to have originated in a newspaper: "Ah! c'est là la question! Telle est effectivement la question: *That is the question!* comme je lisais dernière-ment dans le journal" (p.645) ("Ah! That is it! That is, in fact, the question: *That is the question!* [in English in the French text], as I recently read in the paper").

A quick summary can be given for the other male characters in the novel. Rodolphe understands only the repetition of clichés and cannot perceive that their meaning could be different: "Il ne distinguait pas, cet homme si plein de pratique, la dissemblance des sentiments sous la parité des expressions" (p.639) ("He did not perceive, this man so full of experience, the disparity of feelings below the similarity of expressions"). Emma's (and others') love letters become, in one scene, physical play-things which he lets cascade from one hand to the other (p.642). Lheureux automatically plugs into his financial discourse, and Bournisien plugs into his religious discourse, as do his robotlike catechism students: "—Êtes-vous chrétien? —Oui, je suis chrétien. —Qu'est-ce qu'un chré-tien? —C'est celui qui, étant baptisé . . . , baptisé . . . , baptisé . . ." (p.613) ("'Are you a Christian?' 'Yes, I am a Christian.' 'What is a Christian?' 'It is someone who, being baptized . . . , baptized . . . , baptized . . .'"). Finally, Binet has beautiful handwriting.

[128]

The contrast between the men's and Emma's relations to signifiers and signifieds can be seen in their juxtaposition when each person gives an opinion about a name for Emma's baby. Here a new entity, the baby, exists without a name, without a signifier, and each character reveals his or her relation to language by the manner in which the name is chosen. Charles, of course, wants the baby to be called Emma after her mother in a repetition of the signifier he loves. Homais feels it must be the name of a famous person because for him, the meaning of the thing originates in the word, in the signifier, which itself generates a particular quality: "Car le pharmacien se plaisait beaucoup à prononcer ce mot *docteur,* comme si, en l'adressant à un autre, il eût fait rejaillir sur lui-même quelque chose de la pompe qu'il y trouvait" (p. 630) ("For the pharmacist greatly enjoyed uttering the word *doctor,* as if, by addressing it to another, he could make something of the pomp he found in it rub off on him"). For him, signifiers come first and generate the signified in a second moment. Emma, conversely, thinks of romantic names, the names of literary and historical heroines who somehow know and live the meanings of those words "félicité, passion, ivresse"; she finally settles on a name she heard at the Vaubyessard ball, her dream come true.

To carry this comparison a bit further, we could say that, for the male characters, the plasticity of words takes precedence but that these meaningless physical signifiers then generate the meaning of their lives, as we saw when Emma's meaningless things turn into the center, the happiness of Charles's life. Emma and women, on the other hand, look beneath the signifier for a meaning that presumably exists somewhere, but ironically they unearth only the contingent detail when they attempt to interpret signifiers. The first comical example of this can be seen when one of the minor female characters, Madame Lefrançois, confronts Homais's signifying system. She tries to understand his discourse but unfortunately reads too deeply into his words; in looking for meaning, she comes up with the nonsensical contingent detail: "—Cela vous semble drôle, n'est-ce pas? moi qui reste toujours plus confiné dans mon laboratoire que le rat du bonhomme dans son fromage. —Quel fromage? fit l'aubergiste" (p. 619) ("'It seems odd to you, does it not? I, who remain shut in my laboratory more than the man's rat in his cheese?' 'What cheese?' asked the innkeeper"). Just like Madame Lefrançois, Emma searches for meaning in the signifiers of fiction but finds, as Jonathan Culler has convincingly argued, only contingent details, "things" in their most concrete state. [19] For instance, she extracts from *Paul et Virginie* dreams of bamboo huts, dogs, red fruit, bare feet, birds' nests (p. 586). She locates meaning ironically in the very essence of contingency, in metonymy as that which links by proximity, not by similarity. The most ridiculous instance of this occurs when Emma reads novels about Paris to find out about meaning and life and gleans from these novels details about, of all things, furniture: "Elle étudia, dans Eugène Sue, des descriptions d'ameublements" (p. 594) ("She studied, in Eugène Sue, descriptions of furniture"). Since in novels, meaning and happiness occur in tropical climes, she transfers that meaning and that happiness to the climate: "Il lui semblait que certains lieux sur la terre devaient produire du bonheur" (p. 588) ("It seemed to her that certain places on the earth must produce happiness").

All this discussion of the relation of signifiers to signifieds bring us up against the most basic problem, if not of literature itself, then at least of Flaubert's works and of realism: the second problem, not of the relation of signifiers to signifieds but of the sign to the referent, of fiction and art to reality. Here, men and women line themselves up on either side of the great divide of the present. Emma would like to make the fiction she read in the past become her reality in the present. In an uncanny way, in a very large number of cases, her dream-fictions *do* become reality. As we have seen, what she dreams of are the contingent details of novels, and it appears that she does indeed acquire these details. She dreams of fancy carriages and of a "lévrier [qui] sautait devant l'attelage" (p. 587) ("greyhound [which] frolicked in front of the team of horses"); later she receives a "levrette d'Italie" (p. 589) ("female Italian greyhound") which "vagabondait au hasard" (589) ("roamed about randomly"). She dreams of castles and "un cavalier . . . sur un cheval noir" (p. 587) ("a knight . . . on a black horse"); she later goes riding with Rodolphe and eventually goes to his modest "château" ("castle"). The "djiaours" (p. 587) ("Giaours") of her exotic dreams become "Djali," her dog's name (p. 589). She dreams of lovers in a "chaise de poste" (p. 588) ("post-chaise") and makes love with Léon in the infamous "fiacre" ("cab") of Rouen. Rowing on a lake with Léon by the light of the moon, she makes poetry come alive as she recites: "Un soir, t'en souvient-il? nous voguions" (p. 661) ("One evening, do you remember? we were floating along").

The evening at the Vaubyessard, however, is the crowning point in the realization of her dreams' detailed contingent elements. Having dreamed of "vicomtes" (p. 587) ("viscounts") she dances with one (p. 592). Having dreamed of elegant, gliding swans (p. 587), she sees them at La Vaubyessard (p.592). Having dreamed of "châtelaines . . . le coude sur la pierre et le menton dans la main" (p.587) ("chatelaines . . . their elbows on the stone and chin in hand"), in her room at the castle, after the ball, "Emma . . . ouvrit la fenêtre et s'accouda" (p.592) ("Emma . . . opened the window and rested on her elbows"). Thus the "feminine" position is linked to a certain reversal of representation when fiction becomes reality. If realism and representation privilege seeing, then Emma's identification with the blind man may figure this undermining of representation.

In a later scene in the book, art becomes reality in a different and more immediate way. When Emma and Charles go to the theater in Rouen, the play is described in a rather strange manner. The description centers on the actions of the characters but gives no motivations behind those actions: "Dès la première scène, il enthousiasma. Il pressait Lucie dans ses bras, il la quittait, il revenait, il semblait désespéré: il avait des éclats de colère, puis des râles élégiaques d'une douceur infinie, et les notes s'échappaient de son cou nu, pleines de sanglots et de baisers" (p.650) ("From the very first scene, he generated enthusiasm. He pressed Lucie in his arms, he left her, he came back, he seemed to despair. He went from fits of anger, to elegiac, dying moans of an infinite sweetness, and the notes escaped from his bare throat, notes full of sighs and kisses"). This description exemplifies Emma's method of reading in the sense that, when looking for the meaning, she retains only the details: the costumes, the set, the painted trees, the swords (p.650). Here the Romantic readings of her youth become the detailed theater of her present, and this theater becomes her reality, for just after the scene in which "tout à coup, Edgar-Lagardy parut" ("suddenly Edgar-Lagardy appeared"), who should enter her life but her hero, Léon: "L'ancien clerc d'Yonville entra dans la loge" (p.651) ("The former clerk of Yonville entered the box").

Thus Emma does indeed make her dreams come true; she becomes the heroine of whom she reads: "Elle devenait elle-même comme une partie véritable de ces imaginations et réalisait la longue rêverie de sa jeunesse, en se considérant dans ce type d'amoureuse qu'elle avait tant envié" (p.629) ("She herself became like a real part of these imaginings and she made the dream-saga of her youth come true, seeing herself as that very type of lover which she had so envied"). She does indeed realize the three words "félicité, passion, ivresse" because she has passion and ecstasy with Rodolphe and Léon, and she gets "félicité," albeit in the degraded form of a maid (her maid's name is Félicité).

But as the word *félicité* and the Vaubyessard episode clearly show, the realization of Romantic fiction in reality trivializes the dream. The meaning sought behind the details fails to materialize, and instead the material, the signifier alone, emerges. For, even though the ball at the Vaubyessard makes Emma's dreams come true in a first moment, this dream degenerates in the second and third ball scenes. In the second ball scene, a man passes in front of Emma's house with a box in which miniature dancers waltz around a tiny room: thus the degeneration of the first ball is actually a physical miniaturization at the same time, as if the trivialization itself materialized (p. 596). The thrill of the real ball disintegrates symbolically in its representation here, and in the final ball scene, the other guests of questionable repute degenerate her ideal morally (pp. 672–73).

Another female character in the novel makes fiction into a trivialized reality. Charles's mother makes up her story of what his life should be and makes it come true: "Elle rêvait de hautes positions, elle le voyait déjà grand, beau, spirituel, établi. . . . Mais ce n'était pas tout que d'avoir élevé son fils, de lui avoir fait apprendre la médecine et découvert Tostes pour l'exercer: il lui fallait une femme. Elle lui en trouva une" (pp. 576–78) ("She dreamed of a high position for him; she already saw him tall, handsome, witty, well-established. . . . But it was not everything to have raised her son, to have had him taught medicine, and to have found Tostes where he could practice; he needed a wife. She found him one"). Charles later spoils her dream when he becomes an inept doctor. Thus, for Emma and her mother-in-law, the meaning of fiction becomes a trivial reality, whereas for Charles, a contingent detail in reality generates meaning. This opposition can be seen clearly in the juxtaposition of Emma's and Charles's daydreams. Emma, sitting next to Charles, dreams of her flight with Rodolphe:

> Au galop de quatre chevaux, elle était emportée depuis huit jours vers un pays nouveau, d'où ils ne reviendraient plus. Ils allaient, ils allaient, les bras enlacés, sans parler. Souvent, du haut d'une montagne, ils apercevaient tout à coup quelque cité splendide avec des dômes, des ponts, des navires, des forêts de citronniers, et des cathédrales de marbre blanc, dont les clochers aigus portaient des nids de cigognes. (p. 640) / *To the gallop of four horses, she was carried away for a week toward a new land, from whence they would never return.*

They traveled, they traveled, arms entwined, without speaking. Often from the summit of a mountain, they glimpsed suddenly some splendid city with domes, bridges, ships, forests of citron-wood, and cathedrals of white marble, whose pointed steeples held stork nests.

As usual, she takes Romantic details from fiction and hopes to make them the essence of her reality. Charles, in his daydream, begins with reality, that concrete existence he loves, and grounds his dream there, in the future of his new daughter and Emma. Charles starts from reality to create his secondary fiction from there: "Ah! qu'elle serait jolie, plus tard, à quinze ans, quand, ressemblant à sa mère, elle porterait comme elle, dans l'été, de grands chapeaux de paille!" (p.640) ("Ah! she would be so pretty, later, at fifteen, when, resembling her mother, she would, like her, wear large straw hats in the summertime!").

In one ridiculous scene, Charles seizes upon a contingent detail of reality and tries to extract meaning from it to explain Emma's seizure. The real cause behind it was, of course, that Randolphe had broken off with Emma and had passed by her house, but Charles, unable to know this, knows only that Emma was eating apricots just before the seizure. This metonymic detail is turned into an explanation of the event, into its meaning (p.645). This is, obviously, also Homais's method of creating meaning. He begins with a trivial reality and embellishes it into an elaborate fiction. After the Comices Agricoles, an event mercilessly lampooned by Flaubert, Homais writes an article describing the Comices as the savior of mankind. His style, overflowing with flowery discourse, contrasts humorously with the "discourse" of the event itself (bulls bellowing, pigs oinking, and so on): "Pourquoi ces festons, ces fleurs, ces guirlandes? Où courait cette foule, comme les flots d'une mer en furie, sous les torrents d'un *soleil tropical* qui répandait sa chaleur sur nos guérets?" (p.626; emphasis added) ("Why all these festoons, these flowers, these garlands? Where was this crowd rushing, like the waves of the sea in fury, under the torrents of a *tropical sun* which poured its heat onto our fields?"). If Emma tries to turn the fictional tropical climes of novels into reality, Homais takes the sordid reality of Yonville and turns it into a romantic tropical paradise. And Homais distorts trivial reality into a preferable fiction once again when he describes the fireworks display, which failed completely, as "un brillant feu d'artifice, . . . un véritable kaléidoscope, un vrai décor d'opéra" (p.626) ("brilliant fireworks, . . . a veritable kaleidoscope, a true opera scene"), and yet again when he turns Charles's operation on Hippolyte (which ends in the amputation of his leg) into a resounding humanitarian and scientific success (p.624).

Thus gender and fiction in *Madame Bovary* seem to be related. The men in the text relate reality to storytelling by starting from a specific trivial event and then generating a meaning from it, what one might call the realist (or constative) method. Emma and Charles's mother, on the other hand, begin with a fiction, whether invented by them or taken from literature, and make that fiction into their trivial reality, what one might call the realizing (or performative) method. Homais's journalism begins with reality, history, events and turns them into language; Emma's literature, fiction, poetry descend into her reality. It is uncanny, then, that three of the most interesting readers of Flaubert, two male and one female, line themselves up along this axis of gender difference. For Jonathan Culler and Roland Barthes, signifiers and details become the message, the sense of the text. For Naomi Schor, the real death of Emma at the end of the text originates in an earlier extended metaphor: Emma's death and the death of her desire repeat the metaphor of the dying fire on the steppes of Russia.[20] The present moment of contingent reality seems to orient men to the future, women to a fictional past.

This neat opposition between the genders works most effectively, however, only in the first part of the text, up until the point when Emma has her affair with Léon, for at that point, androgyny manifests itself most clearly in the themes of the text, and our linguistic gender division collapses. As Sartre observes, Emma and Léon, in their affair, seem to reverse gender roles: Emma loves Léon as if he were her mistress: "Il ne discutait pas ses idées; il acceptait tous ses goûts; il devenait sa maîtresse plutôt qu'elle n'était la sienne" (p.668) ("He did not argue with her ideas, he accepted all her tastes; he was becoming her mistress more than she was his").[21] When it comes to signifiers and literature, Léon does not have the same relation as the other men to reality but rather shares Emma's fictional dreams. When Emma chats with Léon that first evening in Yonville, Charles and Homais form a masculine couple and discuss the everyday life of Yonville, whereas Emma and Léon exchange clichés gleaned from fiction (p.601). Like Emma, Léon bases his understanding of life on literature, and he wants to (and does) make that fiction his reality. He dreams of living in a Paris made of the clichés of nineteenth-century novels (and later makes his dreams come true by going to Paris): "Paris alors agita pour lui, dans le lointain, la fanfare de ses bals masqués avec le rire de ses grisettes. . . . *Il se meubla, dans sa tête, un appartement.* Il y mènerait une vie d'artiste! Il y prendrait des leçons de guitare! Il aurait une robe de chambre, un béret basque, des pantoufles de velours bleu" (p.614; emphasis added) ("Paris then summoned him, in the distance, with the fanfare of its masked balls and the laugh of its grisettes. . . . *He furnished for himself, in his head, an apartment.* He would lead the life of an artist there! He would take guitar lessons! He would have a dressing gown, a Basque beret, blue velvet slippers!"). (We must not forget that the third ball scene is a masked ball complete with Emma and *grisettes*.) Thus Léon, like Emma, wants meaning but dreams of furniture. Just as Emma is excited when her dream comes true, when she says: "J'ai un amant! un amant!" (p.629) ("I have a lover, a lover!"), Léon (through the narrator) is elated to think "D'ailleurs, n'était-ce pas *une femme du monde, et une femme mariée!* une vraie maîtresse enfin?" (p.664) ("After all, was she not a *woman of the world,* and a married woman! a real mistress then?"). She is the incarnation of both his and her fictions: "Elle était l'amoureuse de tous les romans, l'héroïne de tous les drames, le vague *elle* de tous les volumes de vers" (p.664) ("She was the lover in all the novels, the heroine of all the dramas, that vague *she* of all the volumes of verses").

Léon, however, does not continue this "feminine" relation to language, which appears to be a childish immaturity later outgrown. He renounces fiction as a basis for reality and takes up the male position in which reality generates his dreams. Like Charles in *Eugénie Grandet,* Léon becomes a man: "Il allait devenir premier clerc: c'était le moment d'être sérieux. Aussi renonçait-il à la flûte, aux sentiments exaltés, à l'imagination" (p.672) ("He was about to become head clerk; it was time to be serious. So he gave up the flute, his exalted feelings, his imagination").

But if Léon is allowed to grow into his masculine stance, Emma's change seems to be permanent, and she becomes more and more masculine in her relation to reality and to language. Her interest in concrete, material things grows, just as Lheureux grows more important in her life. Happiness for her becomes less the romantic dreams of her youth and more the acquisition of money. From the fictional romantic love affairs, she turns to the physical satisfaction of sex. In her relations with Léon and Rodolphe, she slowly abandons the romantic "châtelaine" image to throw herself into the more literal, sensual aspects of love, and this growing corruption parallels her growing masculinization. Physical love coincides with her breaking of rules and with her increasing masculinity (here represented by her clothes) in the following scene:

> [Rodolphe] la traita sans façon. Il en fit quelque chose de souple et de corrompu. C'était une sorte d'attachement idiot plein d'admiration pour lui, de volupté pour elle, une béatitude qui l'engourdissait; et son âme s'enfonçait en cette ivresse et s'y noyait, ratatinée, comme le duc de Clarence dans son tonneau de malvoisie. ¶ Par l'effet seul de ses habitudes amoureuses, madame Bovary changea d'allures. Ses regards devinrent plus hardis, ses discours plus libres; elle eut même l'inconvenance de se promener avec M. Rodolphe une cigarette à la bouche, *comme pour narguer le monde;* enfin, ceux qui doutaient encore ne doutèrent plus quand on la vit, un jour, descendre de l'*Hirondelle,* la taille serrée dans un gilet, à la façon d'un homme." (p.639) / *{Rodolphe} treated her without ceremony. He made of her something flexible and corrupt. It was a kind of idiotic attachment full of admiration for him, voluptuousness for her, a beatitude which sedated her; and her soul sank into this intoxication and drowned there, shriveled, like the Duke of Clarence in his cask of malmsey. ¶ Solely as a result of these amorous ways, Madame Bovary changed her behavior. Her glances became bolder, her speech looser. She even had the indecency to walk with M. Rodolphe with a cigarette in her mouth,* as if in insolent defiance of all. *Finally, those who still doubted, no longer doubted when they saw her one day, emerging from the* Hirondelle, *wearing a tight waistcoat, like a man's.*

This is not to say that Emma no longer dreams of turning fiction into reality: she certainly continues to do so in her relations with both Rodolphe and Léon. But she slowly turns toward a material relation to love, to life, and to signifiers as the book progresses, and she thus seems to become androgynous linguistically and thematically. As her dreams are materialized and trivialized, she seeks contentment in the material— exactly as Charles does. There is a slow erasure of the clear-cut borders between the sexes and between their different relations to representation, a slow androgynization of the text.

Likewise, Charles becomes more and more like Emma toward the end of the novel. From the person who had absolutely no understanding of her, after her death, he becomes the one being who can accurately predict what she would have liked, basing it on her fictions: "Je veux qu'on l'enterre dans sa robe de noces, avec des souliers blancs, une couronne. On lui étalera ses cheveux sur les épaules; trois cercueils, un de chêne, un d'acajou, un de plomb. Qu'on ne me dise rien, j'aurai de la force. On lui mettra par-dessus toute une grande pièce de velours vert (p.685) ("I want her to be buried in her wedding dress, with white shoes, a crown of flowers. You will spread her hair out on her shoulders. Three coffins: one of oak, one of mahogany, one of lead. Let no one try to object to this; I will have the strength to see it through. Finally place over it a large piece of green velvet"). He actually becomes like her: "Pour lui plaire, comme si elle vivait encore, il adopta ses prédilections, ses idées" (p.690) ("To please her, as if she were still living, he adopted her predilections, her ideas"). Finally, after Emma dies, Charles has an unquenchable desire like hers, when, after her death, she becomes a fiction which he would like to return to reality (p.690). The "bovine" in Charles turns into Emma's concept of the "beau" when Charles, at the end of the novel, realizes the most romantic of fictional clichés: he dies of a broken heart.

Thus there seems to be a mechanism in the novel which turns male to female, contingency to essence, female to male, essence to contingency. Charles's opaque *fatalité* generates a certain richness in the repetition of this word by him and by other characters, and Emma's rich fiction turns into a poor maid, a turning described by René Girard: "As Flaubert's novelistic genius ripens his oppositions become more futile; the identity of the contraries is drawn more clearly."[22] Even the two characters who seem most to oppose each other, Homais and Bournisien, the scientist and the cleric, end up resembling each other when they fall asleep over Emma's dead body.

In this way, representation in *Madame Bovary* becomes androgynous, gender turns into a paradoxical, aporetic state, where meaning becomes contingency and contingency meaning when male modes of representation turn to female, and female to male. The text hovers in an androgynous state, being both a text on the most significant question of human existence, the meaning of life, as well as a conglomeration of meaningless signifiers strung together in interesting sounds: "Les*t*ibou*d*ois, le *b*edeau, qui *t*aillait le *b*uis" (p.611), "un *d*uvet *d*'oiseau qui *t*ournoie *d*ans la *t*empête" (p.611), and "*app*uyant sur *d*es *b*a*d*ines à *p*omme *d*'or la *paume t*en*d*ue *d*e leurs *g*ants *j*au*n*es" (p.649; emphasis added) "Lestiboudois, the beadle, who was trimming the boxwood," "the down from a bird which twirls round in the tempest," and "resting the taut palms of their yellow gloves on the gold knobs of canes"). Androgyny thus does not figure representation or the performative undermining of representation but the aporetic co-presence of the one and the other.

This androgyny of representation flows through most of *Bouvard et Pécuchet*. Their "feminine" relation to language can be seen in their projects, which, like Emma's dreams, originate in books. When Bouvard and Pécuchet attempt to turn the ideas in those books into reality, they participate in Emma's "realizing" mode. Like Emma, they read too literally—they invest meaning in the contingent details of texts—and the result of their efforts is disappointing and trivial. For instance, they think that they can make a garden in the fearful "genre terrible" (p. 100) ("terrible, horrifying genre") described in a book by bringing boulders into their yard, and they *do* realize this dream. Yet the reality is anything but fearful: "Au milieu du gazon se dressait un rocher, pareil à une gigantesque pomme de terre" (pp. 101–2) ("In the middle of the lawn stood a rock which looked like a gigantic potato"). On the other hand, they, like Charles and Homais, begin sometimes with the contingent detail of the signifier and go from there to meaning: in one case it is the contingent nature of the signifier that makes them decide to read certain books: "Les noms . . . bizarres ou agréables" (p. 189) ("Words . . . bizarre or pleasing"). Finally, in the sense that they display a figural polarized gender relation of male/female yet are both literally male, they perhaps uncover the underlying structure of the clichéd rhetoric of gender identity (which we saw in Chapter 2), which would seem to distinguish between genders but really bases itself on similarity.

L'Education sentimentale takes an intermediary and more complicated position between the gradual temporal effacement of gender distinction in *Madame Bovary* and the immediate and explicit problematization of gender identity in the opening pages of *Bouvard et Pécuchet*. In the very beginning of *L'Education sentimentale*, in the light of the categories set up in *Madame Bovary*, Frédéric appears to adhere to the male, realist mode and could be considered to be a somewhat more intelligent and cultured Charles. His pleasure originates in a real woman and a real event, which takes place at the very beginning of the novel: he sees and loves Mme Arnoux. As Charles loves Emma's things, Frédéric loves Mme Arnoux's things: when he first meets her, he finds her workbasket "extraordinary," and he ironically wants to see her furniture: "Il souhaitait connaître les meubles de sa chambre" ("He longed to know about the furniture in her room").[23] He, like Charles, takes pleasure in contemplating each tiny detail of her person (p. 106). If one describes *Madame Bovary* as Emma's quest for love, happiness, and meaning in which she ends up finding only contingent things, then one could say that *L'Education sentimentale* reverses this when Frédéric's discovery of a real person and his love for her turns into a quest for things. And it is a tragic quest indeed, for if Frédéric finds and loves Mme Arnoux's things, he also experiences their betrayal and prostitution: "Donc, Sénécal s'étalait, maintenant, au milieu des choses qui provenaient de chez Arnoux! . . . Frédéric se sentit blessé, jusqu'au fond de l'âme" (p. 146) ("So Sénécal sprawled out now in the midst of the things which came from Arnoux's place! . . . Frédéric felt wounded to the depths of his soul"). And he finally experiences the tragedy of their loss when he attends the auction of her possessions. Thus Frédéric is "male" in the categories delineated in *Madame Bovary* in the sense that contingent things become the center of his existence. And, as with Homais, Frédéric thinks that signifiers contain and generate magic meaning: "Les grandes lettres composant le nom d'Arnoux sur la plaque de marbre, au haut de la boutique, lui semblaient toutes particulières et grosses de significations, comme une écriture sacrée" (p. 87) ("The large letters, forming the name of Arnoux on the marble slab above the storefront, seemed to him singular and full of meanings, like a sacred script"). Clearly, then, the meaningless physical signifiers generate meaning for Frédéric, as for the men in *Madame Bovary.*

If in the opening pages of the novel, Frédéric seems to belong to the male mode, troubling similarities between Frédéric and Emma come to light shortly after the beginning of the novel, and Frédéric begins to manifest a nature similar to the aporetic, problematic ones of Emma, Bouvard, and Pécuchet. Like Emma, Frédéric harbors certain clichéd Romantic dreams that contain contingent details: "Ils reviendraient à Paris, ils travailleraient ensemble, ne se quitteraient pas . . . ils auraient des amours de princesses dans des boudoirs de satin" (p. 61). "Il les recevrait chez lui, dans sa maison; la salle à manger serait en cuir rouge, le boudoir en soie jaune" (p. 151) ("They would come back to Paris, they would work together, would never leave each other. . . . They would have gallant love affairs with princesses in satin boudoirs." "He would entertain them at his place, in his house; the dining room would be done in red leather, the boudoir in yellow silk"). And, as in Emma's case, these dreams come true in the very contingency of their details: Frédéric and Deslauriers go to Paris, live and work together, and remain together at the end of the novel. Frédéric gets that room he desired with walls covered in yellow damask silk: "Le dessert était fini: on passa dans le salon, tendu comme celui de la Maréchale, en damas jaune" (p. 198) ("Dessert was over; they went into the drawing room, which was hung, like the Maréchale's, in yellow damask"). And, of course, Madame Arnoux comes to him at the end of the novel. But again, as in Emma's case, somehow the realizations of Frédéric's dreams do not meet his expectations. Thus he has a "feminine" position, too, in the sense that his fictions turn into a trivial reality.

This androgyny of representation becomes extremely complicated in *L'Education sentimentale*. If real yet contingent things, such as furniture, generate meaning in the male mode, and if the Romantic dreams of fiction become trivialized in contingent things in the female mode, then these two modes are inextricably intertwined when Frédéric first dreams of the sale of Mme Arnoux's furniture ("Et il aperçut Mme Arnoux, ruinée, pleurant, vendant ses meubles" (p. 200) ("And he envisioned Mme Arnoux, ruined, weeping, selling her furniture"), and when that dream later comes true (p. 499). Furthermore, if Frédéric's love for Mme Arnoux originates in the opening scene, when he first sees her and her things in reality, it is suggested later in the novel that he falls in love with her in that scene because she conforms to a preexisting image of Romantic heroines: "Elle ressemblait aux femmes des livres romantiques" (p. 55) ("She resembled the women in romantic books"). Thus do his fictions become reality or does reality turn into fiction?

Perhaps the most important androgynous structure of representation in *L'Education sentimentale*, when male realist modes mix with female realizing modes, is that of the hallucination. Although John Lapp studies hallucination in Flaubert's life and relates it to *Madame Bovary*,[24] it becomes important in a different way in our context of realities and fictions, because hallucination represents an ambiguous, aporetic place between the two. Frédéric's dreams of a daughter become a fictional reality in his hallucination: "Et sa rêverie devint tellement profonde, qu'il eut une sorte d'hallucination. Il voyait là, sur le tapis, devant la cheminée, une petite fille. Elle ressemblait à Mme Arnoux et à lui-même, un peu" (p. 436) ("And he was so deep in his reverie that he had a kind of hallucination. He saw there, on the rug, in front of the fireplace, a little girl. She resembled Mme Arnoux, and him a bit"). For a moment, fiction becomes reality, reality becomes fiction: the two, male and female modes, join together and are one. There is a second important androgynous couple in *L'Education sentimentale*. Frédéric and Deslauriers, like Bouvard and Pécuchet, form a kind of male/female couple. Frédéric, at the beginning, is the "petit," Deslauriers the "grand." Frédéric likes what are called "less serious" pursuits—drawing, drama, memoirs; Deslauriers likes philosophy. Frédéric is even seen to seduce Deslauriers in a specifically feminine way: "Puis, il [Deslauriers] songea à la personne même de Frédéric. Elle avait toujours exercé sur lui un charme presque féminin" (p.311) ("Then he [Deslauriers] thought of Frédéric himself, who had always exerted an almost feminine charm over him"). There is a hierarchical distinction between big, serious male and smaller, less serious female.

But, as with Bouvard and Pécuchet, the differences are somewhat leveled out by similarities: both Frédéric and Deslauriers are men, both pursue politics, both even pursue the same women. One could even say that Deslauriers "becomes" Frédéric in his attempted seduction of Mme Arnoux, in his interest in Louise Roque, and in the substitution of his point of view for Frédéric's in the middle section of the novel. And their gender differences finally end up in sameness when Frédéric and Deslauriers face and mirror each other at the end of the novel, when Deslauriers repeats Frédéric's words, and when they rehearse together a memory of that infamous trip to the brothel in their youth. The male/female couple is set up and then dissolved into similarity.

Let us now take an overview of the relation of gender to representation in Flaubert. On the one hand, Charles and Homais, representing the male mode, tend to create their fictions from a preexisting reality: this is certainly the standard understanding of the function of words and texts, they *re*present an original idea or thing. Jacques Derrida shows that this belief that representation, *mimesis,* represents an original presence has at its heart a familiar hierarchization. The present comes first, the imitation follows:

That which is, the being-present . . . is distinguished from the appearance, the image, the phenomenon, etc., that is, from anything that, presenting it *as* being-present, doubles it, re-presents it, and can therefore replace and de-present it. There is thus the 1 and the 2, the simple and the double. The double comes *after* the simple; it multiplies it as a *follow-up* . . . the image *supervenes* upon reality, the representation upon the present in presentation, the imitation upon the thing, the imitator upon the imitated.[25]

The male mode in Frédéric's representation could then be seen as the realist mode, which represents reality. Emma's feminine mode, her realizing technique, is then the uncanny double of the male mode, the reverse mirror image of his mirroring technique. Her mode is thus a "fantastic" one in the sense that in it, fiction has the power to literalize itself in reality.[26] The problematics of androgyny and representation, however, make the distinction between genders and between reality and fiction undecidable. When we ask, Which comes first, reality or fiction? these texts sometimes do not permit an answer but leave us in an aporia between the two, in an androgynous state. This undecidability is best exemplified in Frédéric's projected novel. The content of his novel implies that it is based on the previous reality of his life: "Il se mit à écrire un roman intitulé: *Sylvio, le fils du pêcheur*. . . . Le héros, c'était lui-même; l'héroïne, Mme Arnoux" (p.72) ("He began to write a novel entitled, *Sylvio, the Fisherman's Son*. . . . The hero was himself, the heroine, Mme Arnoux"). But its title implies that the book has not descended from reality, but rather, that its father is *"Gaspardo le Pêcheur"* (p.176) (*"Gaspardo the Fisherman"*), an already existing text, a melodrama written by Bouchardy (p.519). Thus in gender as in representation, the hierarchical polarity is upset when one cannot tell which is which, which comes first. At this point, I must agree with Jonathan Culler, who sees in *Madame Bovary* a similar undecidability between representation and antirepresentation: "Flaubert's vealism puts us in the position of trying to interpret— without adequate means—the collision and collusion of the representational and antirepresentational."[27]

My analysis showed that the feminocentric *Madame Bovary* moves toward androgyny, but in the androcentric novels *Bouvard et Pécuchet* and *L'Education sentimentale,* the protagonists renounce their feminine modes of representation in the end: Frédéric no longer dreams of making fiction into reality but contents himself with repeating real (although unrealized) past moments with his male friend, Deslauriers. Bouvard and Pécuchet renounce their projects, no longer try to realize books in reality, and end up (in the projected end of the novel) simply copying, repeating, physical signifiers. Androgynous gender in androcentric fiction seems to need to return to a homogeneous male mode as well as to a mirroring reflection of sameness when two male characters face each other at the ends of both novels. [28] When the feminocentric *Madame Bovary* turns to androgyny and the androcentric novels move from androgyny to masculinity, we should perhaps see here an embodiment of Freud's theory of bisexuality (which is perhaps a cliché belonging to our general culture): females can be bisexual, but males and desire must be masculine. "Male" androgyny does exist for an uncanny moment, however, even though these two androcentric novels of Flaubert, *L'Education sentimentale* and *Bouvard et Pécuchet,* do (or plan to) return to the realist mode in the end.

REPRESENTATION'S OTHERS:

Monsieur Vénus and Decadent Reversals

> Strictly speaking,
> it is only themselves that such women love with an intensity comparable to
> that of the man's love for them. . . . The charm of a child lies to a great
> extent in his narcissism, his self-contentment and inaccessibility, just as
> does the charm of certain animals which seem not to concern themselves
> about us, such as cats and the large beasts of prey.—SIGMUND FREUD,
> "On Narcissism: An Introduction"

JULIEN SOREL'S feminine persona, Mignonne's phallic attributes, and *Madame Bovary*'s androgynous representations subvert conventional gender categories, but only in a limited way, for, in the texts by realist authors, society eventually suppresses their subversions by means of death, renunciation, or irredeemable ! s Just as the Freudian repressed must be forced back into the depths when it surfaces, so too it seems that any ambiguities of gender must be radically repressed as if they were intolerable to the proper functioning of society and of realist texts. [29] This parallel between the repressed of society and Freud's unconscious is very close to Jameson's concept of the political unconscious. In a Jamesonian analysis, the polarization and hierarchization of the sexes represent one of the oldest modes of production: "In our present perspective, it becomes clear that sexism and the patriarchal are to be grasped as the sedimentation and the virulent survival of forms of alienation specific to the oldest mode of production of human history, with its division of labor between men and women, and its division of power between youth and elder."[30]

Yet a few texts do not repress these acts of subversion: rather, they seem to be the very subject of their plots. The final two texts to be considered center on gender as their main problematic and shed new light on the issues encountered in the previous chapters. *Monsieur Vénus,* a decadent text by Rachilde, centers its textual play on the institutional nature of gender and fiction; and *Séraphîta,* a fantastic/marvelous text (in Tzvetan Todorov's categorization)[31] explores the floral abyss of woman's (and all) gender identity. That these two texts belong to genres outside of realism will be particularly important to the analysis.

The term "literary decadence" conjures up images of gloom, perversions and inversions, dissatisfaction with existence, rebellion against social codes. Recent theories of decadence, however, rather than mapping out its social and thematic elements, see it more as a reaction to a new understanding of language. In the nineteenth century, the recognition of an autonomy of language, and of the problematic relation of language to reality, engendered what has been called the "cult of artifice" in decadent style.[32] Thus certain problematic areas that previously have been seen as related to gender identity, and that are only partially dealt with in realism, find a full expression in decadent texts. For instance, Flaubert problematizes the relation between reality and fiction and reveals the autonomous power of a language and a fiction that can sometimes create a secondary reality; Balzac, in *Le Lys dans la vallée,* reveals the always already "artificial" and clichéd essence of the natural, floral woman and, in *Sarrasine,* the clichéd essence of the ideal woman herself. But whereas realist texts, as we have seen, seem to need to suppress those problematic areas with the restoration of the clichés of gender identity or, at the very least, to counterbalance them with the realist mode, decadent texts make those problematic areas their very center.

I will next investigate a decadent text that centers on gender identity, *Monsieur Vénus* by Rachilde (a pen name for Marguérite Eymery), and that explores the artifice of language, literature, and gender. This text describes gender and desire from a woman's point of view, both in the sense that the author is a woman and that the main character is a woman who desires. Written in 1889, firmly situated in the decadent mode by its scandalous erotic content and by its inversion of moral codes, this novel begins with artifice as Raoule de Vénérande enters an artificial flower shop to order a decoration for a ball gown. There she sees a beautiful, effeminate man, Jacques Silvert, surrounded by the flowers he is making. She feels immediately attracted to him, particularly to the soft, golden-red hair that covers his body. Discovering that he is a poor artist (in both senses of the word *poor*), she obtains for him and his ailing prostitute sister, Marie, a secret atelier where he can work and where Raoule can visit him at will.

As their affair progresses, Raoule becomes more and more masculine: called by men's names, she begins to dress in men's clothes, practices fencing, and reveals an increasingly violent nature. Conversely, Jacques's masculine nature is slowly eclipsed by his feminine one, a change symbolized in the following description of his body: "Les cuisses, un peu moins fortes que des cuisses de femme, possédaient pourtant une rondeur solide qui effaçait leur sexe" ("His thighs, a bit less full than a woman's thighs, did have, however, a solid roundness which effaced their sex").[33] Thus the two of them form a perverse inverted couple composed of two beings with aporetic gender identities but still in a "normal" female/male union.

Raoule finally decides to marry Jacques to make an "honest man" of him, but because he is not a noble, both upper and lower classes ostracize them. They find their only friend in Raittolbe, one of Raoule's former suitors, who is horrified to find that he, too, desires the effeminate Jacques. Hoping to return Jacques to masculinity to eliminate his own desire for him, Raittolbe takes Jacques to Marie's brothel. There Jacques, discovering he can no longer love women, tries to seduce Raittolbe. When Raoule learns about this betrayal, she makes Raittolbe challenge Jacques, a very poor swordsman, to a duel. Jacques dies, and the novel ends with Raoule kissing a mannequin made in part from a cadaver's body, presumably Jacques's, in particular, from the golden-red hair she so loved.

Thus this text tells the story of a woman's desire (however ambiguous a woman she might be), and Raoule's search for the florist in the beginning of the text represents an allegorical search for the object of that desire. In the rhetoric of the text, however, when Raoule looks for the object of her desire, what she finds is a metaphor for her own female gender, both in the cliché of the flower and in another specific metaphor: "Mlle de Vénérande cherchait à tâtons une porte dans l'étroit couloir. . . . Puis, la clef étant sur la porte, elle entra; mais sur le seuil, une odeur de pommes cuisant la prit à la gorge et l'arrêta net" (p. 23) ("Mlle de Vénérande groped for a door in the narrow corridor. . . . Then, since the key was in the door, she went in. But on the threshold, a strong odor of apples struck her and stopped her short"). This description of her entry into the florist's, typically decadent in its eroticism, depicts in vivid metaphorical terms the entry into the female body. In searching for her desire, Raoule ends up by finding herself in these metaphorical images and, in a more general sense, in the body of the effeminate Jacques, for it is precisely his femininity that attracts her: "Et depuis quand Raoule de Vénérande, qu'une orgie laisse froide, se sent-elle bouillir le crâne devant un homme faible comme une jeune fille?" (p. 56) ("And since when is Raoule de Vénérande, left cold by an orgy, set on fire at the sight of a man as weak as a girl?").

This decadent text about a woman's desire parallels and prefigures certain of Freud's texts on female sexuality (texts which Kofman believes approach a radical questioning of gender identity). Freud claims that, in the case of certain women, desire remains narcissistic, whereas man's desire turns to object-choice: "A different course is followed in the type of female most frequently met with, which is probably the purest and truest one. With the onset of puberty the maturing of the female sexual organs, which up till then have been in a condition of latency, seems to bring about an intensification of the original narcissism, and this is unfavour-able to the development of a true object-choice with its accompanying sexual overvaluation."[34] Such a woman desires herself, and indeed this link between femininity and narcissism emerges clearly in *Monsieur Vénus* in two parallel mirror scenes. In the first, when the masculine woman, Raoule, looks at her own image in a reflection, it makes her feel feminine: "La glace du coupé lui renvoyait son image, son corsage ruisselant de dentelles allait bien, elle se sentait *femme* jusqu'au plaisir" (p. 71) ("The coupé's mirror reflected her image back to her; the bodice of her dress, overflowing with lace, fitted just right; she felt like a *woman* even in her pleasure"). Similarly, Jacques, the effeminate man, looks in the mirror at Raoule's urging, and they both see that he is pretty (in the feminine, as well as the masculine, grammatical form), as Raoule says to him: "—Tu es si beau, chère créature, que tu es plus belle que moi! Regarde là-bas dans la glace penchée, ton cou blanc et rose" (p. 102) ("'You are so handsome, dear creature, that you are more beautiful than I! Look down there, in that mirror leaning from the wall, at your neck so white and pink' ").

Yet it is also important that Jacques be a man because, in remaining male, he can reflect for Raoule a narcissistic image of her other, masculine nature. In the midst of all the descriptions of Jacques's femininity, we find "Ce n'est pas même un hermaphrodite, pas même un impuissant, c'est un beau mâle de vingt et un ans" (p.89) ("He is not even a hermaphrodite, not even an impotent, he is a handsome male twenty-one years old"). But most important, Raoule loves his bisexuality, which reflects and reverses her own: "Ce souvenir de mâle frais et rose comme une fille la hantait cruellement" (p.33) ("This memory of a male fresh and pink like a girl obsessed her cruelly"). The two members of the couple therefore reflect each other in a reversed mirror image and permit a paradoxical narcissistic object love.

Kofman notes that, as Freud explores feminine identity, he becomes "panic-stricken . . . in the face of the reappearance of what he believed he had overcome in himself, narcissism and femininity."[35] To escape this fearful return, "he flees, dragging women with him in his retreat: he leads them along the path of salvation, the path that, despite their basic narcissism, can lead them to fully realized object love—the path of pregnancy" (Kofman, p.57). It is therefore no surprise that Jacques is characterized more and more often as a child: "Il avait l'air d'un petit enfant" (p.45). "Il avait un rire d'enfant très doux" (p.73) ("He had the look of a young child." "He had the laugh of a child, very sweet"). Raoule's relation to him develops into one that resembles the relation between a mother and her son: "Elle le serrait en le berçant entre ses bras, le calmant comme on calme les enfants au maillot" (p.126). "Elle le força à se coucher de suite, alla chercher une fiole d'arnica et le pansa, comme s'il se fût agi d'un enfant au berceau" (p.144) ("She held him tightly while rocking him in her arms, calming him as one calms children in swaddling clothes." "She made him lie down right away, went to find a vial of arnica and bandaged him, as if he were a child in a cradle"). In this text, as in Freud's, when the woman has a child, her narcissism turns to object-choice, and she becomes more masculine. Raoule becomes masculine in her cultural attributes and, by turning her narcissistic desire to object-choice, she desires as a man: "Loving the other, overvaluing the object—for woman this is loving according to the masculine type, this means becoming a man" (Kofman, p.58). We are back to the same problematic place, for desire must always be masculine when it is desire for the other. But if this text parallels the plot of Freud's narrative on female narcissism and its resolution in object-choice, it also subverts it, for, until the end of the novel, Raoule remains essentially bisexual, both male and female (even though she leans more toward masculinity). She continues to desire narcissistically (because Jacques remains a woman for her), yet she also loves as a man in the sense that she loves Jacques as a child/man. She seems to manifest both female narcissistic desire and male object-desire and to find the perfect narcissistic object of her bisexual desire in Jacques. She does not need to return to pure narcissism or to convert to object love but finds fulfillment in both.

Jacques, too, develops a bisexual desire, and as a couple they rewrite the story of Plato's androgyn:

> Il ne cherchait pas à soutenir sa danseuse, mais il ne formait avec elle qu'une taille, qu'un buste, qu'un être. A les voir pressés, tournoyants et fondus dans une étreinte où les chairs, malgré leurs vêtements, se collaient aux chairs, on s'imaginait la seule divinité de l'amour en deux personnes, l'individu *complet* dont parlent les récits fabuleux des brahmanes, deux sexes distincts en un unique monstre. (p. 171) / *He did not try to support his dance partner, but rather formed with her one waist, one torso, one being. To see them pressed together, twirling and joined in an embrace in which, flesh, despite their clothes, clung to flesh, one took them for the one deity of love in two people, that* complete *being of which the fabulous stories of the brahmans speak, two distinct sexes in one unique monster.*

Instead of Plato's two "homosexual" beings, one male and one female,[36] who split in two, along with the third heterosexual being, who splits into male and female, in this case, each split element was already itself split into two, and the "unity" formed by the couple is a differential, fluid combination of all possibilities. It would seem that instead of the normal realist scenario in which male plenitude unites with female lack, here the split woman relates to the split man in a strange nonunion in the sense that they remain split in themselves as well as between each other. Lacan's radical split phallus (not Freud's literal, penile phallus) functions in this text.

Of course, this bisexual relation is not tendered as a wonderful utopian relation between the sexes but is condemned both implicitly and explicitly: implicitly in the atmosphere of debauchery and decadent dissolution that pervades the novel; explicitly in the transgression of social codes, for Raoule and Jacques belong to different classes. Raittolbe says of their marriage: "C'est impossible! c'est monstrueux! c'est . . . c'est révoltant même! Vous! épouser ce misérable? Allons donc!" (p. 154) ("It is impossible! It is monstrous! It is . . . It is even revolting! You! Marry this wretch? Come now!"). What is monstrous is the crossing over of society's boundaries; and like Julien Sorel, Jacques Silvert (who bears Julien's initials) is killed by the classes and groups in power.

Thus as Jacques threatens Raittolbe's masculinity, he threatens society's structure in the sense that he represents the forbidden desire to cross class as well as gender boundaries. At the ball, the other noblemen succumb to this desire, too, even as they despise Jacques's background:

Jacques, la tête renversée, avait encore son sourire de fille amoureuse; ses lèvres relevées laissaient voir ses dents de nacre, ses yeux, agrandis d'un cercle bleuâtre, conservaient une humidité rayonnante, et, sous ses cheveux épais, sa petite oreille, épanouie comme une fleur de pourpre, leur donna, à tous, le même frisson inexplicable. Jacques passa, ne les ayant pas remarqués; sa hanche, cambrée sous l'habit noir, les frôla une seconde . . . et d'un même mouvement, ils crispèrent leurs mains devenues moites. (p. 173) / *Jacques, his head thrown back, still wore his smile of a girl in love; his raised lip showed his pearly teeth; his eyes, enlarged by a bluish circle, retained a radiant moisture; and beneath his thick hair, his small ear, open like a crimson flower, inspired in them all the same, inexplicable shiver. Jacques went by, not having noticed them. His hip, shapely under his black clothes, brushed them for an instant . . . and with one movement, they all clenched their fists, which had become moist.*

But is not another, more basic law being broken in the men's desire for Jacques? One could see in Raittolbe's violent desire (and in that of the other nobles with their clenched fists) a hidden side of the Oedipus complex, for Raittolbe, often alluded to metaphorically as Jacques's father, threatens the son, Jacques, because he *desires* him, and he kills the son to eliminate that desire: "—Je suis un misérable! fit-il avec l'accent d'un père qui, par mégarde, aurait assassiné son fils" (p. 222) (" 'I am a wretch!' " he said with the same tone as would a father who had inadvertently killed his son"). Perhaps this is a horrifying taboo that can make its appearance only in a text written by a woman.

A second taboo seems to be too great even for this text to tolerate: the revelation of man's bisexuality. For, after Raoule introduces Jacques to narcissistic desire, he leans to the other, feminine side and loses his ability to desire women: "Pas une de ces filles, tu m'entends? pas une n'a pu faire revivre ce que tu as tué. . . . Je les déteste, les femmes, oh! je les déteste!" (p. 209) ("Not one of those wenches, do you hear me, not one has been able to revive what you killed. . . . I detest them, women. Oh, I detest them!"). Feminine desire takes over, and Jacques tries to seduce Raittolbe, a male corresponding paradoxically to Jacques's "female" desire, as his narcissistic desire for the image of his own male body. This turn is couched in metaphors of symbolic castration when he, like Julien Sorel, receives a neck injury, here inflicted by the furious Raittolbe.

It is as if the man's bisexuality poses too great a threat (as in Flaubert and in "Une Passion dans le désert") by showing that, when a man accepts the narcissism of his desire, he risks losing all masculinity. Raoule can take over the man's role and dress as a man, but Jacques cannot take over the woman's role, for, significantly, when Jacques arrives at Raittolbe's dressed as Raoule, his own wife, the game must end: at that point, Raoule arrives (dressed as Jacques), and when she discovers Jacques's attempted seduction of Raittolbe, she and Jacques switch clothing, switch back to their prescribed social roles, she arranges for the duel to take place, and they leave as the traditional man and wife. Jacques becomes too feminine, and the delicate balance of his relation with Raoule is destroyed. Gender aporia seems to return to convention.

Even though the relationship between Raoule and Jacques ends, the reversals that take place between gender roles in that relationship generate a different effect that endures. Let us rehearse some of these reversals briefly. Raoule sends Jacques flowers, he makes flowers, thereby becoming associated with the metaphor traditionally associated with women. He veils himself (p. 11), she undresses herself. He is natural, she is degraded (p. 107). She lifts him up and carries him (p. 115); she is the one solicited by a female prostitute; she is challenged to a duel; she is called the "honnête homme" (p. 70), the "monsieur" (p. 84), the "maître" (p. 103) ("master"). He is called the "épouse" (p. 115) ("wife"), the "fiancée" (p. 84) ("woman betrothed"). Finally, she calls him "Mme de Vénérande": it is the woman who gives the man his name in marriage (p. 172).

As these examples show, the reversals are so mechanical as to be humorous and the gender identities so clichéd as to be ludicrous. The constant reversals point less to the horrors or wonders of bisexuality and androgyny than to the clichéd nature of gender identity and to the process of reversal. Gender is so superficial, so artificial, that one can assume and discard it at will.[37]

Indeed, what Rachilde seems to have hit upon in this text of feminine desire is that woman's gender identity and desire are involved with decadent, belated reversals of normal (masculine) identity and desire. Here woman desires but in a "male" way by being a man who desires a woman. As Irigaray asks: "Does female bisexuality not figure as an *inverted recapitulation of the 'program' masculine sexuality writes for itself?* As a projection, upside down and backward, of the end—the telos—of male sexuality's history?"[38]

Yet these reversals spiral out to include reversals of the man's position, too. If woman becomes man in becoming a mother, here masculine object-choice becomes narcissistic desire in Jacques's case. In a sense, Jacques reveals the narcissism of male object-choice, as Kofman notes in speaking of Freud's theory: "In short, they [women] are fascinating because of their narcissism, which constitutes the basis of all desire" (Kofman, p. 53). This reversal goes on to become a reversal in which the man comes second, the woman first. In *Monsieur Vénus,* it is Jacques, not the woman, who is weak and powerless, and in Freud's text, penis envy is reversed: "It is no longer the woman who envies man his penis, it is he who envies her for her unassailable libidinal position, whereas he himself—one may wonder why—has been impoverished, has been emptied of this original narcissism in favor of the love object" (Kofman, p. 52).

In *Monsieur Vénus,* however, so many reversals take place, so many roles are exchanged, that after a while, one can no longer tell what is being reversed, which gender is which, whether one should be scandalized or not, whether the subject of this text is a woman's love for a man, a man's love for a woman, a woman's love for herself or for another woman, or a man's love for himself or for another man. In one case, Raittolbe ironically becomes scandalized by this tale's very *unscandalous* nature, for when Raoule tells him that she (albeit in the masculine grammatical form) loves a man in the "normal" code of desire ("Je suis *amoureux* d'un homme et non pas d'une femme!" (p. 88) ("I am [a man] in love with a man and not with a woman!"), he exclaims: "—Elle est *amoureux* d'un . . . hom . . . mme! Dieux immortels! s'exclama-t-il, prenez pitié de moi! Je crois que ma cervelle s'écroule!" (p. 89) (" 'She is [a man] in love with a . . . a . . . man! Immortal gods!' he exclaimed, 'Take pity on me! I think my brain is crumbling!' "). The decadent, upside-down world turns itself around so many times that one loses one's bearings and after a while notices only the artificial machine of reversal, the artificial nature of gender identity itself.

If readers of *Frankenstein* found it monstrous that a woman should have written such a monstrous text,[39] so readers of Rachilde find monstrous her text of desire. What seems to be universally astonishing, if not scandalous, about this text in the opinion of the critics is that it was written by an innocent twenty-year-old woman:

> Ce qui est tout à fait délicat dans la perversité de ce livre, c'est qu'il a été écrit par une jeune fille de vingt ans. . . . Toute cette frénésie tendre et méchante, et ces formes d'amour qui sentent la mort, sont l'oeuvre d'une enfant, de l'enfant la plus douce et la plus re-tirée! . . . Ce vice savant, éclatant dans le rêve d'une vierge, c'est un des problèmes les plus mystérieux que je sache. / *What is completely delicate in the perversity of this book, is the fact that it was written by a twenty-year-old girl. . . . All that tender and wicked frenzy, and those forms of love which smack of death, are the work of a girl child, of the gentlest and the most retiring child! . . . This knowledgeable vice, breaking out in the dream of a virgin; this is one of the most mysterious problems I know.*[40]

The enigmatic conjunction of innocence, woman, writing, and desire shocks. But if we look closely at another inversion in this text, this scandal reverses itself and it, too, becomes unscandalous.

Just as this text plays with gender stereotypes, so it plays with literary clichés. To construct its plot, it blatantly uses certain clichés of plot construction (in a Proppian sense). Here an upper-class woman takes a lower-class man for a lover, hoping to marry him, as does Mathilde de la Mole (we must not forget the initials, J.S.). The young painter kept by a more experienced woman makes up the plot of *La Cousine Bette*. Raoule's perverse nature, like Emma Bovary's, results from her reading of books. This overuse of conventionality culminates in the frequent mythological allusions and in this text's patent adherence to the code of decadence.

But often when this novel uses narrative master texts, it inverts one of the elements in the master text; the title itself shows this clearly. Like Paquita in *La Fille aux yeux d'or*, Jacques is kept in a secluded, haremlike environment; in the Balzac text, a masculine woman keeps a feminine woman; but in *Monsieur Vénus,* masculine Raoule keeps an effeminate man. The traditional scenario in which a poor, destitute woman, trying to earn money to support herself and a dependent family member, falls into the wrong hands, is reversed here when the destitute woman is a destitute man trying to support his sick sister. In *La Peau de Chagrin,* Raphael spies on the woman he loves from behind a curtain; here, Raoule peeks at Jacques. If, as we saw in *Le Lys dans la vallée,* the flower metaphor figures women's imprisonment in a rhetorical structure, in this text it is Jacques who is associated with the flowers, which—in light of the constant, artificial reversals—are as artificial as the structure itself.

Whether these master narratives originate in these precise texts or merely in the corpus of standard plot structures (one could list other texts in which hidden men peek at beautiful women, helpless women are locked up in a haremlike prison, or an upper-class character desires a lower-class one) is not important. What is significant is that Rachilde takes standard plot elements and inverts them, and literature takes its own artificial nature as its subject. In a typical eighteenth-century plot, described by Nancy K. Miller, a vulnerable heroine falls into a sensuality not condoned by society and eventually dies because of it (Manon Lescaut, for instance).[41] This plot, so tame and acceptable when heroines are the victims, becomes curiously intolerable when the victim is the hero. Rachilde's heroines are, in the critics' eyes, sadomasochists, who, like Raoule de Vénérande, always "control, corrupt, and destroy their pliable men."[42] The approval of the control, corruption, and destruction of female victims and the disapproval of that same fate for male victims should give us pause, and Rachilde's inversion does just that. Similarly, desire, sadistic behavior, and writing are all acceptable when associated with men but not when associated with innocent, virginal women such as Rachilde.

In any case, the innocent Rachilde's invention of this erotic, sadistic plot becomes less scandalous for she simply inverts the canon of gender and narrative and thereby points out the repetitive, coded nature of both. This text, in fact, alludes in a strange way to the artificial nature of its own textuality. Raoule is called at one point a man handsome "comme tous les héros de roman que rêvent les jeunes filles" (p. 191) ("like all the heroes in novels of which young women dream"). This odd metaphor points out its own fictional nature in a *structure en abyme* in which the hero (Raoule) of the novel becomes the hero of the novel (of the young women).

Taken one step further, Raoule is indeed a "hero" dreamed up by the young woman, Rachilde.

This text thematizes its own fictionality most clearly in the image of Jacques as a work of art (text or statue) created by Raoule, just as this text is written by the young woman, Rachilde. Raoule needs, as she says, to create a work of art, to "write her book," a creation she relates to her own sexual desire: "—Il est certain, monsieur, reprit Raoule haussant les épaules, que j'ai eu des amants. Des amants dans ma vie comme j'ai des livres dans ma bibliothèque, pour savoir, pour étudier. . . . Mais je n'ai pas eu de passion, je n'ai pas écrit mon livre, moi!" (p.85) (" 'It is certain, sir,' resumed Raoule shrugging her shoulders, 'that I have had lovers. I have had lovers in my life as I have books in my library, in order to know, to study. . . . But I have never experienced passion; *I* have not written my book!' "). (She is, after all, an artist in the text.) Woman's exclusion from desire (Raoule's passionless affairs) figures her exclusion from language (her unwritten text), and when Raoule finally does desire, she can then write her text, Jacques. She creates him, brings out his femininity more and more, makes him more and more like a statue: "Son visage pâle dans les ténèbres lui fit l'effet d'une face de statue" (p.130) ("His pale face in the shadows seemed to her to be like the face of a statue"). Finally, she turns him into the mannequin (even though another, a German, actually creates him). The book she writes, here called a poem, is Jacques's body, his bisexuality, his paradoxical nature of a text to be read: "Jacques, dont le corps était un poème, savait que ce poème serait toujours lu avec plus d'attention que la lettre d'un vulgaire écrivain comme lui" (p.139) ("Jacques, whose body was a poem, knew that this poem would always be read with closer scrutiny than the letter of a common writer like him"). Here, woman's writing, both Raoule's and Rachilde's, does not imitate nature but points out its own invention (it turns reality into the mannequin), as it plays with conventions. It is a writing of dislocation resulting from woman's place of reversal, a reversal so repetitious as to end up in undecidability. The end product of this writing is the artificial machine-doll as work of art, the machinelike nature of fiction and gender, a doll that is itself undecidable in the sense that it is both real and artificial, Jacques's real body and a simulacrum.

Even though this text is written by a woman, woman's writing is monstrous here; it is a deformation of the natural. For Raoule's desire and her desire to write end up in the death of the child (Jacques), the death of woman's natural production, and the birth of the monster, half-human, half-machine. This might explain the bizarre statement made by Raoule when she, attracted to Jacques, tries to cover up her troubled desire by saying that she had just witnessed the death of a child: "Troublée, voilà tout. J'ai vu tomber un enfant sous un omnibus, rue de Rivoli" (p.35) ("Troubled, that is all. I saw a child fall beneath an omnibus on the Rue de Rivoli"). With the death of the real, natural child comes the birth of woman's art and desire, the birth of the monster at the end, an artificial mannequin that moves but by means of an interior spring. In the century in which realism reigned, woman's writing can be but a decadent, unnatural, and monstrous inversion.

Séraphîta, the Fantastic, and Undecidable Gender

Ce qui est
ainsi levé, ce n'est donc pas la différence mais le différent, les différents,
l'extériorité décidable des différents. – JACQUES DERRIDA, *La Dissémina-
tion / What is lifted, then, is not difference but the different, the differends, the
decidable exteriority of differing terms.*

FANTASTIC TEXTS, in Todorov's classic definition, create an essential undecidability (or aporia in my terms) between categories, and this undecidability can exist between the gender categories of male and female.[43] Indeed, the last text considered here, Balzac's *Séraphîta*, is perhaps the one that most clearly presents the deconstruction of imprisoning gender identities in a literal manner. It takes the moments of aporia encountered in the previous texts and turns them into its very subject. Yet at first sight, the title of the text, *Séraphîta*, would seem to situate it securely in standard gender traditions because it bears, first, an angelic connotation (*séraphin* in French, *seraph* in English) and at the same time implies femininity in the final letter *a*. A story about an angelic woman would hardly seem likely to undermine institutional gender categories because, as we have seen, this is one of the most prevalent of images for women in the nineteenth-century texts studied here.

The second word in the text, the subtitle of the first section, "Séra-phîtüs," immediately destroys the security of these presuppositions, however, for it connotes masculinity, especially since it follows the name *Séraphîta*. This juxtaposition of titles raises the issue of gender identity from the outset because one must ask the question: Who is the subject of this story, a man or a woman? It also calls attention to one way in which gender is differentiated, in this case, by means of the three letters, *a* and *üs*, suggesting that sexual difference corresponds to textual difference. Furthermore, the masculinity implied in the subtitle tends to contaminate the conventional image of the angelic woman. So early in the text, then, we confront the problem of gender identity in several ways.

The first section of the story describes the young man, Séraphîtüs, and his relation to a beautiful young woman, Minna, and ends as Séraphîtüs falls asleep, a "blanking-out" represented in the text by a blank space between the first two sections. Then, in the second section entitled "Séraphîta," in one of the strangest moments in literature, Séraphîtüs wakes up as Séraphîta, with no accompanying explanation in the text. Here Séraphîta's relations with a young man, Wilfrid, are described. In the third section, whose title, "Séraphîta/Séraphîtüs," combines the two names and genders into one, the main character is called alternately "he" and "she." Again, the text does not account for this fantastic gender switch but simply continues the narration as if nothing unusual had happened. Her unexplained gender has given rise to two conflicting theories: one is that she is an androgyn, espoused by Gaston Bachelard, Albert Béguin, and Lucienne Frappier-Mazur; the other, espoused by Pierre Castex, that she simply has no sex.[44]

To be sure, the religious connotation of the androgyny of angels (or at least of the problematic nature of their gender) and the philosophical aspect of the story (a large part of it explicates Swedenborg's philosophy more or less accurately) render the sex change of the main character more "traditional," more symbolic, and certainly more tolerable. Nonetheless, this change cannot be dismissed as a conventional metaphor, for it functions too literally and ostentatiously, and thereby calls out for a closer reading of the way in which the text describes this change and why it does so.

The gender change in fact creates a dilemma for the literary critic, who does not know whether to refer to this character as a "he" or a "she." I label Séraphîta/Séraphîtüs a "she" because of the force of the title of the text and also because it is the prevalent form used in the story. But more important, as we have seen, the question of *woman's* identity rather than man's seems to draw out the problematic nature of all concepts of identity, be they human, male, or female. Hence I call her a woman in the sense that the concept of "woman" has already been put into question.[45] Logically, the first step in the study of Séraphîta's gender identity would be the observation of her body. One would normally think sex could easily be verified physiologically, yet Séraphîta's physical characteristics pose some interesting problems. The very first description of her omits any reference to gender, when she and Minna, illuminated by a light that does not penetrate the mystery of their identity, climb the mountain named the Falberg: "Par une matinée où le soleil éclatait au sein de ce paysage en y allumant les feux de tous les diamants éphémères produits par les cristallisations de la neige et des glaces, deux personnes passèrent sur le golfe, le traversèrent et volèrent le long des bases du Falberg, vers le sommet duquel elles s'élevèrent" ("One morning when the sun shone brightly on the heart of this landscape, lighting the fires of all the ephemeral diamonds produced by the crystallizations of the snow and ice, two people crossed the bay, traversing it and flying along the base of the Falberg, toward whose summit they climbed").[46] Immediately after this vague introduction, the narrator questions their identities: "Etait-ce deux créatures, était-ce deux flèches?" (p.736) ("Were they two creatures; were they two arrows?"). Here, distance prevents the determination of identity, and space or distance will continue to play an important role in its problematization (as we saw once already, when the interval of sleep and its textual representative, the white space, represented the moment of gender change).

Following these initial descriptions of Séraphîta as a neutral being (as an "être," a "créature," a "personne" ["a being," "a creature," "a person"]), the text shifts to a heterogeneous description, which portrays her alternately as a male and a female. On the one hand, Séraphîta "paraissait être un jeune homme de dix-sept ans," (p.741) ("seemed to be a young man of seventeen years"), but on the other, she has a body "mince et grêle comme celui d'une femme" (p.741) ("slim and slight like that of a woman"). The oscillation of these perspectives (both of which belong to the narrator) is one way in which the text describes the simultaneous presence of contradictory elements.

A typical, extremely detailed Balzacian portrait is never given of Séraphîta; instead we see a body so diaphanous that it almost disappears.[47] "Nitescence," "fluide phosphorique," "ces lueurs contenues dans une coupe d'albâtre," "diaphanes," "attitude aérienne" (p.741) ("luminosity," "phosphoric fluid," "those glimmers contained in an alabaster cup," "diaphanous," "airy attitude"): such are the words used to describe the angelic Séraphîta in her limited portrait. Air and light compose a body lacking weight and mass. Superimposed, however, over this almost translucent torso appear isolated body parts, usually extremities: her feet in the skis, her tapering hands, the gold of her hair, her red lips; yet none of these body parts specifies her gender (as the possession of the phallus or lack thereof would). From these details emerges the final portrait of an airy, centerless, literally decentered being composed of isolated limbs and members, which appear one by one but never unite into a whole. It must be stressed that the narrator never categorically states her gender in the beginning but says only what she *seems* to be or compares her to something else.

In fact, the text precludes the possibility of any physical gender identity because, as Minna's father says: "Jamais Séraphîta n'a été vue dans sa nudité, comme le sont quelquefois les enfants; jamais elle n'a été touchée ni par un homme ni par une femme; elle a vécu vierge sur le sein de sa mère, et n'a jamais crié" (p.787) ("Séraphîta has never been seen naked, as children are sometimes; she was never touched by man or woman. She lived virginal on the breast of her mother, and never cried"). This prohibits any referential definition of sexual identity, and consequently one cannot arrive at the truth of Séraphîta's sex; gender here does not fit into a neat system of well-defined, closed categories. It is not biological, it cannot be verified in the literal realm. If, in the psychoanalytic sense, the male has the phallus, and the female does not, then Séraphîta cannot have a sex, for one cannot tell whether she has the phallus or not. Thus it is neither that woman has nothing, as in *La Cousine Bette,* nor that the real woman never appears, as in *Sarrasine,* but that seeing and woman's gender identity are incompatible.

The impossibility of a literal identity naturally does not prevent Séraphîta from being defined in a rhetorical way. As *Le Lys dans la vallée,* "Une Passion dans le désert," and *Sarrasine* show, the metaphorical seems to be woman's fate. As is so often the case in Balzac texts, one of the principal means of gaining insight into Balzacian characters is to study their environment. The metonymic relationship between character identity in Balzac's texts and the milieu surrounding them turns into a metaphoric one, particularly in this story, where the leap from the name

"Séraphîtüs" in the subtitle to a landscape description in the first paragraph links character to environment. In this first section the landscape symbols do indeed represent in a surprising way the problematic identity of the main character.

The first paragraph introduces the concept of delimitation in a description of the coastline of Norway, the dividing line between land and sea: "A voir sur une carte les côtes de la Norvège, quelle imagination ne serait émerveillée de leurs fantasques découpures, longue dentelle de granit où mugissent incessamment les flots de la mer du Nord?" (p. 729) ("Perceiving the coastlines of Norway on a map, whose imagination would not marvel at their fantastic indentations, a kind of long granite lace where the waters of the North Sea ceaselessly roar?"). Attention focuses on the "découpures" ("indentations"), on the complicated pattern that delimits land from sea, on the borders between two elements that oppose each other in a veritable struggle, which presents "l'image d'une lutte entre l'Océan et le granit, deux créations également puissantes: l'une par son inertie, l'autre par sa mobilité" (p. 730) ("the image of a struggle between the Ocean and the granite, two creations equally strong, one because of its inertia, the other because of its mobility"). The dividing line between these two elements, the place where the land meets the sea, is an abyss or a chasm: "un abîme profond de cent toises" (p. 730) ("an abyss one hundred fathoms deep"). These "rivages sans grèves" ("shores without beaches") offer no gradual change from sea to land along a flat and sandy stretch of beach but only an unbreachable abyss. Thus the divisions between sea and land are, unsurprisingly, spaces, and dangerous ones at that: "abîmes sans chemins" (p. 729) ("pathless abysses"). In this introduction to the landscape two elements oppose each other and again remain separated by a distance, here frightening and dangerous.

In a second moment in the text this initial clear-cut distinction between land and sea gives way to a different structure. As the description proceeds by moving away from the coast to the gulf inland, a new relation between land and sea emerges; and as the typical initial Balzacian bird's-eye view moves in closer to the characters' dwellings and finally to the characters themselves, the relation between polarities changes. The events take place in a special time, at the dividing line between two centuries, at the time of a very special winter: "L'hiver de 1799 à 1800 fut un des plus rudes dont le souvenir ait été gardé par les Européens; la mer de Norvège se prit entièrement dans les Fiords, où la violence du ressac l'empêche ordinairement de geler" (p.734) ("The winter of 1799 and 1800 was one of the harshest which the Europeans have kept in memory. The Norwegian Sea was entirely iced over in the fjords, where the violence of the surf normally keeps it from freezing"). Just at this liminal turning point between centuries, an extreme winter freezes the sea making it like the land, entangling the polarities. From the initial chasm that divided land from sea develops the chiasmus that mixes up the two elements by exchanging their properties. In a similar way, the land and sea combine in the gulf inland:

> En cet endroit, le golfe est assez large pour que la mer, refoulée par le Falberg, vienne expirer en murmurant sur la dernière frange de ces collines, rive doucement bordée d'un sable fin, parsemé de mica, de paillettes, de jolis cailloux, de porphyres, de marbres aux mille nuances amenés de la Suède par les eaux de la rivière, et de débris marins, de coquillages, fleurs de la mer que poussent les tempêtes, soit du pôle, soit du midi. (p.731) / *In this place, the bay is wide enough so that the sea, pushed back by the Falberg, can expire murmuring on the last slopes of the hills, on a shore softly bordered with a fine sand, scattered with mica, with crystals, with pretty stones, with porphyry, with marbles of a thousand hues brought from Sweden by the waters of the river, and with marine debris, with shells, with flowers of the sea driven in by tempests, either from the north pole, or from the south.*

Here a gradual and continuous change from land to sea along the shoreline, a change from solid to liquid, mixes together solid pieces of land brought to the gulf by the river (liquid) with bits of solid landlike substances (shells) that come from the sea (liquid). Such a confusion of solid and liquid elements turns the beach into the union of what were formerly opposing elements and culminates in the metaphor "flowers of the sea," which in an oxymoron, unites sea and land.

The evolution of these structures, from the chasm that completely separates one element from another, to the chiasmus that puts into question the radical split between them, echoes the evolution of gender, for the sequence of titles, "Séraphîtüs," "Séraphîta," "Séraphîta/Séraphîtüs," tells the story of the polarity male/female (the chasm) that ends up in aporia (the chiasmus). In looking for clues to Séraphîta's identity in her rhetorical relation to her environment, we find that, in the landscape details, the very existence of contradictory structures informs us about her enigmatic being.

Another detail in Séraphîta's environment, an unusual flower, represents her in several interesting ways. First, the flower mixes up different categories, as she does, in that it is a hybrid; like Mme de Mortsauf's lily, it is essentially double. In addition, the flower's physical structure resembles that of Séraphîta herself:

> Il lui donna soudain une plante hybride que ses yeux d'aigle lui avaient fait apercevoir . . . véritable merveille éclose sous le souffle des anges. Minna saisit avec un empressement enfantin la touffe d'un vert transparent et brillant comme celui de l'émeraude, formée par de petites feuilles roulées en cornet, d'un brun clair au fond, mais qui, de teinte en teinte, devenaient vertes à leurs pointes partagées en découpures d'une délicatesse infinie. Ces feuilles étaient si pressées qu'elles semblaient se confondre, et produisaient une foule de jolies rosaces. (p.739) / *Suddenly he gave her a hybrid plant which his eagle eyes had spotted . . . a veritable marvel brought to bloom by the breath of angels. With a childish eagerness Minna seized the tuft of a brilliant, transparent green like that of the emerald, which was formed of small leaves rolled like a cornet, light brown at the base, but which, from hue to hue, changed to green at their tips which were notched in indentations of an infinite delicacy. These leaves were pressed in so tightly that they seemed to blend together, and they produced a mass of pretty rosettes.*

Here the flower displays two distinct colors, which change from one to the other, just as Séraphîta alternately displays masculine and feminine traits. What is more, its tiny leaves combine in a muddled heap, in the same manner that Séraphîta's body forms a loose conjunction of parts rather than a coherent entity. Here, as in the chasm and chiasmus structures, Séraphîta's identity is given in metaphors, a fact that is extremely important, as we saw in Chapter 2. Hence, since a literal, one-to-one mapping of identity onto things or people never occurs, the illusion of identity can never take hold. Identity always remains at a distance because of the space of symbolism, and distance or difference thus paradoxically marks identity. Identity is, in a certain way, always rhetorical and relational, and this text points out the linguistic nature of institutional categories of identities.

Actually, the relationships between Séraphîta and others determine gender in this text because they determine the use of gender pronouns. Women call Séraphîta a man; it is Minna who, as the text makes explicit, names her Séraphîtüs: "La personne que Minna nommait Séraphîtüs s'appuya sur son talon droit pour relever la planche" (p.736) ("The person whom Minna named Séraphîtüs rested on his right heel to lift off the plank"). Minna names Séraphîta in order to name herself, for, when she begins to doubt whether Séraphîtüs is an earthly being, she cries: " 'Qui donc es-tu? dit-elle avec un sentiment de douce terreur. Mais je le sais, tu es ma vie' " (p.738) (" 'Who are you then?' she asked with a feeling of gentle terror. 'But I know; you are my life' "). As her life, as her very being, Séraphîta *is* her identity. Just as the soldier in "Une Passion dans le désert" uses the panther, Minna uses Séraphîta as a mirror with which to construct her own female identity by seeing in Séraphîta the "other," the male. It is not a coincidence that at the beginning of the story Minna and Séraphîta are walking along the abyss, along the line of demarcation between the polar opposites of land and sea. For Minna to name Séraphîta is to place herself on the "proper" side of the abyss. In speaking of the literal abyss she claims: "Je n'ai voulu regarder que toi en côtoyant les murailles de ce gouffre; autrement que serais-je devenue?" (p.736) ("I wanted to look only at you while skirting the high walls of this chasm, otherwise what would I have become?"). In other words, if she had not looked at Séraphîta, she would have literally been drawn into the abyss to fall to her death; and symbolically, if she cannot use Séraphîta as a point of reference, she cannot keep from dying in the figural sense of losing her identity or of never being able to establish it. In psychoanalytic terms, she thus cedes the phallus to Séraphîta, accepts her own loss, and gives herself a false identity.

Hence Minna assigns both to Séraphîta and to herself an identity based completely on a relational foundation: one could call it a differential identity. Significantly, in the text, Minna is not the only one to call Séraphîta a man; the narrator also refers to her as a young man and thus the gender change does not result from a limitation of the point of view of one or of several of the characters. Furthermore, and most surprising, Séraphîta refers to herself in the masculine form in the following quotation in which the verb *arriver,* whose past participle agrees in gender with the subject, has a masculine form: "Je suis arrivé au dégoût de toutes choses" (p.745) ("I have come to disgust all things"). Thus Séraphîta actually assumes the identity given to her by Minna.

Even though Séraphîta does play the role of a man for a while, she eventually stops doing so when she refuses to be Minna's partner: "Je ne saurais être ton compagnon" (p.743) ("I could not be your companion"). Here, she refuses her love and refuses to be her masculine counterpart, to assume fully the masculine identity assigned to her. Thus she suspends the process of gender determination and does not allow her masculine identity to take hold.

Just after this scene Séraphîta changes from Séraphîtüs to Séraphîta during her nap, and again, others define Séraphîta's identity, since all of the men call her a woman. This second section, entitled "Séraphîta," mirrors the first section, for here, a young man, Wilfrid, loves her. Séraphîta, too, refers to herself in the feminine gender: "J'en suis sûre, Wilfrid" (p.749) ("I am sure of it, Wilfrid"). But she finally refuses this identity also: "Vous voyez bien, mon ami, que je ne suis pas une femme" (p.750) ("You can well see, my friend, that I am not a woman"). By assuming both masculine and feminine identities, then neither one nor the other, she frustrates attempts to define her gender. Because of the impossibility of categorizing her sex, she uncannily suspends the ability to differentiate between male and female, calling their very definitions into question. Thus although Séraphîta accepts provisionally, perhaps playfully (in the Derridean sense), the identities given to her by others, in a second moment she refuses to be labeled either as a man or as a woman and affirms her difference from the definition.

The third section of the story, entitled "Séraphîta/Séraphîtüs," by characterizing her as both male and female at once, affirms her paradoxical identity. A perfect distinction between the genders in the first two sections of the story never really exists, for near the place where her gender changes, both masculine and feminine pronouns describe her. When she descends the mountain at the end of section one, in which she is a man, she begins to "laisser sa force mâle" (p.747) ("leave his male strength"), and although she is still called Séraphîtüs, Minna calls her "chère" (p.747) ("dear"), and Séraphîta speaks of herself as being "trop lasse" (p.748) ("too weary"), both words with feminine genders. Thus even the boundaries set up by the text's most basic structures break down, for, as Séraphîta says, she simply cannot fit into a polarized structure: "Moi, je suis comme un proscrit, loin du ciel; et comme un monstre, loin de la terre" (p.746) ("I, I am like an exile, far from heaven, and like a monster, far from earth").

Hence, in her relations with others, Séraphîta assumes the identity given to her but assumes it only in a playful way, not in earnest: she plays at being a man, then at being a woman, but she does not settle into either category. In identifying Séraphîta, the others can identify themselves, can give themselves a seemingly stable identity not attainable without her; indeed, Séraphîta knows that those who love her do not love *her* but merely use her as a mirror to create their own illusory self-identity, as she says, "vous m'aimez pour vous et non pour moi" (p.751) ("you love me for yourself and not for me"). Both men and women use the imaginary self (in the Lacanian sense), the fictional mirror-self, on which to base their identity. Séraphîta would like Minna and Wilfrid to love each other, something the two of them refuse at first to do, because as mirror, Séraphîta lets them see and love an image they themselves create in an odd form of narcissism, but through which they cannot see to the real other. In the text, this stage is surpassed only with the breaking of the mirror, with the death of Séraphîta, at which point Minna and Wilfrid can turn to each other, not because of a fictional sexual difference, but because of the experience they share in common. In a sense, this is an extremely negative moment because Minna and Wilfrid can wake to the "truth" about Séraphîta (and themselves) only through her death.

This mirror seems to be necessary, however, because acting as a mirror, Séraphîta always seems to protect the two characters from danger by breathing on them (in the religious sense, this is like the breath, the "souffle" of God). Her breath acts like a potion to induce amnesia, in one instance, keeping Minna from dying: "'Je meurs, mon Séraphîtüs, n'ayant aimé que toi,' dit-elle en faisant un mouvement machinal pour se précipiter. Séraphîtüs lui souffla doucement sur le front et sur les yeux. Tout à coup, semblable au voyageur délassé par un bain, Minna n'eut plus que la mémoire de ses vives douleurs, déjà dissipées par cette haleine carressante" (pp.737–38) ("'I am dying, my Séraphîtüs, having loved only you,' she said, making a mechanical movement to throw herself off. Séraphîtüs breathed softly on her forehead and on her eyes. Suddenly, like a traveler refreshed by a bath, Minna retained only the memory of her bitter woes, already dissipated by that caressing breath"). Her breath also revives Wilfrid from a deathlike swoon: "Wilfrid était tombé demi-mort sur le tapis, mais Séraphîta souffla sur le front de cet homme qui s'endor-mit aussitôt paisiblement à ses pieds" (p.753) ("Wilfrid had fallen half-dead on the rug, but Séraphîta breathed on the forehead of this man, who immediately fell asleep at her feet").

Thus Séraphîta, again following a traditionally feminine path, veils certain frightening truths about her own identity, as she says: "Je ne me trouve pas assez de voiles et crains que tu ne me voies encore trop: tu frémirais si tu me connaissais mieux" (p.745) ("I find I do not have enough veils and I fear that you still see too much of me; you would tremble if you knew me better"). The other characters aim to discover this truth of Séraphîta's identity, or, as Wilfrid says, the truth about truth (just as in *Sarrasine,* one looks for truth and woman), but she keeps veiling herself and does not permit them to see: "Elle se montre et se retire comme une vérité jalouse" (p.763) ("She shows herself and withdraws herself like a jealous truth"). What is this dangerous truth that she must hide? When Séraphîta prevents Minna from seeing the abyss of nonidentity, this veiled abyss is *Séraphîta herself:* "Séraphîtüs laissa Minna cramponnée au granit, et, comme eût fait une ombre, il alla se poser sur le bord de la table, d'où ses yeux plongèrent au fond du Fiord en en défiant l'éblouissante profondeur; son corps ne vacilla point, son front resta blanc et impassible comme celui d'une statue de marbre: abîme contre abîme" (p.738) ("Séraphîtüs left Minna clinging to the granite, and, as would a shadow, he went to stand on the edge of the slab; from there his eyes plumbed the depths of the Fjord defying the dazzling depth. His body did not waver, his forehead remained white and impassive like that of a marble statue, abyss facing abyss"). Furthermore, the other metaphor for Séraphîta, the flower, is also called an abyss: " 'Voilà qui est surnaturel, dit le vieillard en voyant une fleur éclose en hiver. —Un abîme! s'écria Wilfrid exalté par le parfum' " (p.764) (" 'That is something supernatural,' said the old man seeing a flower blooming in winter. 'An abyss!' cried Wilfrid, exalted by its scent"). If she does not carefully veil herself, she causes others to experience the abyss, their own abyss of nonidentity, as when Wilfrid goes to see her and catches a glimpse of the truth, the religious truth of the "abîmes supérieurs" (p.758) ("superior abysses" in a religious sense of a higher, spiritual knowledge) as well as the truth of Séraphîta as abyss: "Depuis quelques jours, lorsque Wilfrid entrait chez Séraphîta, son corps y tombait dans un gouffre" (p.757) ("For several days, when Wilfrid entered Séraphîta's home, his body fell there into a chasm").

This identification of Séraphîta with the abyss generates several important meanings. Since the figure of the abyss functions in two contradictory ways, its equation with Séraphîta underscores in a more structural way the questioning of gender identity which she introduces thematically. In representing, on the one hand, the unbreachable chasm between opposites and unique entities, that between male and female, solid and liquid (and also in the philosophical aspect of the text, between mind and body, matter and spirit), the abyss functions as difference and alterity. In a sense, it functions as Sarrasine's discovery of castration. On the other hand, its contradictory role as chiasmus complicates matters a great deal. Since Séraphîta, being both male and female, incorporates these supposedly mutually exclusive entities within her own unique self (she contains the abyss), she undermines the unity of the self-present subject, revealing the split therein. In a sense, Séraphîta, containing this split, always remains at a distance from herself, in the sense that she can never secure her own gender identity. And, as the abyss, she *is* distance, the gap of the symbolic, for her very equation with the abyss and with the flower points out the essentially symbolic nature of any identity and shows that it can exist only in language.

As a consequence, this text exposes a certain tendency to interpret the world in terms of metaphorical polarities, while at the same time putting these polarities into question, a "deconstruction" of gender, which, of course, does not go beyond it, for that is impossible. But if it does not go beyond it, at least from Séraphîta's deconstruction of the opposition between male and female emerges a different concept of woman, one that helps to understand why it is so often a woman who brings about a questioning of gender. In this view of woman, man does not reign at the top of a hierarchical polarity, nor does woman in a reversal of power, but rather this conventional polarization of male and female is undermined by the "other" woman. It must be stressed that this "woman" is not elevated into an Other preferable to her masculine counterpart. Rather, this concept of woman belongs to the very juxtaposition of male with female, to the process of differentiation, to the place where borderlines are not fixed but are in the process of becoming, where hierarchy cannot exist.

As this "woman," Séraphîta marks a significant difference from the characters studied in earlier chapters who undermine gender identity but who are subsumed back into the polarized structure. Like these others, Séraphîta dies, but at the end of the text, in becoming an angel, she rises from the dead to ascend to heaven, neutralizing the previous negative moment of death through rebirth. She rewrites the ending of the texts that define the selfless "angel in the house." This ascension (and consequently the entire religious aspect of the story), along with the new-found love between Minna and Wilfrid, symbolizes perhaps a certain overcoming of a repressive and essentially improper polarized structure. Clearly, this overcoming does not somehow do away with dichotomous oppositions but instead points out the system's limitations and inconsistencies and allows for an identity *in and of difference.*

Here Séraphîta as "woman" (one could just as well call her "man," since both sexes are affected), functions not as difference but as Derrida's concept of *différance,* as that which cannot be situated in a traditional opposition.[48] For Séraphîta shows that sexual difference is indeed textual difference, the difference between the letters *a* and *üs* in her names. This "sextual" difference cannot be located in the sensible (or here biological realm), nor is it an idea or concept in the sense that it can be clearly defined (male clearly distinguished from female) but is a process of production in the system of language. No unique masculinity or femininity exists as a plenitude, for they are constructed only within a system of differences, and they contain this difference within.

Finally, Séraphîta radically questions the psychoanalytic definition of gender identity in which man has the phallus and woman has lost it. For, as we have seen, Séraphîta cannot find a place there, since the question of her possession of the phallus is undecidable. She challenges the very existence of castration by suspending her relation to it. Here, Séraphîta as woman does not veil the fact that she does not have the phallus (is castrated) but rather veils the fact that castration does not have a place in this text, that gender identity does not exist as a real or representable thing. Séraphîta plays with castration in the sense that she assumes a gender identity only to discard it and reveal its fictional nature.

That these two texts, *Monsieur Vénus* and *Séraphîta,* which most clearly problematize gender identity, lie outside of the realist mode is no coincidence. It seems that gender identity can be problematized on a literal level only in nonrealist texts. On the one hand, decadent texts take the artifice of language as their subject, thus reversing the realist understanding of language (as defined by Barthes),[49] in which language is believed to re-present reality, to denote reality in an immediate way. Instead, in the decadent text, as in (Barthes's notion of "modernity"), the referent is eclipsed from view and the sign becomes the subject. Thus decadent texts take gender out of the "real" world to situate it in language. Fantastic texts, on the other hand (in Todorov's definition), render the limits between elements ambiguous and thus unlocatable in the real: in *Séraphîta* it is the limit between genders (although *Séraphîta* is more generally a "merveilleux" ["marvelous"] text in Todorov's schema, in terms of gender identity it is "fantastique" ["fantastic"]). It is the problematic relation of gender identity to realist ideology that I will explore in the conclusion.

CONCLUSION

Realism

AND FETISHISM

Disparu est

le sujet. Le disparu *apparaît*. . . . Titre, donc, d'un (tableau) absent: d'un
disparu. —JACQUES DERRIDA, *La Vérité en peinture* / *Disappeared* [*disparu*]
is the subject. What has disappeared *appears*. . . . Title, then, of one
absent (picture): of one disappeared.

WHAT EMERGES from our readings of realist texts is the notion
that they define gender on the basis of *sameness:* woman is just like
a man missing only one thing. The two texts belonging to literary genres
outside of realism, however, do not define feminine gender as a mirror of
man's, but rather emphasize and problematize difference in their explora-
tions of the linguistic and artificial basis of gender identity. It would
seem, then, that a realist theory of representation is itself an institution,
which promotes a particular notion of gender identity—one based on
similarity.

Let us now explore this problem of gender identity and realism in a
text which itself explores the relation of gender to representation and
modernism. In the short story "Le Chef d'oeuvre inconnu" by Balzac, the
young painter Poussin meets the great master Frenhofer and learns that
this master painter has been working on a portrait of a woman for many
years but will allow no one to see it. Poussin, whose mistress/model is
extremely beautiful, arranges a "trade" with Frenhofer: Frenhofer will
allow Poussin to look at his master portrait, *Catherine Lescaut,* if Poussin
will allow Frenhofer to look at Poussin's mistress, Gillette.

The descriptions of the techniques of these two painters reveal that
they have different strategies of painting. Poussin strives to represent

reality on the canvas as convincingly as possible. Art must appear to be reality, and the master Frenhofer's previous paintings (which are for Poussin ideals) do just that: "Cette figure offrait, en effet, une telle puissance de réalité, que Nicolas Poussin commença dès ce moment à comprendre le véritable sens des confuses paroles dites par le vieillard" ("This figure produced, in fact, such a powerful effect of reality that Nicolas Poussin began at that moment to understand the real meaning of the obscure words uttered by the old man").[1] Poussin thus obviously espouses a fundamental mimetic or representational ideology: art imitates nature. This imitation should take one beyond a simple copying of what one sees, however: "Vous autres, vous croyez avoir tout fait lorsque vous avez dessiné correctement une figure et mis chaque chose à sa place d'après les lois de l'anatomie! . . . Vous croyez avoir copié la nature" (p.416) ("You others, you believe you have done everything when you have drawn a figure correctly and have put everything in its place according to the laws of anatomy! . . . You believe you have copied nature"). Imitating nature and reality does not entail merely approximating them, but entails making the copy so good that one cannot tell it from the real thing: art functions as a *trompe l'oeil*, an optical illusion. This is Frenhofer's (and thus Poussin's) goal: to make his portrait so lifelike that one confuses it with a real person. Frenhofer actually believes he has achieved this, for when Porbus (a third artist) and Poussin examine the masterpiece, Frenhofer affirms: "Ce n'est pas une toile, c'est une femme!" (p.431) ("It is not a canvas, it is a woman!"). One can discern that it is art only by the frame, the easel, and the tools of painting that surround it: " 'Oui, oui, c'est bien une toile, leur disait Frenhofer en se méprenant sur le but de cet examen scrupuleux. Tenez, voilà le châssis, le chevalet, enfin voici mes couleurs, mes pinceaux' " (p.436) (" 'Yes, yes, it is indeed a painting,' Frenhofer said mistaking the goal of this scrupulous investigation. 'Look, here is the canvas-stretcher, the easel, and here my colors, my brushes' ").

Frenhofer adheres to this realist ideology so slavishly that he pushes it beyond representation, beyond the concept of art as realism and imitation. He understands that art involves something more than copying and translating: "—La mission de l'art n'est pas de copier la nature, mais de l'exprimer!" (p.418) ("The mission of art is not to copy nature, but to express it!"). A mission to express nature rather than to copy it: what could this be? For Frenhofer it is Pygmalion's dream of creating life itself, of creating reality, rather than imitating it: "Mabuse seul possédait le secret de donner de la vie aux figures" (p.421) ("Mabuse alone possessed the secret of giving life to figures"). Frenhofer takes seriously the old realist cliché that art should "give life" to images and, in a sense, makes the cliché real by literalizing it, by trying to create reality. For him, art is a doing, a creating, a "faire" (p.427), not a passive process of copying (similar to Emma Bovary's realizing mode).

The story's plot dramatizes the confrontation of Poussin's and Frenhofer's two artistic goals in the exchange of "viewings," which takes place between the two artists. Poussin, pursuing standard representative art, wants to see Frenhofer's portrait, the *represented* woman, *Catherine Lescaut,* and agrees to trade a glance at the real woman, Gillette, for a glance at this painted image. In fact, when we first see Poussin at work, he is not copying the real woman, Gillette, but a portrait of a woman painted by Porbus. In a sense, the "realist" Poussin proliferates representations of woman and does not see Gillette, the real woman, at all: "Ne voyant plus que son art, le Poussin pressa Gillette dans ses bras" (p.430) ("Seeing nothing but his art, Poussin pressed Gillette in his arms"). Frenhofer, on the other hand, in his attempt to take representation through itself to an unknown beyond, wants to see the *real* woman, Gillette, thus trading in his representation, and the two artists exchange gazes and mistresses.

Frenhofer's glance at the real woman results in a perfect painting in his eyes. Instead of seeing a representation of woman, one sees woman herself: "Vous êtes devant une femme et vous cherchez un tableau" (p.435) ("You stand before a woman and you seek a painting"). But when this painting is directed at the gaze of the representational artists, they, significantly, see *nothing:* "—Apercevez-vous quelque chose? demanda Poussin à Porbus. —Non. Et vous? —Rien" (p.435) ("'Do you see anything?' Poussin asked of Porbus. 'No, and you?' 'Nothing'"). In looking at Frenhofer's painting, created after he glanced at the real woman (Gillette), Poussin and Porbus can see only a chaos of colors and tones, a formless fog (p.436). In the perspective of representation the real woman is invisible; in terms of gender, she has nothing to see. For these representational artists who always look for the *same,* Frenhofer and his painting are intolerable, for nonrepresentational art in this text signifies Frenhofer's madness and brings him death.

Significantly, when Frenhofer looks at the real woman, Gillette, this gaze is *not* represented in the text. Instead we get a secondary representation of the scene through the eyes of the representational artists, who, locked outside the studio, do not see the gaze but look at each other, only imagining Gillette's story:

> Porbus et Poussin restèrent à la porte de l'atelier, se regardant l'un l'autre en silence. Si, d'abord, le peintre de la Marie égyptienne se permit quelques exclamations: "Ah! elle se déshabille. Il lui dit de se mettre au jour! Il la compare!" bientôt il se tut à l'aspect du Poussin dont le visage était profondément triste. . . . Le jeune homme avait la main sur la garde de sa dague et l'oreille presque collée à la porte. (p.434) / *Porbus and Poussin remained at the door of the studio, looking at each other in silence. If, at first, the painter of the Egyptian Mary allowed himself to proclaim: "Ah! She is getting undressed. He is telling her to move into the light! He is comparing her!"; soon he stopped speaking because of the look on Poussin's face, deeply saddened. . . . The young man had his hand on the hilt of his dagger and his ear glued to the door.*

The revelation of the real woman is unrepresentable, and one gets in its place the two men's invention and a mirroring of maleness (as in the end of *L'Education sentimentale* and in *Bouvard et Pécuchet*).

What could be more significant, then, when these two men, who do not see the real woman but only their own story, their own representation of what this gaze might be, end up seeing something in Frenhofer's chaotic picture after all: "Dans un coin de la toile le bout d'un pied nu qui sortait de ce chaos . . . mais un pied délicieux, un pied vivant!" (p.436) ("In a corner of the canvas, the end of a bare foot which emerged from this chaos . . . but a delicious foot, a living foot!"). The glance at the woman is like the Freudian "glanz auf der Nase" in the sense that all the representational artists see of the woman is a fetishized foot/phallus.

This is analogous to one of the roles played by the fetish in Freudian analysis: it reassures that the woman has a phallus and that castration has not taken place. The fetishist, although he has seen that the woman (specifically the mother) does not have a penis, denies that fact and selects an object of desire that stands in for her phallus, be it a foot, a nose, an undergarment, or some other object, often one that bears a metonymical relation to the woman's genitals (it is next to them) and/or a metaphoric link to the male organ (shoes, noses). In this same way, the fetishistic naming of woman as flower, panther, machine, or other traditional metaphors in nineteenth-century texts covers her up with a metaphorical undergarment through which one cannot see the real woman but can see only one's own symbol of what she is. Substituting metaphors for woman and substituting objects for the maternal phallus amount to the same thing in realist texts. Castration and its threat can be disavowed when these fetishistic veils hide woman, whose absence echoes the "aversion, which is never absent in any fetishist, to the real female genitals [which] remains a *stigma indelibile* of the repression that has taken place."[2] Since the phallus is always on the scene, if female desire ever emerges, it must be masculine, phallic—witness Mignonne, Bette, and Valérie.

Once one covers over the woman with metaphors, she remains veiled and remains phallic, the pure mother on the throne of respect—the ideal Mme de Mortsauf. The veil of realist metaphors *is* the fetish, is Sarrasine's fascination with La Zambinella's veils as well as with her feminine submissiveness and weakness; in short, the fetish stands for an ideal femininity that hides the real woman so that castration can be disavowed. Just as in their paintings, the realists of "Le Chef d'oeuvre inconnu" represent woman by making the canvas imitate nature as accurately as possible; when they interpret art, they again reproduce the same (an image of their own phallus). Woman (as art) reproduces them. In their eyes, the non-representational painting (the real woman) is chaotic nonsense that can but veil their idealized woman, the perfect mirror beneath the nonrepresentational painting: "'Il y a une femme là-dessous,' s'écria Porbus en faisant remarquer à Poussin les diverses couches de couleurs que le vieux peintre avait successivement superposées en croyant perfectionner sa peinture" (p.436) ("'There is a woman underneath,' exclaimed Porbus, calling Poussin's attention to the various coats of paint which the old painter had successively superimposed on his painting while thinking he was perfecting it").

But at the same time, there is a negative moment in this act of representation because the attempt to represent woman fails. To tear the veil, "déchirer le voile" (p.431), and to render woman always result in imperfection, for there is always something that is not quite right, something is always *missing:* "Qu'y manque-t-il? *Un rien, mais ce rien est tout.* Vous avez l'apparence de la vie, mais vous n'exprimez pas son trop-plein qui déborde, ce je ne sais quoi qui est l'âme peut-être et qui flotte nuageusement sur l'enveloppe" (p.419; emphasis added) ("What is missing? *A nothing, but that nothing is everything.* You have the semblance of life, but you do not express its fullness which overflows, that indescribable something which is the soul, perhaps, and which floats like a cloud around the outside of the body"). Once the artist tears the veil in the search for the same, he sees only woman's lack (of phallus), her incompleteness. The represented woman always lacks something, here in representational art, a "little something," a "nothing" that is, of course, "all"; represented woman is "not-all."

This is, then, the second, contradictory role of the fetish. It preserves castration: "The horror of castration has set up a memorial to itself in the creation of this substitute" (Freud, "Fetishism," p. 154). Fetishists do, in fact, know that the woman does not have a penis: "It is not true that after the child has made his observation of the woman, he has preserved unaltered his belief that women have a phallus" (Freud, "Fetishism," p. 154). Thus, as Freud says, fetishists simultaneously express "two contrary premises. On the one hand, they are disavowing the fact of their perception—the fact that they saw no penis in the female genitals—and on the other hand they are recognizing the fact that females have no penis and are drawing the correct conclusions from it."[3] In the same way, when gender serves institutions, it reveals the woman's castration: she is the one who has less (she does not have the phallus). The woman's place in *Le Rouge et le noir* is that of the headless, in *Eugénie Grandet* that of the moneyless, in *La Cousine Bette* that of the powerless. Fetishism and realism oscillate between presenting an image of the ideal phallic mother and an image of the powerless, castrated woman.

In any case, it would seem that at the basis of nineteenth-century French fiction, as at the basis of the fetish, lies a secret, an enigma,[4] that of woman's identity, and these texts sometimes reveal and confirm, sometimes hide and deny the answer to that enigma. Freud himself manifests this need to hide in his own writings on fetishism, as Guy Rosolato says: "Ainsi perçoit-il la nécessité de préserver, mais aussi de mettre en évidence, un *secret*" ("Thus he perceives the need to preserve, but also to make evident, a *secret*").[5] What is this secret feminine identity in the nineteenth-century text? It is the original tale of woman's castration; when these texts lift the veil, that is what they see. In fetishism, the mother's phallus is the invisible object that gives perspective to the picture; like the point of infinity in realist painting, it is the absent center that organizes everything.[6] In realism, the mother's phallus, by permitting one to see gender on the basis of sameness (the male phallus), distributes both sexes around it. The laming of woman that sees her as castrated or veils her as phallic, her taming into a frigid, passionless state by a fetishistic naming, both amount to, if we might be permitted to invent a word, the "saming" of woman.

Charles Bernheimer, speaking of *Bouvard et Pécuchet* as a "fetishistic solution to the problem of sexual difference," explains that fetishism is "a kind of desperate effort to salvage the narcissistic theory of sexual sameness just when it is about to be revealed as a fiction."[7] Indeed, the gender wars we have seen played out in these texts aim at a leveling out of gender difference or at its repression, in the sense that they reduce gender to male terms, to the presence or absence of the phallus. Thus it is understandable that realism is a world view based on the mirror reflection of reality, since it plays out the problem of sexual difference on the level of similarity. It is interesting in this context that, as Rosolato says, the fetish is often a kind of mirroring veil: in the literal sense, like the shiny shoes, it reflects and reveals the absent penis of the woman and comes to stand in for it; and in the figural sense, it mirrors man's phallus.

Just as seeing is important in fetishism, realist narratives highlight seeing by presenting innumerable visual details, by presenting a vision of sameness, a reflection of reality to the reader. If, as Rosolato shows, the glance at the woman produces the fetishistic shine (glanz) on the nose, which covers over the woman's absent penis (glans) (Rosolato, p. 35), then, in a similar way, in Balzac's "Le Chef d'oeuvre inconnu," the glance at the woman by the realist artist produces the perfect foot that covers over the real woman. The linguistic chain "glanz/glance/glans" parallels the realist textual reflection of reality and the fetishistic cover-up of feminine identity.

Thus my argument here is not simply that realist texts can be fetishistic, for this has been amply documented,[8] but rather that the entire realist project is itself about the fetish, about a phallic strategy, which, in its peek-a-boo problematic of castration, can keep things on phallic terms. Whether the woman has the phallus, or whether she originally had it and lost it, she is always defined around that phallus, which can therefore remain on center stage. As Freud himself shows, the fetish, like a screen memory created to cover up the real problem, takes the place of the normal aim, just as the fetishistic woman takes the real woman's place.[9]

The fetish and realism end up with the abolition of difference: not only the difference between the sexes but also the difference in language. By making woman mirror man, the mimetic enterprise eliminates difference just as it sees language as a transparent reflection of reality. [10] The belief in a clear, unproblematic, and transparent language glosses over the opaque and worrisome difference of woman and language. What Rosolato says of the fetish, one could say also of realism: "Mieux il réfléchit, *plus il se fait oublier*" (Rosolato, p.36) ("The better it reflects, *the better it makes itself forgotten*"). In this way, the realist and fetishist concretization of objects (the seemingly gratuitous description of things in realist texts and the concentration of desire on an object in fetishism) can make gender, language, and their problems disappear behind a reflecting veil: "Si le langage est la mise à mort de la chose, avec le fétiche cet ordre se renverse, et l'objet fige et supplante les séquences signifiantes qui aboutissent à lui" (Rosolato, p.37) ("If language is the putting to death of the thing, with the fetish this order is reversed, and the object fixes and supplants the signifying sequences which lead to an end in it."). In the nineteenth century, when French society sought a new identity as the state, society, and literature underwent radical changes, realism perhaps provided a comfortable sameness and a protection against the fearful difference of gender, self, and language.

If these texts have shown us anything, however, it is the inadequacy of this fetishistic understanding of gender. Something in gender does not fit into the polarized structure of possess or be possessed: consider the androgyny of Julien, Bette, Emma, Raoule, and Séraphîta; the ambiguous nature of Mme de Mortsauf and Mignonne; the undecidability of La Zambinella. Something is slightly askew in the realist *trompe l'oeil;* sometimes it malfunctions to reveal the opacity of language, most notably in Flaubert.

The recognition of the autonomous nature of art and language is, in fact, how representation deconstructs itself in "Le Chef d'oeuvre inconnu." As Poussin does not paint the real woman but paints instead one of Porbus's paintings, art imitates its *own techniques*. Representation reveals itself as a technical machine in the paragraphs that profusely describe technique and also in the machinelike nature of the artist, Frenhofer, called several times a demon, a man ruled by a machinelike force (p.422). The text itself becomes a machine which produces more and more text on technique, in the sense that much of the story is spent describing the various strategies used by Frenhofer. The machine of representation runs faster and faster until it runs out of control and shows itself as technique. [11] In the end, the painting created by pushing realist techniques to their limits and beyond shows its own productive nature, shows the work of art as process and technique, as the swatches of color. It reveals that the ostensible reality reproduced by the painting is merely an effect of certain techniques, realism reveals itself as a *trompe l'oeil* when Frenhofer's step beyond representation turns out to be an exaggerated performative pursuit of his own realist technique.

Of the various techniques discussed, the most important is that Frenhofer draws no lines for his figures: "Le corps humain ne finit pas par des lignes" (p. 424) ("The human body is not delimited by lines"); he uses light and shadow instead. This lack of outline and the undermining of representation produce fearful and uncanny effects in this text by rendering borderlines imperceptible. In Frenhofer's pictures, one cannot tell just where the human body ends. This loss of borders appears also in Frenhofer's desire to create life, for in so doing, he effaces the borders between reality and fiction, figural and literal. Art, no longer a result derived from an external source, becomes the source that itself creates the reality supposedly imitated (thus upsetting art's secondariness). Frenhofer, representing art itself "ce vieillard était devenu, par une transfiguration subite, l'art lui-même" (p. 426) ("this old man had become, in a sudden transfiguration, art itself"), derives from a work of art, from a Rembrandt painting; in describing him, the narrator says: "Vous eussiez dit une toile de Rembrandt marchant silencieusement et sans cadre dans la noire atmosphère que s'est appropriée ce grand peintre" (p. 415) ("One might have thought he was a Rembrandt portrait walking silently without a frame in the dark atmosphere which that great painter adopted"). Here Frenhofer's reality (and through the allegory, that of art itself) originates in a painting that comes before that reality. Not surprisingly, then, the canonical notion that the mimetic artist stands by the side of the road holding a mirror up to reality is reversed in this text when what is held up to the mirror is a work of art: "'Oui, je la signerais (l'oeuvre), ajouta-t-il en se levant pour prendre un miroir dans lequel il la regarda'" (p. 422) ("'Yes, I would sign it [the work],' he added, rising to pick up a mirror in which he looked at it"). [12] As in *Madame Bovary,* reality originates in art; in more general terms, what we see as reality is always already a representation.

The imperceptible borderlines in the painting become more uncanny in the sense that, since women serve as the objects of representation, one cannot tell where the woman's body ends. If, in representational art, woman's lack reflects man's properness, here, as in Mignonne's case, the borderless woman threatens all integrity. In a sense, then, when Frenhofer paints the undecidability of the woman's body in its lack of limits, he paints lack itself as this undecidability. Instead of trying to eliminate the missing element which always mars representation, "the nothing which is missing," Frenhofer instead *reveals* the lack of borders and paints it as the deconstruction of mimesis in nonrepresentation.

Thus realism, even as it reassures the primacy of the phallus in the false problematic of castration and adheres to the second, conventional trajectory of gender identity, also shows the aporia of gender identity, shows that behind this screen lies the real woman, woman's difference and nonphallic nature; nonphallic not in the sense that she lost it but in the sense that castration does not take place. Thus in this "fetish-once-removed," it is not simply that the woman oscillates between being castrated or not castrated, but that this dialectical, oscillating problematic of castration (dialectical because it is synthesized by the phallus) itself oscillates with its other, with the undecidable other of castration as woman's unknowable, aporetic difference.[13] This is not to say that the problematic of castration can simply be discarded, or that the nature of gender difference could be known. If that were the case, there would be no problem: one would simply be able to say woman's difference or say that she is castrated in fact. Rather, the undecidability of woman's castration (she is and is not castrated in fetishism and in realism) alternates with the undecidable, groundless state in which castration is always already a fiction.

But, of course, in "Le Chef d'oeuvre inconnu," written by the realist Balzac, mimesis returns to power in the end, and Frenhofer destroys his paintings, thereby reestablishing the supremacy of realist art and reinstating the conventional trajectory of gender identity. Nothing of the undermining of mimesis remains. And what of the woman? She too is symbolically destroyed when she asks Poussin to kill her. The real woman must return to invisibility in this text and cannot be "represented," is that which is missing in a representational text. We see her only in the destroyed unknown painting and in the "holes" in this text's representation, in the places where things fall apart and do not make sense in the perspective of mimesis. The missing dedication, for example, is indeed very odd:

À un Lord

. . . .
. . . .
. . . .
. . . .
. . . .

1845 (p.413)

One could almost see the text's missing dedication as a dedication to the missing element, to the missing woman and to the missing unknown painting, which, rather than presenting the woman as castrated in order to reflect through her lack the plenitude of the phallus/foot, emphasizes the fallacy of the representational system that sees the woman as a reflection of man, that sees art as a reflection of reality. Do we not hear echoes of another missing woman in the name of the represented "painted" woman, Catherine Lescaut? The "real" Manon Lescaut, that other courtesan who strangely lacks a body, who is strangely missing from the book that now bears her name as its title, never appears to us but is always filtered through Des Grieux's eyes, through his representation of her. In the dominance of the ideology of *seeing,* and of seeing sameness, woman can appear only as absence, as "other."

If, as in *Sarrasine,* the real woman cannot appear on the stage of this theater of phallic representation in the nineteenth century except in the aporetic and paralyzing moments of the text, she perhaps remains to be written (or to write) in our modernity when a different perspective on difference can allow her to emerge. Perhaps a study of the linguistic detours, those involved in the creation of the fetish and of those aporetic moments which contradict the realist project, may lead to a new understanding of gender.

NOTES

Introduction

1 Honoré de Balzac, *La Cousine Bette*, in *La Comédie humaine*, vol. 7 (Paris: Pléiade, 1977), p. 80. All further references to this work appear in the text.

2 "The grammatical mode of the question becomes rhetorical not when we have, on the one hand, a literal meaning and on the other hand a figural meaning, but when it is impossible to decide by grammatical or other linguistic devices which of two meanings (that can be entirely incompatible) prevails" (Paul de Man, *Allegories of Reading* [New Haven: Yale University Press, 1979], p. 10).

3 Sigmund Freud, "Femininity," in *New Introductory Lectures* (New York: Norton, 1965), p. 113. All further references to this essay appear in the text.

4 It must be emphasized that in Freud's theory, repression is not coherently linked to biology: a biological woman does not necessarily repress her masculine impulses, nor does a biological male his feminine ones. Freud claims in a criticism of Wilhelm Fliess: "I decline to sexualize repression in this way— that is, to explain it on biological grounds" (Freud, "Analysis Terminable and Interminable," in the *Standard Edition of the Complete Psychological Works of Sigmund Freud* [London: Hogarth, 1953–74], 23: 251. All further references to the *Standard Edition* appear in the text, as *SE*).

5 Jonathan Culler, *On Deconstruction: Theory and Criticism after Structuralism* (Ithaca: Cornell University Press, 1982), p. 171. The concept of bisexuality existed already in the literature of the 1890s, and Wilhelm Fliess first brought it to Freud's attention. Freud is, however, credited with introducing the notion into psychoanalysis. See J. Laplanche and J.-B. Pontalis, *The Language of Psycho-analysis*, trans. Donald Nicholson-Smith (New York: Norton, 1973), p. 52.

6 For a detailed analysis of active/passive in Freud's essays on female sexuality, see Sarah Kofman, *The Enigma of Woman: Woman in Freud's Writing*, trans. Catherine Porter (Ithaca: Cornell University Press, 1985), pp. 148–58.

7 Quotations from the German are taken from "Über die Weibliche Sexualität," in *Gesammelte Werke* (London: S. Fischer Verlag, 1948), 14:522.

8 Freud, "Die Weiblichkeit," in *Gesammelte Werke*, 15:120. The translation is a bit misleading here, for in Heine's poem, heads confront the riddle, but in Freud's text it is a question only of man brooding over the riddle.

9 Sigmund Freud, "The Uncanny," in *On Creativity and the Unconscious: Papers on the Psychology of Art, Literature, Love, Religion* (New York: Harper & Row, 1958), p. 141.

10 For two slightly different perspectives

on Freud's work on feminine sexuality see Luce Irigaray's critique of Freud in her *Speculum of the Other Woman,* trans. Gillian C. Gill (Ithaca: Cornell University Press, 1985), and Sarah Kofman's deconstructive reading in *Enigma of Woman.*

11 Jacques Lacan, "The Signification of the Phallus," in *Ecrits: A Selection,* trans. Alan Sheridan (New York: Norton, 1977), pp. 287, 288, 285. All further references to this translation appear in the text.

12 Lacan emphasizes that this notion of a negativity inherent in sexuality originates in Freud's thought: "In *Civilization and Its Discontents* Freud, as we know, went so far as to suggest a disturbance of human sexuality, not of a contingent, but of an essential kind" (Lacan, "Signification," p. 281).

13 Juliet Mitchell and Jacqueline Rose, *Feminine Sexuality: Jacques Lacan and the école freudienne* (New York: Pantheon, 1982), p. 40. The introduction by Jacqueline Rose is an extremely helpful introduction to Lacan's writings on woman. All further references to this work appear in the text.

14 Jacques Lacan, "The Subversion of the Subject and the Dialectic of Desire in the Freudian Unconscious," in *Ecrits,* p. 312.

15 Jacques Lacan, "Les Formations de l'inconscient," *Bulletin de Psychologie* 11 (1957–58): 293. "L'objet du désir humain est l'objet de désir de l'autre et le désir toujours désir d'autre chose (de ce qui manque à l'objet primordialement perdu)."

16 In Lacan's theory, the notions of the radical phallus and the real phallus are constantly confused, for they both play a role at the same time. Thus the explanation here is necessarily reductive, for it is much simplified for clarity.

17 Jacques Lacan, "God and the *Jouissance* of The Woman," trans. Juliet Mitchell and Jacqueline Rose, in *Feminine Sexuality,* p. 144. All further references to this work appear in the text.

18 Jacques Lacan, *Encore* (Paris: Seuil, 1975), "A Love Letter," trans. Mitchell and Rose, in *Feminine Sexuality,* p. 150. All further references to this translation appear in the text. "C'est par la fonction phallique que l'homme comme tout prend son inscription" (Lacan, *Encore,* "Une Lettre d'âmour," p. 74).

19 In *Ecrits,* pp. 146–78.

20 Jacques Lacan, "Séminaire of the 21 January, 1975," trans. Mitchell and Rose, in *Feminine Sexuality,* p. 168. The French version appears in *Ornicar?,* no. 3 (1973), p. 109.

21 Jane Gallop's frolicking essay "Of Phallic Proportions: Lacanian Conceit" points out Lacan's willful and pointed assumption of phallocentrism and shows how one cannot and should not simply dismiss him on account of it, but must confront it face to face, must "knock one's head against it" (*The Daughter's Seduction: Feminism and Psychoanalysis* {Ithaca: Cornell University Press, 1982}).

22 Catherinne Clément and Hélène Cixous, *The Newly Born Woman* trans. Betsy Wing, in *Theory and History of Literature,* vol. 24 (Minneapolis: University of Minnesota Press, 1986), p. 63.

23 Jacques Derrida, *Positions,* trans. Alan Bass (Chicago: University of Chicago Press, 1981), p. 41.

24 The logic of the supplement is analyzed in Jacques Derrida, *Of Grammatology,* trans. Gayatri Spivak (Baltimore: Johns

Hopkins University Press, 1976); that of the origin in *Positions;* and that of the hymen and pharmakon in *Dissemination,* trans. Barbara Johnson (Chicago: University of Chicago Press, 1981). See Culler, *On Deconstruction,* for a clear analysis of these strategies of deconstruction.

25 Barbara Johnson, "The Frame of Reference: Poe, Lacan, Derrida," *Yale French Studies: Literature and Psychoanalysis* 55–56 (1977): 457–505. Although the radical side does exist rather covertly in the early writings, as shown in the previous discussion of the phallus, Lacan evolved later to a more explicitly radical position, even though he still played upon his phallocentrism. Rose analyzes his renunciation of the concept of the *parole pleine* as a turn away from a conservative stance (Mitchell and Rose, *Feminine Sexuality,* pp. 45–46).

26 Jacques Derrida, "The Purveyor of Truth," trans. Willis Domingo, James Hulbert, Moshe Ross, and Marie Rose-Logan, in *Yale French Studies: Graphesis: Perspectives in Literature and Philosophy* 52 (1975): 45. All further references to this article appear in the text.

27 Jacques Derrida, *Spurs: Nietzsche's Styles,* trans. Barbara Harlow (Chicago: University of Chicago Press, 1979), p.61. All further references to this work appear in the text.

28 The illustration in Lacan's "A Love Letter" shows this double orientation clearly when one arrow of the diagram points from the woman to the phallus on the man's side, and another arrow points to the Other.

29 Derrida, *Glas,* trans. John P. Leavey, Jr., and Richard Rand (Lincoln: University of Nebraska Press, 1986), p. 229. All further references to this work

appear in the text.

30 Sarah Kofman, *Lectures de Derrida* (Paris: Editions Galilée, 1984), p.144.

31 "Mais cette opposition (Sé/Sa), comme toutes les oppositions du reste, la sexuelle en particulier, par chance régulière, se compromet, chaque terme en deux divisé s'agglutinant à l'autre" (Derrida, *Glas* [Paris: Galilée, 1974], advertising insert which describes the text and is signed J.D.).

32 William C. Dowling, *Jameson, Althusser, Marx: An Introduction to the Political Unconscious* (Ithaca: Cornell University Press, 1984), pp.129–30.

33 Ruth Amossy and Elisheva Rosen, *Le Discours du cliché* (Paris: SEDES-CDU, 1982), p.5.

34 See Pierre Grimal, ed., *Histoire mondiale de la femme* (Paris: Nouvelle Librairie de France, 1967), 4:118–20; and Claire Goldberg Moses, *French Feminism in the Nineteenth Century* (Albany: State University of New York Press, 1984), pp.17–18. All further references to Moses's book appear in the text.

35 Marie-Henriette Faillie, in her book, *La Femme et le Code civil dans la 'Comédie humaine' de Honoré de Balzac* (Paris: Didier, 1968), discusses the role of the Civil Code in Balzac and the attitudes about it reflected in his works. Moses, in *French Feminism,* summarizes de Gouges's fate on pages 10–13. Marilyn Boxer, in "Foyer or Factory: Working Class Women in Nineteenth-Century France, in *Proceedings of the Second Meeting of the Western Society for French History, November 21–23, 1974,* ed. Brison D. Gooch (College Station: Department of History, Texas A and M University, 1975), provides the statistics on nineteenth-century working women.

36 Julia Kristeva, "La Femme ce n'est

jamais ça," *Tel Quel*, no. 59 (Autumn 1974), p. 19.

37 Michel Foucault, *La Volonté de savoir*, vol. 1 of *Histoire de la sexualité* (Paris: Gallimard, 1976).

38 Kamuf, *Fictions of Feminine Desire: Disclosures of Heloise* (Lincoln: University of Nebraska Press, 1982); Miller, *The Heroine's Text: Readings in the French and English Novel, 1722–1782* (New York: Columbia University Press, 1980); Schor, *Breaking the Chain: Women, Theory, and French Realist Fiction* (New York: Columbia University Press, 1985).

39 Jacqueline Rose translates this unpublished typescript of the 21st seminar, Mitchell and Rose, *Feminine Sexuality*, p. 47.

40 Both Alice Jardine and Sarah Kofman play with this genderization of hysteria and paranoia, respectively, in *Gynesis: Configurations of Woman and Modernity* (Ithaca: Cornell University Press, 1985) and *Enigma of Woman*.

Chapter One

1 F. W. J. Hemmings, *Stendhal: A Study of His Novels* (London: Oxford University Press, 1964), p. 84.

2 Peter W. Stearns, *Paths to Authority: The Middle Class and the Industrial Labor Force in France, 1820–48* (Urbana: University of Illinois Press, 1978), p. 3.

3 André Granou, *La Bourgeoisie financière au pouvoir et les luttes de classes en France* (Paris: François Maspero, 1977), pp. 13–17.

4 Fernand Braudel and Ernest Larousse, *Histoire économique et sociale de la France* (Paris: Presses Universitaires de France, 1976), tome 3, vol. 1, p. 132.

5 Ibid., tome 3, vol. 2, p. 749.

6 Henri Martineau, Preface to *Lamiel*, in Stendhal, *Romans* (Paris: Pléiade, 1952), 2:861. All further references to this edition of the novel appear in the text.

7 Stendhal, *La Chartreuse de Parme*, in ibid., 2:431, 467. All further references to this novel appear in the text.

8 Stendhal, *Le Rouge et le noir*, in ibid., 1:614; emphasis added. All further references to this novel appear in the text.

9 Stendhal, *Armance*, in ibid., 1:105. All further references to this novel appear in the text.

10 Geneviève Mouillaud, *Le Rouge et le noir de Stendhal* (Paris: Larousse, 1973), p. 198.

11 Moses, *French Feminism*, p. 19.

12 Peter Brooks studies the relation of paternity to authority and decapitation in his article "The Novel and the Guillotine; or, Fathers and Sons in *Le Rouge et le noir*," *PMLA* 97 (May 1982): 348–62.

13 William J. Palmer sees decapitation as castration and as society's punishment: "The metaphor of castration is Stendhal's image of society's method of devitalizing the individual" ("Abelard's Fate: Sexual Politics in Stendhal, Faulkner and Camus," *Mosaic* 7, no. 3 [1974]: 29).

14 The image of the machine as representing a status quo that demands "conformity to utilitarian modes of thought and behavior" is studied by James F. Hamilton in "Romantic Heroism in Stendhal's *Le Rouge et le noir*: A Victory over the 'Machine,'" in *Voices of Conscience: Essays on Medieval and Modern*

French Literature in Memory of James O. Powell and Rosemary Hodgins, ed. Raymond J. Cormier (Philadelphia: Temple University Press, 1977), p.202.

15 Luce Irigaray, This Sex Which Is Not One, trans. Catherine Porter (Ithaca: Cornell University Press, 1985), p. 173.

16 Moses, French Feminism, p.26.

17 Mathilde too could be said to defy the law and order of society when she seduces Julien: "Par sa rébellion contre les lois de sa caste elle est une récusation vivante du système de valeurs sur lequel repose une aristocratie vieillie" ("In her rebellion against the laws of her caste, she is a living objection to the system of values upon which rests an obsolete aristocracy") (Richard Bolster, Stendhal, Balzac et le féminisme romantique [Paris: Minard, 1970], p.91).

18 Naomi Schor analyzes Lamiel's galloping in Breaking the Chain.

19 Hélène Cixous, "Castration or Decapitation?" trans. Annette Kuhn, Signs: Journal of Women in Culture and Society 7, no. 1 (1981): 42–43; emphasis added.

20 Stendhal's "feminism," his delicate linking of gender to political struggle that appears in the rhetoric of this text, has, of course, been noted several times, most significantly by Simone de Beauvoir in Le Deuxième sexe. Stendhal's women, for Beauvoir, "are not angels, nor demons, nor sphinxes: merely human beings reduced to semislavery by the imbecile ways of society" ("Stendhal or the Romantic of Reality," in Stendhal: A Collection of Critical Essays, ed. Victor Brombert [Englewood Cliffs, N.J.: Prentice-Hall, 1962] p.148). Schor also analyzes Stendhal's feminism in Breaking the Chain.

21 Honoré de Balzac, Le Père Goriot, in La

Comédie humaine, vol. 3 (Paris: Pléiade, 1976), p.275.

22 Moses, French Feminism, pp.18, 19.

23 Braudel and Larousse, Histoire Economique et sociale de la France, tome 3, vol. 2, pp.791, 751.

24 Moses, French Feminism, p.34.

25 Bonnie Smith, Ladies of the Leisure Class: The Bourgeoises of Northern France in the Nineteenth Century (Princeton: Princeton University Press, 1981), pp.32, 49.

26 John W. Shaffer, "Family, Class, and Young Women: Occupational Expectations in Nineteenth-Century Paris," in Family and Sexuality in French History, ed. Robert Wheaton and Tamara K. Hareven (Philadelphia: University of Pennsylvania Press, 1980), pp.195–96.

27 Balzac, La Cousine Bette, p.55. All further references to this novel will appear in the text.

28 Moses, French Feminism, p.19.

29 Ibid., p.20.

30 Braudel and Larousse, Histoire économique et sociale de la France, tome 3, vol. 2, pp.846–47.

31 Nicole Mozet interprets the conflict of La Cousine Bette as the struggle of the family to survive the onslaught of courtesans and prostitutes (La Cousine Bette de Balzac [Paris: Editions Pédagogie Moderne, 1980]).

32 Irigaray here speaks of female homosexual desire, and, as we shall see, Bette and Valérie form a subliminal homosexual couple (This Sex Which Is Not One, p. 196).

33 For a discussion of La Cousine Bette as a novel of women's power, see Nicole Mozet, "La Cousine Bette, Roman du pouvoir féminin?" in Balzac et les parents pauvres, ed. Françoise van Rossum

Guyon and Michel van Brederode (Paris: SEDES, 1981), pp. 33–45.

34 Irigaray, *This Sex Which Is Not One*, p. 30.

35 Frederic Jameson, "*La Cousine Bette* and Allegorical Realism," *PMLA* 86 (1971): 248.

36 John Vernon, *Money and Fiction: Literary Realism in the Nineteenth and Early Twentieth Centuries* (Ithaca: Cornell University Press, 1984), p. 35.

37 *Eugénie Grandet* (1833), written around the same time as Balzac's more fantastic stories (which will be discussed in Chapter 3), perhaps partakes of a different and earlier code, which permits certain gender ambiguities impossible in *La Cousine Bette* (1846) as Balzac's realism increased and his romanticism decreased.

38 Honoré de Balzac, *Eugénie Grandet*, in *La Comédie humaine*, vol. 3 (Paris: Pléiade, 1976), p. 1039. All further references to this novel appear in the text.

39 William T. Conroy, Jr., studies the change from the machinelike routine to a more spontaneous life form in "Imagistic Metamorphosis in Balzac's *Eugénie Grandet*," *Nineteenth-Century French Studies* 7 (1979): 192–201.

40 Schor, *Breaking the Chain*, p. 91.

41 Ibid., pp. 90–107.

42 The literal, nonalliterated translation would be "to fondle, caress, brood over, ferment (or, in another sense, dissipate his own intoxication with), and encircle (in small casks) his gold."

43 It is only with his last words, when he faces death and the loss of his money in the present, that he speaks of an afterlife.

44 Derrida, *Of Grammatology*, p. 12.

45 Roland Le Huenen and Paul Perron see this as a narrative strategy in the text (whereas I see it as Eugénie's strategy) that sets up a position in opposition to Grandet's: "Alors que Grandet s'efforce de compter les bijoux de Charles au seul poids de l'or, négligeant les façons, le narrateur en d'autres occasions s'empresse de promouvoir un ordre de la finition et de l'ouvragé" ("Whereas Grandet endeavors to figure out the worth of Charles's valuables in their gold value, disregarding the workmanship, the narrator on other occasions is eager to promote a different order of finely finished and well wrought work)" ("Le Système des objets dans *Eugénie Grandet*," *Littérature* 26 [1977]: 110).

46 Ruth Amossy and Elisheva Rosen analyze the opposition between dandyism and Grandet's avarice in "La Configuration du dandy dans *Eugénie Grandet*," *L'Année balzacienne*, 1975, p. 247.

47 Irigaray, *This Sex Which Is Not One*, p. 172.

48 Roland Le Huenen and Paul Perron, *Balzac. Sémiotique des personnages romanesques: L'Exemple de "Eugénie Grandet"* (Montreal: Les Presses de l'Université de Montréal, 1980), p. 196. The "genderized" symbolism is summarized by Freud: "Boxes, cases, chests, cupboards and ovens represent the uterus"; "It is a fact that the imagination does not admit of long, stiff objects and weapons being used as symbols of the female genitals, or of hollow objects, such as chests, cases, boxes, etc., being used as symbols for the male ones" (*The Interpretation of Dreams* [New York: Avon, 1965], pp. 389, 394).

49 For an analysis of the Sleeping Beauty image in descriptions of female protagonists, see Sandra Gilbert and Susan Gubar, *The Madwoman in the Attic: The Woman Writer and the Nineteenth-Century*

Literary Imagination (New Haven: Yale University Press, 1979), p.23. For a more specific analysis of Sleeping Beauty in *Eugénie Grandet,* see John Gale, "Sleeping Beauty as Ironic Model for *Eugénie Grandet,*" *Nineteenth-Century French Studies* 10 (1981–82): 28–36.

50 Elizabeth Janeway, "Who is Sylvia? On the Loss of Sexual Paradigms," *Signs: Journal of Women in Culture and Society* 5 (1980): 580.

51 Ibid., p.574.

52 Moses, *French Feminism,* p.6.

53 Jules Simon, *L'Ouvrière* (Brionne, France: Gérard Montfort, 1977), p.v. Jules Michelet, of course, also links the *ouvrière* to the destruction of the family (*La Femme* [Paris: Flammarion, 1981]).

54 Michel Foucault, ed., *Herculine Barbin: Being the Recently Discovered Memoirs of a Nineteenth-Century French Hermaphrodite,* trans. Richard McDougall (Brighton, Sussex: Harvester, 1980), p.151.

55 This problematic identity is played out in Balzac's texts not only on the level of gender but also on the level of one's general social identity, as in "Le Colonel Chabert." When Chabert's existence is denied by the state, he ceases to exist as a human being and subsists only as a numbered body.

56 Michel Foucault, ed., *Herculine Barbin dite Alexina B.* (Paris: Gallimard, 1978), p.119.

57 Quoted in Pierre Grimal, ed., *Histoire mondiale de la femme,* vol. 4 (Paris: Nouvelle Librairie de France, 1967), p. 103.

Chapter Two

1 Smith, *Ladies of the Leisure Class,* pp.81–82.

2 Margery Sabin, "The Life of English Idiom, the Laws of French Cliché," *Raritan* 1 (Fall 1981): 54.

3 Schor, *Breaking the Chain,* p.137.

4 Honoré de Balzac, *Le Lys dans la vallée,* in *La Comédie humaine,* vol. 9 (Paris: Pléiade, 1978), p.998; emphasis added. All further references to this novel appear in the text.

5 Nina Auerbach, *Woman and the Demon: The Life of a Victorian Myth* (Cambridge, Mass.: Harvard University Press, 1982).

6 Sarah Kofman, *Le Respect des femmes* (Paris: Galilée, 1982). My English translation will appear in the text and the original French in the notes; all further references to this study appear in the text.

7 Nancy K. Miller studies Blanche de Mortsauf and the problem of the mother's desire in relation to Rousseau's Julie in "'Tristes Triangles': *Le Lys dans la vallée* and Its Intertext," in *Pre-Text/Text/Context: Essays on Nineteenth-Century French Literature* ed. Robert L. Mitchell (Columbus: Ohio State University Press, 1980), pp.67–77.

8 "C'est, en effet, la nature qui, éprouvant de la crainte pour le maintien de l'espèce, aurait enraciné dans la nature de la femme la crainte devant les atteintes corporelles et la timidité devant les dangers physiques."

9 "Les comédiennes, en effet, sont dépourvues de toute pudeur: elles cherchent les regards des hommes, se montrent en public—ce qui déjà les déshonore; elles sont des filles publiques."

10 Their desire is often interpreted, and feared, as "a sort of insatiable hunger, a

voracity which will engulf you entirely" (Irigaray, *This Sex Which Is Not One*, p.29). One will be reminded of the Baudelaire of the cat poems and the poem "Sed non satiata" throughout this chapter.

11 "La femme le tient désormais dans ses fers, tente de l'enfermer dans l'ombre de sa clôture; au lieu d'être une mère, de lui *donner le jour,* de le laisser au grand jour, elle veut le garder dans son antre, le faire rentrer de nouveau dans son ventre; *l'étouffer* par manque d'air et de mobilité." "C'est lui [le sexe masculin] qu'il faut protéger d'une dépense excessive, de l'avidité sexuelle des femmes, de leur toute-puissance phallique et castratrice." "Car telle est l'avidité des femmes! Elles n'abandonnent l'homme que lorsqu'il n'est plus en vie."

12 "Etre une femme, tel est peut-être la crainte, le désir le plus profond de Rousseau."

13 "Et cette perte des vertus propres à son sexe est plus redoutable que ne semble le dire Saint-Preux, puisqu'elle fait courir non seulement le risque de l'extinction de l'espèce humaine tout entière, mais aussi le risque pour l'homme d'y perdre ses caractères propres; la femme, devenue homme, pourrait bien vouloir prendre sa *place.*"

14 "Car placer les femmes sur un trône, en faire des déesses ou des reines, c'est aussi se garder de découvrir qu'elles n'ont pas de phallus."

15 Nicole Mozet, Introduction to *Le Lys dans la vallée* (Paris: Garnier, 1972), p.27.

16 This uncrossable barrier is, for Kofman, that of a respect for women which forbids the fulfillment of immediate desire: "Respect is—in every sense—a cover; at the heart of the most tender union, it still maintains a certain distance by suspending a veil, a 'sacred vestment,' a supplementary piece of clothing, invisible, which, even when the woman is totally uncovered, stripped of every veil, never leaves her. It is a brake that comes to stop the most impetuous transports by imposing an uncrossable and insurmountable barrier" (Kofman, pp.66–67) ("Le respect est—en tous sens—une couverture: au sein de l'union la plus tendre, il maintient encore une certaine distance en étendant un voile, un 'vêtement sacré,' un vêtement supplémentaire, invisible, qui même lorsque la femme est totalement découverte, dépouillée de tout voile, ne l'abandonne jamais. Il est un frein qui vient arrêter les transports les plus impétueux en imposant une barrière infranchissable et insurmontable").

17 Moses, *French Feminism*, p.3.

18 André Lorant in "Pulsions Oedipiennes dans *Le Lys dans la vallée,*" *L'Année balzacienne* 3 (1982): 247–56, convincingly maps Freud and Klein onto this Balzac text, thus bringing the Oedipal configuration to light, but he does not go beyond the symmetries of the three texts.

19 Naomi Schor has pointed out that woman's desire is often punished by the death of her children in the nineteenth-century novel (*Breaking the Chain*, p. 39).

20 "Les respecter, c'est toujours les tenir en respect, à distance, afin de ne pas être tenté de lever leur voile."

21 "acte coupable à cause de l'interdit de l'inceste, mais surtout dangereux et doublement dangereux."

22 "La levée du voile risquerait de terrasser l'homme, de l'écraser, de le paralyser, *et*

d'ôter à la femme, la mère, toute sa dignité phallique, de l'emasculer. Placer les femmes/les mères bien haut, les respecter, c'est éviter de voir qu'elles n'ont pas de pénis, 'qu'elles n'ont rien à cacher.' L'économie que réalise le respect serait celle de l'angoisse de castration, et elle communiquerait avec un geste fétichiste."

23 "Le désir chez Rousseau est contraint de prendre une position fétichiste, voire perverse, qui lui permet de s'assouvir en se reportant sur le substitut symbolique de la personne convoitée en laissant intact Rousseau lui-même et la femme aimée. Il la dévore du regard ou par l'intermédiaire d'une glace—médiation supplémentaire—il ne la possède pas . . . il s'arrange pour introduire entre lui et elle un voile, une barrière qui au dernier moment maintient la distance et la séparation salvatrices."

24 The similarity between Rousseau's Julie and Mme de Mortsauf is studied by Nicole Mozet, Introduction to *Le Lys dans la vallée,* p. 2, and by Nancy K. Miller in "'Tristes Triangles.'"

25 "De plus, alors que de façon générale Rousseau déplore l'usage des signes qui se substituent aux choses mêmes, pour les femmes c'est l'inverse: il faut, dans ce cas, que le représentant se substitue au représenté, le signe à la chose même."

26 "La distance respectueuse, en effet, est un moyen pour conserver les véritables rapports naturels, rapports les plus sacrés, les seuls sacrés, grâce auxquels chaque sexe se trouve maintenu à la place que lui aurait assignée la nature."

27 Most scandalously, the image of water under pressure appears several times in a very sensual image of pleasure: "Ce fut pour moi, je n'ose dire pour elle,

comme ces fissures par lesquelles jaillissent les eaux contenues dans un barrage invincible" (p. 1057) ("It was, for me [I would not dare say for her], like one of those fissures through which waters, held back by an invincible dam, burst forth"); "L'amour n'est-il pas dans les espaces infinis de l'âme, comme est dans une belle vallée le grand fleuve où se rendent les pluies, les ruisseaux et les torrents, où tombent les arbres et les fleurs, les graviers du bord et les plus élevés quartiers de roc; il s'agrandit aussi bien par les orages que par le lent tribut des claires fontaines" (pp. 1129–30) ("In the infinite spaces of the soul, is not love like the great river in a beautiful valley, to which flow the rains, the streams, and the torrents, into which fall trees and flowers, gravel from its bank and sections of the highest rock; it grows as much by storms as by the slow contribution of clear fountains").

28 Leyla Perron-Moisés, in "Balzac et les fleurs de l'écritoire," *Poétique,* no. 43 (September 1980), p. 305, says that in this novel we find "the most erotic pages written by Balzac," because the images of flowers parallel descriptions of male and female sex organs. The image of a flower opened corresponds almost scandalously to that of a woman abandoning herself: "Mettez ce discours dans la lumière d'une croisée, afin d'en montrer les frais détails, les délicates oppositions, les arabesques, afin que la souveraine émue y voie une fleur plus épanouie et d'où tombe une larme; elle sera bien près de s'abandonner, il faudra qu'un ange ou la voix de son enfant la retienne au bord de l'abîme" (Balzac, p. 1057) ("Place this message in the light of a window, in order to show its

fresh details, its delicate oppositions, its arabesques, so that the queen of your heart, moved, might see one particular flower opened wider, from which a tear falls; she will be ready to yield. Only an angel or the voice of her child can retain her on the brink of the abyss").

Peter Brooks studies this rhetoric in psychoanalytic terms in "Virtue Tripping: Notes on *Le Lys dans la vallée*," *Yale French Studies: Intoxication and Literature* 50 (1974): 155.

29 Doris Y. Kadish links Félix's blindness to this willful imposition of a false, subjective rhetoric on nature and on Mme de Mortsauf in "The Ambiguous Lily Motif in Balzac's *Le Lys dans la vallée*," *International Fiction Review* 10 (1983): 8–14.

30 L'interdit de l'inceste introduit un clivage entre la tendresse et la sensualité, entre les deux figures de la mère, la vierge et la putain."

31 Perron-Moisés speaks of the hermaphroditic nature of these flowers. She also sees the flowers as metaphors for sex scenes that cannot appear in the literal text of the novel ("Balzac et les fleurs de l'écritoire," pp. 306–8). Brooks links the flowers' double nature to the breakthrough of the repressed ("Virtue Tripping," p. 157).

32 "ne saurait être une personne morale digne de respect . . . objet sexuel suffisamment rabaissé pour ne pas évoquer la mère."

33 Honoré de Balzac, "Une Passion dans le désert," in *La Comédie Humaine*, vol. 8 (Paris: Pléiade, 1977), p. 1226. All further references to this story appear in the text.

34 Patrick Berthier, Introduction to ibid., p. 1215.

35 Berthier also suggests that the more the

panther resembles a woman, the less scandalous the story becomes (Introduction, p. 1217). Janet Beizer, however, claims the opposite in *Family Plots: Balzac's Narrative Generations* (New Haven: Yale University Press, 1986).

36 See Auerbach, *Woman and the Demon*, and Gilbert and Gubar, *Madwoman in the Attic*.

37 For an interesting analysis of Plato's cave see Irigaray, *Speculum of the Other Woman*. Kofman also analyzes the smothering cave in Rousseau's discussion of the theater in *Le Respect des femmes*. Freud, of course, links hollowness in general to the woman's body (*Interpretation of Dreams*, p. 389).

38 Karen Horney, *Feminine Psychology* (New York: Norton, 1967), p. 134.

39 Melanie Klein, *Love, Guilt and Reparation* (New York: Delacorte, 1975), p. 249.

40 Ibid., p. 208.

41 Leo Bersani, *Balzac to Beckett: Center and Circumference in French Fiction* (New York: Oxford University Press, 1970), p. 40.

42 Klein, *Love, Guilt and Reparation*, p. 187.

43 Her phallic attributes could be seen to reflect an image of the phallic mother (formed before the onset of the Oedipus conflict), and her being both friend and foe could represent the good and bad mother of Melanie Klein. The two levels of narration in this text, studied by Léon-François Hoffman in "Eros camouflé: En Marge d'*Une Passion dans le désert*," *Hebrew University Studies in Literature* 5 (1977): 19–34, correspond to the panther's ambiguous nature.

44 Beizer, *Family Plots*, p. 77. Beizer's chapter on "Une Passion dans le dé-

sert," which appeared after this analysis was written, emphasizes the same details of the story: the sea, the images of cutting and devouring, the panther's tail. The congruence of her choice of details and mine shows how the lens of psychoanalysis makes certain themes stand out in a literary text. Our readings diverge, however, when concluding about these details, most generally when Beizer reads the tale as "Balzac's version of the Oedipus story" (p.90). As we will see later, my analysis moves away from this reading.

45 For an analysis of the implications of this type of historical reading see Shoshana Felman's reading of Balzac's "Adieu" in "The Critical Phallacy," *Diacritics* 5 (Winter 1975): 2–10.

46 Honoré de Balzac, *Sarrasine,* in *La Comédie humaine,* vol. 6 (Paris: Pléiade, 1977), p.1060. All further references to this story appear in the text.

47 Roland Barthes, *S/Z* (Paris: Seuil, 1970).

48 Barbara Johnson, *The Critical Difference: Essays in the Contemporary Rhetoric of Reading* (Baltimore: Johns Hopkins University Press, 1980).

49 Kofman, *Enigma of Woman,* p.141.

50 Similarly, Gilbert and Gubar in *The Madwoman in the Attic* note: "While they sometimes tore aside the veil, the Romantics also advised themselves to 'lift not the painted veil' because of their common dread of what would be glimpsed behind it" (p.469).

51 Barthes, *S/Z,* pp.216–18.

52 Johnson, *Critical Difference,* p.8.

53 For a sensitive analysis of Sarrasine's relation to art and storytelling, see Ross Chambers, "*Sarrasine* and the Impact of Art," *French Forum* 5 (1980): 218–30.

54 The word *folle* here means a frivolous, reckless gaiety, but it is also used in the nearby context to describe the narrator's companion, in the stronger sense of her "mad" or "crazy" actions.

55 Derrida, "Purveyor of Truth," p.61.

56 Ibid., pp.62–63.

Chapter Three

1 Charles Bernheimer, *Flaubert and Kafka: Studies in Psychopoetic Structure* (New Haven: Yale University Press, 1982), p.106.

2 Claudine Gothot-Mersch, "Bouvard et Pécuchet: Sur la genèse des personnages," in *Flaubert à l'oeuvre,* ed. Raymonde Debray-Genette (Paris: Flammarion, 1980), p.154.

3 Gustave Flaubert, *Madame Bovary,* in *Oeuvres complètes,* vol. 1 (Paris: Seuil, 1964), p.611. All further references to this novel appear in the text.

4 Jonathan Culler, "The Uses of Madame Bovary," in *Flaubert and Post-Modernism,* ed. Naomi Schor and Henry Ma-

jewski (Lincoln: University of Nebraska Press, 1984), p.3.

5 Charles Baudelaire, *Oeuvres complètes* (Paris: Pléiade, 1961), p.652.

6 Elizabeth Ermath also sees Emma as a casualty of the realist consensus that defines just what a woman can be and do, and because Emma tries to break out of these confines, she dies ("Fictional Consensus and Female Characters," in *The Representation of Women in Fiction,* ed. Carolyn G. Heilbrun and Margaret R. Higonnet [Baltimore: Johns Hopkins University Press, 1983], pp.1–18).

7 "What she lacks in order to write are

neither words nor pen, but a phallus" (Schor, *Breaking the Chain*, p. 17).

8 Culler, "Uses of *Madame Bovary*," p. 2.

9 Baudelaire, *Oeuvres complètes*, p. 652; emphasis added.

10 Jean Paul Sartre, *L'Idiot de la famille* (Paris: Gallimard, 1971), p. 723.

11 Schor, *Breaking the Chain*, p. 12.

12 Schor, in her investigation of androgyny in *Madame Bovary*, links it to reading and writing, but in so doing she does not really consider the characters' literal sexes.

13 Translation of this phrase from Paul de Man's edition of *Madame Bovary* (New York: Norton, 1965), p. 6.

14 Naomi Schor attributes the first use of this word to Rodolphe in his dear John letter to Emma, but it makes an earlier and more ambiguous appearance in Charles's vocabulary in a passage written in indirect discourse: "Bovary, pendant ce temps-là, n'osait bouger de sa maison. Il se tenait en bas, dans la salle, assis au coin de la cheminée sans feu, le menton sur sa poitrine, les mains jointes, les yeux fixes. Quelle mésaventure! pensait-il, quel désappointement! Il avait pris pourtant toutes les précautions imaginables. La *fatalité* s'en était mêlée. N'importe! si Hippolyte plus tard venait à mourir, c'est lui qui l'aurait assassiné" (p. 636; emphasis added) ("Bovary, during that time, did not dare budge from his house. He remained downstairs, in the sitting room, by the flameless hearth, his chin on his chest, his hands joined, his eyes staring. 'What a mishap!' he thought, 'what a disappointment!' He had, however, taken all the precautions imaginable. *Fate* had taken a hand in it. In any case, if Hippolyte were to die later, he would be the one who murdered him").

15 Roland Barthes, "L'Effet de réel," in *Littérature et réalité*, ed. Tzvetan Todorov (Paris: Seuil, 1982), pp. 81–90.

16 Jean Ricardou, *Nouveaux problèmes du roman* (Paris: Seuil, 1978), pp. 37–39.

17 In French "mettre la charrue devant les boeufs" means literally to put the plow in front of the oxen; or in the English idiom, to put the cart before the horse.

18 Translations of the medicines, pharmacy paraphernalia, and script styles were taken from de Man's edition of *Madame Bovary*, p. 51.

19 Jonathan Culler, *Flaubert: The Uses of Uncertainty*, rev. ed. (Ithaca: Cornell University Press, 1985), p. 141.

20 Culler's argument appears in *Flaubert: The Uses of Uncertainty;* Barthes's in his article "L'Effet de réel"; and Schor's in "Details and Decadence: End-Troping in *Madame Bovary*," *SubStance* 9, no. 26 (1980): 30–33. Culler has since modified his stance to a more androgynous one in his article "The Uses of Madame Bovary" and in the Afterword of the aforementioned book.

21 Sartre, *L'Idiot de la famille*, pp. 708–10.

22 René Girard, *Deceit, Desire, and the Novel: Self and Other in Literary Structure*, trans. Yvonne Freccero (Baltimore: Johns Hopkins University Press, 1965), p. 152.

23 Gustave Flaubert, *L'Education sentimentale* (Paris: Gallimard Flammarion, 1985), p. 51. All further references to this novel appear in the text.

24 John C. Lapp, "Art and Hallucination in Flaubert," in *Flaubert: A Collection of Critical Essays*, ed. Raymond Giraud (Englewood Cliffs, N.J.: Prentice-Hall, 1964).

25 Derrida, *Dissemination*, p. 191.

26 For an analysis of the performative nature of fantastic language, see my "The

Ghost of Meaning: Language in the Fantastic," *SubStance* 11 (Winter–Spring 1982): 46–55.

27 Culler, "The Uses of Madame Bovary," p. 9.

28 This tendency of the novel in the eighteenth century is noted by Nancy Miller in "The Exquisite Cadavers: Women in Eighteenth-Century Fiction," *Diacritics* 5 (Winter 1975): 37–43.

29 *Sarrasine* is one text in which the character who undermines polarities does not die, but that novel could be considered a fantastic text.

30 Frederic Jameson, *The Political Unconscious: Narrative as a Socially Symbolic Act* (Ithaca: Cornell University Press, 1981), pp. 99–100.

31 Tzvetan Todorov, *Introduction à la littérature fantastique* (Paris: Seuil, 1970).

32 Three interesting studies that deal with new concepts of decadence are Linda Dowling, *Language and Decadence in the Victorian Fin de Siècle* (Princeton: Princeton University Press, 1986); Gayatri Spivak, "Decadent Style," *Language and Style* 7 (1974): 227–34; and Michael Riffaterre, "Decadent Features in Maeterlinck's Poetry," *Language and Style* 7 (1974): 3–19.

33 Rachilde, *Monsieur Vénus* (Paris: Flammarion, 1977), p. 55. All further references to this novel appear in the text.

34 Freud, "On Narcissism," in *SE*, 14:88.

35 Kofman, *Enigma of Woman*, p. 57. All further references to this study appear in the text.

36 Carolyn Heilbrun in *Toward a Recognition of Androgyny* (New York: Knopf, 1973), discusses the homosexual side of the circular being (p. xiii).

37 This text appears to reverse "Une Passion dans le désert." If in that text, the woman who brought out man's bisexual

nature was killed, in this text, it is the bisexual man who dies.

38 Irigaray, *Speculum of the Other Woman*, p. 111.

39 Barbara Johnson discusses monstrosity and woman's writing in "My Monster My Self," *Diacritics* 12 (Summer 1982): 2–10.

40 Maurice Barrès, Preface to *Monsieur Vénus*, pp. 5–6.

41 In Miller's words: "The memoir—whose author is most often an orphan—usually opens with an exposition/exposure of the heroine's vulnerability: coded as lack of experience, protection, money. Think of Fanny Hill, fifteen-year-old orphan on her way to seek her fortune in London, or Justine, twelve-year-old orphan seeking work in Paris. Young, beautiful, ignorant, poverty-stricken and of course virginal, the combination is irresistible. The advent of the seducer, inevitable. . . . Death is the highest calling of the fictional woman" ("Exquisite Cadavers," pp. 39–40).

42 George Ross Ridge, *The Hero in French Decadent Literature* (Athens: University of Georgia Press, 1961), p. 138.

43 Todorov, *Introduction à la littérature fantastique*, pp. 138–39.

44 See Lucienne Frappier-Mazur, "Balzac et l'androgyne," *L'Année balzacienne*, 1973, pp. 253–77; Albert Béguin, *Balzac lu et relu* (Paris: Seuil, 1965); Gaston Bachelard, *Poétique de la rêverie* (Paris: Presses Universitaires de France, 1960), and Pierre Castex, *Le Conte fantastique en France de Nodier à Maupassant* (Paris: José Corti, 1951). See also Lucienne Frappier-Mazur, "Balzac and the Sex of Genius," *Renascence* 27 (1974): 23–30, for a study of the relation of androgyny to genius.

45 My notion of this other concept of woman parallels several points in Jacques Derrida's *Spurs*.

46 Honoré de Balzac, *Séraphîta*, in *La Comédie humaine*, vol. 11 (Paris: Pléiade Gallimard, 1980), pp.735–36. All further references to this story appear in the text.

47 Geneviève Delattre observes the unusual nature of this Balzacian portrait in "De 'Séraphîta' à 'La Fille aux yeux d'or,'" *L'Année balzacienne*, 1970, pp. 183–226.

48 In Jacques Derrida's "Différance," the opposition is between sensible and intelligible: "But, from this point of view, that the difference marked in the 'differ()nce' between the *e* and the *a* eludes both vision and hearing perhaps happily suggests that here we must be permitted to refer to an order which no longer belongs to sensibility. But neither can it belong to intelligibility, to the ideality which is not fortuitously affiliated with the objectivity of *theōrein* or understanding. Here, therefore, we must let ourselves refer to an order that resists the opposition, one of the founding oppositions of philosophy, between the sensible and the intelligible" (Derrida, *Margins of Philosophy*, trans. Alan Bass [Chicago: University of Chicago Press, 1982], p.5).

49 Barthes, "L'Effet de réel," p.89.

Conclusion

1 Honoré de Balzac, "Le Chef d'oeuvre inconnu," in *La Comédie humaine*, vol. 10 (Paris: Pléiade, 1979), p.423. All further references to this story appear in the text.

2 Freud, "Fetishism," in *SE*, 21:154. All further references to this article appear in the text.

3 Freud, *An Outline of Psychoanalysis*, in *SE*, 23:203.

4 This enigma of Freud's is studied by Sarah Kofman in *The Enigma of Woman*.

5 Guy Rosolato, "Le Fétishisme dont se dérobe l'objet," *Nouvelle Revue de psychanalyse*, no. 2 (Fall 1970), p.31. All further references to this article appear in the text.

6 This is the metaphor Rosolato uses in "Le Fétishisme dont se dérobe l'objet."

7 Bernheimer, *Flaubert and Kafka*, p.108.

8 It is, in particular, Flaubert's fetishism that has been studied: in Bernheimer's *Flaubert and Kafka* and in Schor's *Breaking the Chain*.

9 Freud, "Three Essays," p.154.

10 Rosolato emphasizes that the fetish is "le surpassement de *la différence des langues* et de la *différence des sexes*" (p.37) ("going beyond *the difference between languages* and the *difference between the sexes*").

11 J. Hillis Miller follows this line of argument: "The procedures of realism dismantle themselves by being systematically exploited, taken to their limits, transported to that hyperbolic point where they reverse themselves and become something else" ("'Herself Against Herself': The Clarification of Clara Middleton," in *The Representation of Women in Fiction*, ed. Heilbrun and Higonnet, p.104).

12 This is, of course, a technique used by artists to check on their technique by examining a reversed image of the painting.

13 This parallels Derrida's argument, outlined by Sarah Kofman: "Une certaine

indécidabilité du fétiche laisse osciller entre une dialectique (de l'indécidable et de la dialectique) ou une indécidabilité (entre la dialectique et l'indécidable)" ("A certain undecidability of the fetish permits an oscillation between dialectics [of the undecidable and dialectics] and an undecidability [between dialectics and the undecidable]") (Kofman, *Lectures de Derrida,* p. 133).

BIBLIOGRAPHY

AMOSSY, RUTH, and ROSEN, ELISHEVA
"La Configuration du dandy dans *Eugénie Grandet.*" *L'Année balzacienne,* 1975, pp.247–61.
Le Discours du cliché. Paris: SEDES-CDU, 1982.

AUERBACH, NINA
Woman and the Demon: The Life of a Victorian Myth. Cambridge, Mass.: Harvard University Press, 1982.

BACHELARD, GASTON
Poétique de la rêverie. Paris: Presses Universitaires de France, 1960.

BALZAC, HONORÉ DE
"Le Chef d'oeuvre inconnu." In *La Comédie humaine,* vol. 10. Paris: Pléiade, 1979.
La Cousine Bette. In *La Comédie humaine,* vol. 7. Paris: Pléiade, 1977.
Eugénie Grandet. In *La Comédie humaine,* vol. 3. Paris: Pléiade, 1976.
Le Lys dans la vallée. In *La Comédie humaine,* vol. 9. Paris: Pléiade, 1978.
"Une Passion dans le désert." In *La Comédie humaine,* vol. 8. Paris: Pléiade, 1977.
Le Père Goriot, In *La Comédie humaine,* vol. 3. Paris: Pléiade, 1976.
Sarrasine. In *La Comédie humaine,* vol. 6. Paris: Pléiade, 1977.
Séraphîta. In *La Comédie humaine,* vol. 11. Paris: Pléiade, 1980.

BARRÈS, MAURICE
Preface to *Monsieur Vénus,* pp.5–21. Paris: Flammarion, 1977.

BARTHES, ROLAND
"L'Effet de réel." In *Littérature et réalité,* edited by Tzvetan Todorov, pp.81–90. Paris: Seuil, 1982.
S/Z. Paris: Seuil, 1970.

BAUDELAIRE, CHARLES
Oeuvres complètes. Paris: Pléiade, 1961.

BEAUVOIR, SIMONE DE
"Stendhal or the Romantic of Reality." In *Stendhal: A Collection of Critical Essays,* edited by Victor Brombert, pp.147–56. Englewood Cliffs, N.J.: Prentice-Hall, 1962.

BIBLIOGRAPHY

BÉGUIN, ALBERT
Balzac lu et relu. Paris: Seuil, 1965.

BEIZER, JANET
Family Plots: Balzac's Narrative Generations. New Haven: Yale University Press, 1986.

BERNHEIMER, CHARLES
Flaubert and Kafka: Studies in Psychopoetic Structure. New Haven: Yale University Press, 1982.

BERSANI, LEO
Balzac to Beckett: Center and Circumference in French Fiction. New York: Oxford University Press, 1970.

BERTHIER, PATRICK
Introduction to "Une Passion dans le désert." In Honoré de Balzac, *La Comédie humaine,* 8:1215–18. Paris: Pléiade, 1977.

BOLSTER, RICHARD
Stendhal, Balzac et le féminisme romantique. Paris: Minard, 1970.

BOXER, MARILYN
"Foyer or Factory: Working Class Women in Nineteenth-Century France." In *Proceedings of the Second Meeting of the Western Society for French History, November 21–23, 1974,* edited by Brison D. Gooch. College Station: Department of History, Texas A and M University, 1975.

BRAUDEL, FERNAND, and LAROUSSE, ERNEST
Histoire économique et sociale de la France. Tome 3, vols. 1 and 2. Paris: Presses Universitaires de France, 1976.

BROOKS, PETER
"The Novel and the Guillotine; or, Fathers and Sons in *Le Rouge et le noir.*" *PMLA* 97 (May 1982): 348–62.
"Virtue Tripping: Notes on *Le Lys dans la vallée. Yale French Studies: Intoxication and Literature* 50 (1974): 150–62.

CASTEX, PIERRE
Le Conte fantastique en France de Nodier à Maupassant. Paris: José Corti, 1951.

CHAMBERS, ROSS
"*Sarrasine* and the Impact of Art." *French Forum* 5 (1980): 218–38.

CIXOUS, HÉLÈNE
"Castration or Decapitation?" Translated by Annette Kuhn. *Signs: Journal of Women in Culture and Society* 7 (1981): 41–55.

CLÉMENT, CATHERINE, and CIXOUS, HÉLÈNE
The Newly Born Woman. Translated by Betsy Wing. In *Theory and History of Literature,* vol. 24. Minneapolis: University of Minnesota Press, 1986.

CONROY, WILLIAM T., JR.
"Imagistic Metamorphosis in Balzac's *Eugénie Grandet.*" *Nineteenth-Century French Studies* 7 (1979): 192–201.

CULLER, JONATHAN
Flaubert: The Uses of Uncertainty. Rev. ed. Ithaca: Cornell University Press, 1985.
On Deconstruction: Theory and Criticism after Structuralism. Ithaca: Cornell University Press, 1982.
"The Uses of Madame Bovary." In *Flaubert and Post-Modernism,* edited by Naomi Schor and Henry Majewski, pp. 1–12. Lincoln: University of Nebraska Press, 1984.

DELATTRE, GENEVIÈVE
"De 'Séraphîta' à 'La Fille aux yeux d'or.'" *L'Année balzacienne,* 1970, pp. 183–226.

DERRIDA, JACQUES
Margins of Philosophy. Translated by Alan Bass. Chicago: University of Chicago Press, 1982.
Dissemination. Translated by Barbara Johnson. Chicago: University of Chicago Press, 1981.
Glas. Paris: Galilée, 1974. Translated by John P. Leavey, Jr., and Richard Rand. Lincoln: University of Nebraska Press, 1986.
Of Grammatology. Translated by Gayatri Spivak. Baltimore: Johns Hopkins University Press, 1976.
Positions. Translated by Alan Bass. Chicago: University of Chicago Press, 1981.
"The Purveyor of Truth." Translated by Willis Domingo, James Hulbert, Moshe Ross, and Marie Rose-Logan. In *Yale French Studies: Graphesis: Perspectives in Literature and Philosophy* 52 (1975): 31–113.
Spurs: Nietzsche's Styles. Translated by Barbara Harlow. Chicago: University of Chicago Press, 1979.

DOWLING, LINDA
Language and Decadence in the Victorian Fin de Siècle. Princeton: Princeton University Press, 1986.

DOWLING, WILLIAM C.
Jameson, Althusser, Marx: An Introducton to the Political Unconscious. Ithaca: Cornell University Press, 1984.

ERMATH, ELIZABETH
"Fictional Consensus and Female Characters." In *The Representation of Women in Fiction,* edited by Carolyn G. Heilbrun and Margaret R. Higonnet, pp. 1–18. Baltimore: Johns Hopkins University Press, 1983.

BIBLIOGRAPHY

FAILLIE, MARIE-HENRIETTE
La Femme et le Code civil dans la 'Comédie humaine' de Honoré de Balzac.
Paris: Didier, 1968.

FELMAN, SHOSHANA
"The Critical Phallacy." *Diacritics* 5 (Winter 1975): 2–10.

FLAUBERT, GUSTAVE
Bouvard et Pécuchet. Paris: Gallimard, 1979.
L'Education sentimentale. Paris: Gallimard Flammarion, 1985.
Madame Bovary. In *Oeuvres complètes,* vol. 1. Paris: Seuil, 1964.
Madame Bovary (English ed.). Edited by Paul de Man. New York: Norton, 1965.

FOUCAULT, MICHEL
Ed. *Herculine Barbin: Being the Recently Discovered Memoirs of a Nineteenth-Century French Hermaphrodite.* Translated by Richard McDougall. Brighton, Sussex: Harvester, 1980.
Ed. *Herculine Barbin dite Alexina B.* Paris: Gallimard, 1978.
La Volonté de savoir. Vol. 1 of *Histoire de la sexualité.* Paris: Gallimard, 1976.

FRAPPIER-MAZUR, LUCIENNE
"Balzac and the Sex of Genius." *Renascence* 27 (1974): 23–30.
"Balzac et l'androgyne." *L'Année balzacienne,* 1973, pp.253–77.

FREUD, SIGMUND
"Analysis Terminable and Interminable." In *Standard Edition of the Complete Psychological Works of Sigmund Freud,* 24 vols. London: Hogarth, 1953–74. 23:216–53.
" 'A Child Is Being Beaten': A Contribution to the Study of the Origin of Sexual Perversions." In *Standard Edition of the Complete Psychological Works.* 24 vols. London: Hogarth, 1953–74. 23:216–53.
"Female Sexuality." In *Standard Edition of the Complete Psychological Works.* 24 vols. London: Hogarth, 1953–74. 21:221–43.
"Femininity." In *New Introductory Lectures,* pp.112–35. New York: Norton, 1965.
"Fetishism." In *Standard Edition of the Complete Psychological Works.* 24 vols. London: Hogarth, 1953–74. 21:152–57.
The Interpretation of Dreams. New York: Avon, 1965.
"On Narcissism: An Introduction." In *Standard Edition of the Complete Psychological Works.* 24 vols. London: Hogarth, 1953–74. 14:73–102.
An Outline of Psychoanalysis. In *Standard Edition of the Complete Psychological Works.* 24 vols. London: Hogarth, 1953–74. 23:144–207.
"Some Psychical Consequences of the Anatomical Distinction between the Sexes." In *Standard Edition of the Complete Psychological Works.* 24 vols. London: Hogarth, 1953–74. 19:248–58.

Three Essays on the Theory of Sexuality. In *Standard Edition of the Complete Psychological Works.* London: Hogarth, 1953–74. 7:135–243.

"The Uncanny." In *On Creativity and the Unconscious: Papers on the Psychology of Art, Literature, Love, Religion,* pp. 122–61. New York: Harper & Row, 1958.

"Über die Weibliche Sexualität." In *Gesammelte Werke,* 14:517–37. London: S. Fischer Verlag, 1976.

"Die Weiblichkeit." In *Gesammelte Werke,* 15:119–45. London: S. Fischer Verlag, 1979.

GALE, JOHN
"Sleeping Beauty as Ironic Model for *Eugénie Grandet.*" *Nineteenth-Century French Studies* 10 (1981–82): 28–36.

GALLOP, JANE
The Daughter's Seduction: Feminism and Psychoanalysis. Ithaca: Cornell University Press, 1982.

GILBERT, SANDRA, and GUBAR, SUSAN
The Madwoman in the Attic: The Woman Writer and the Nineteenth-Century Literary Imagination. New Haven: Yale University Press, 1979.

GIRARD, RENÉ
Deceit, Desire, and the Novel: Self and Other in Literary Structure. Translated by Yvonne Freccero. Baltimore: Johns Hopkins University Press, 1965.

GOTHOT-MERSCH, CLAUDINE
"Bouvard et Pécuchet: Sur la genèse des personnages." In *Flaubert à l'oeuvre,* edited by Raymonde Debray-Genette, pp. 135–67. Paris: Flammarion, 1980.

GRANOU, ANDRÉ
La Bourgeoisie financière au pouvoir et les luttes de classes en France. Paris: François Maspero, 1977.

GRIMAL, PIERRE, ED.
Histoire mondiale de la femme, vol. 4. Paris: Nouvelle Librairie de France, 1967.

HAMILTON, JAMES F.
"Romantic Heroism in Stendhal's *Le Rouge et le noir:* A Victory over the 'Machine.'" In *Voices of Conscience: Essays on Medieval and Modern French Literature in Memory of James D. Powell and Rosemary Hodgins,* edited by Raymond J. Cormier, pp. 201–14. Philadelphia: Temple University Press, 1977.

HEILBRUN, CAROLYN
Toward a Recognition of Androgyny. New York: Knopf, 1973.

HEMMINGS, F. W. J.
Stendhal: A Study of His Novels. London: Oxford University Press, 1964.

BIBLIOGRAPHY

HOFFMAN, LÉON-FRANÇOIS

"Eros camouflé: En Marge d'*Une Passion dans le désert.*" *Hebrew University Studies in Literature* 5 (1977): 19–36.

HORNEY, KAREN

Feminine Psychology. New York: Norton, 1967.

IRIGARAY, LUCE

Speculum of the Other Woman. Translated by Gillian C. Gill. Ithaca: Cornell University Press, 1985.

This Sex Which Is Not One. Translated by Catherine Porter. Ithaca: Cornell University Press, 1985.

JAMESON, FREDERIC

"*La Cousine Bette* and Allegorical Realism." *PMLA* 86 (1971): 241–54.

The Political Unconscious: Narrative as a Socially Symbolic Act. Ithaca: Cornell University Press, 1981.

JANEWAY, ELIZABETH

"Who Is Sylvia? On the Loss of Sexual Paradigms." *Signs: Journal of Women in Culture and Society* 5 (1980): 573–89.

JARDINE, ALICE

Gynesis: Configurations of Woman and Modernity. Ithaca: Cornell University Press, 1985.

JOHNSON, BARBARA

The Critical Difference: Essays in the Contemporary Rhetoric of Reading. Baltimore: Johns Hopkins University Press, 1980.

"The Frame of Reference: Poe, Lacan, Derrida." *Yale French Studies: Literature and Psychoanalysis* 55–56 (1977): 457–505.

"My Monster My Self." *Diacritics* 12 (Summer 1982): 2–10.

KADISH, DORIS Y.

"The Ambiguous Lily Motif in Balzac's *Le Lys dans la vallée. International Fiction Review* 10 (1983): 8–14.

KAMUF, PEGGY

Fictions of Feminine Desire: Disclosures of Heloise. Lincoln: University of Nebraska Press, 1982.

KELLY, DOROTHY

"The Ghost of Meaning: Language in the Fantastic." *SubStance* 11, no. 2 (1982): 46–55.

KLEIN, MELANIE

Love, Guilt and Reparation. New York: Delacorte, 1975.

KOFMAN, SARAH

The Enigma of Woman: Woman in Freud's Writing. Translated by Catherine Porter. Ithaca: Cornell University Press, 1985.

Lectures de Derrida. Paris: Editions Galilée, 1984.

Le Respect des femmes. Paris: Galilée, 1982.

KRISTEVA, JULIA
"La Femme ce n'est jamais ça." *Tel Quel,* no. 59 (Autumn 1974), pp. 19–25.

LACAN, JACQUES
"The Agency of the Letter in the Unconscious or Reason since Freud." In *Ecrits: A Selection,* translated by Alan Sheridan, pp. 146–78. New York: Norton, 1977.

Encore. Paris: Seuil, 1975.

"Les Formations de l'inconscient." *Bulletin de Psychologie* 11 (1957–58): 293–96.

"God and the *Jouissance* of The Woman." Translated by Juliet Mitchell and Jacqueline Rose. In *Feminine Sexuality: Jacques Lacan and the 'école freudienne,'* pp. 137–48. New York: Pantheon, 1982.

"A Love Letter." Translated by Juliet Mitchell and Jacqueline Rose. In *Feminine Sexuality: Jacques Lacan and the 'école freudienne,'* pp. 149–61. New York: Pantheon, 1982.

"Séminaire of the 21 January, 1975." Translated by Juliet Mitchell and Jacqueline Rose. In *Feminine Sexuality: Jacques Lacan and the 'école freudienne,'* pp. 162–71. New York: Pantheon, 1982. The French version appears in *Ornicar?* no. 3 (1975), pp. 104–10.

"The Signification of the Phallus." In *Ecrits: A Selection,* translated by Alan Sheridan, pp. 281–91. New York: Norton, 1977.

"The Subversion of the Subject and the Dialectic of Desire in the Freudian Unconscious." In *Ecrits: A Selection,* translated by Alan Sheridan, pp. 292–325. New York: Norton, 1977.

LAPLANCHE, J. and PONTALIS, J.-B.
The Language of Psycho-analysis. Translated by Donald Nicholson-Smith. New York: Norton, 1973.

LAPP, JOHN C.
"Art and Hallucination in Flaubert." In *Flaubert: A Collection of Critical Essays,* edited by Raymond Giraud, pp. 75–87. Englewood Cliffs, N.J.: Prentice-Hall, 1964.

LE HUENEN, ROLAND, and PERRON, PAUL
Balzac. Sémiotique des personnages romanesques: L'Exemple de "Eugénie Grandet." Montreal: Les Presses de l'Université de Montréal, 1980.

"Le Système des objets dans Eugénie Grandet." *Litterature* 26 (1977): 94–119.

LORANT, ANDRÉ
"Pulsions Oedipiennes dans Le Lys dans la vallée." *L'Année balzacienne* 3 (1982): 247–56.

MAN, PAUL DE
Allegories of Reading: Figural Language in Rousseau, Nietzsche, Rilke, and Proust, pp.3–19. New Haven: Yale University Press, 1979.

MARTINEAU, HENRI
Preface to *Lamiel*. In Stendhal, *Romans*, vol. 2. Paris: Pléiade, 1952.

MICHELET, JULES
La Femme. Paris: Flammarion, 1981.

MILLER, J. HILLIS
"'Herself Against Herself': The Clarification of Clara Middleton." In *The Representation of Women in Fiction*, edited by Carolyn G. Heilbrun and Margaret Higonnet, pp.98–123. Baltimore: Johns Hopkins University Press, 1983.

MILLER, NANCY K.
"The Exquisite Cadavers: Women in Eighteenth-Century Fiction." *Diacritics* 5 (Winter 1975): 37–43.
The Heroine's Text: Readings in the French and English Novel, 1722–1782. New York: Columbia University Press, 1980.
"'Tristes Triangles': *Le Lys dans la valée* and Its Intertext." In *Pre-Text/Text/Context: Essays on Nineteenth-Century French Literature*, edited by Robert L. Mitchell, pp.67–77. Columbus: Ohio State University Press, 1980.

MITCHELL, JULIET, and ROSE, JACQUELINE
Feminine Sexuality: Jacques Lacan and the école freudienne. New York: Pantheon, 1982.

MOSES, CLAIRE GOLDBERG
French Feminism in the Nineteenth Century. Albany: State University of New York Press, 1984.

MOUILLAUD, GENEVIÈVE
Le Rouge et le noir de Stendhal. Paris: Larousse, 1973.

MOZET, NICOLE
La Cousine Bette de Balzac. Paris: Editions Pédagogie Moderne, 1980.
"*La Cousine Bette*, Roman du pouvoir féminin?" In *Balzac et les parents pauvres*, edited by Françoise van Rossum Guyon and Michel van Brederode, pp.33–45. Paris: SEDES, 1981.
Introduction to *Le Lys dans la vallée*, pp.17–33. Paris: Garnier, 1972.

PALMER, WILLIAM J.
"Abelard's Fate: Sexual Politics in Stendhal, Faulkner and Camus." *Mosaic* 7, no. 3 (1974): 29–41.

PERRON-MOISÉS, LEYLA
"Balzac et les fleurs de l'écritoire." *Poétique*, no. 43 (September 1980), pp.305–23.

RACHILDE
Monsieur Vénus. Paris: Flammarion, 1977.

RICARDOU, JEAN
Nouveaux problèmes du roman. Paris: Seuil, 1978.

RIDGE, GEORGE ROSS
The Hero in French Decadent Literature. Athens: University of Georgia Press, 1961.

RIFFATERRE, MICHAEL
"Decadent Features in Maeterlinck's Poetry." *Language and Style* 7 (1974): 3–19.

ROSOLATO, GUY
"Le Fétishisme dont se dérobe l'objet." *Nouvelle revue de psychanalyse*, no. 2 (Fall 1970), pp. 31–39.

SABIN, MARGERY
"The Life of English Idiom, the Laws of French Cliché." *Raritan* 1 (Fall 1981): 54–72.

SARTRE, JEAN PAUL
L'Idiot de la famille. Paris: Gallimard, 1971.

SCHOR, NAOMI
Breaking the Chain: Women, Theory, and French Realist Fiction. New York: Columbia University Press, 1985.
"Details and Decadence: End-Troping in *Madame Bovary*." *SubStance* 9, no. 26 (1980): 27–35.

SHAFFER, JOHN W.
"Family, Class, and Young Women: Occupational Expectations in Nineteenth-Century Paris." In *Family and Sexuality in French History*, edited by Robert Wheaton and Tamara K. Hareven, pp. 179–200. Philadelphia: University of Pennsylvania Press, 1980.

SIMON, JULES
L'Ouvrière. Brionne, France: Gérard Montfort, 1977.

SMITH, BONNIE
Ladies of the Leisure Class: The Bourgeoises of Northern France in the Nineteenth Century. Princeton: Princeton University Press, 1981.

SPIVAK, GAYATRI
"Decadent Style." *Language and Style* 7 (1974): 227–34.

STEARNS, PETER W.
Paths to Authority: The Middle Class and the Industrial Labor Force in France, 1820–48. Urbana: University of Illinois Press, 1978.

STENDHAL
Armance. In *Romans*, vol. 1. Paris: Pléiade, 1952.
La Chartreuse de Parme. In *Romans*, vol. 2. Paris: Pléiade, 1952.

Le Rouge et le noir. In *Romans,* vol. 1. Paris: Pléiade, 1952.

TODOROV, TZVETAN

Introduction à la littérature fantastique. Paris: Seuil, 1970.

VERNON, JOHN

Money and Fiction: Literary Realism in the Nineteenth and Early Twentieth Centuries. Ithaca: Cornell University Press, 1984.

INDEX

Active and passive: in Freud, 5–6, 8–9, 18; in Kofman, 181 n.6; in *Sarrasine*, 76; and woman, 78

Amossy, Ruth, 186 n.46

Androgyny: and angels, 156; in Balzac, 1, 116, 156, 193 n.44; in Flaubert, 120, 121, 122, 137, 138; of Julien, 176; in *Monsieur Vénus*, 148, 151; as neutral gender, 157; as oscillation between genders, 157; and representation, 140–41, 143

Angel: in *Le Lys dans la vallée*, 81–94 passim; in *Seraphita*, 155–56, 166. *See also* Good mother; Woman

Aporia: in *Bouvard et Pécuchet*, 124, 138; and castration, 111; in *La Cousine Bette*, 56; and deconstruction, 14; in Derrida, 14–16, 21; as double bind of femininity, 93; in *L'Education sentimentale*, 140; and the fantastic, 155; in Freud, 4, 21; of gender, 2, 20, 21, 74, 115, 150, 154, 167; of gender in *Eugénie Grandet*, 65–67, 71; of gender in *Herculine Barbin*, 74; of gender in *Le Lys dans la vallée*, 80, 94; of gender in *Madame Bovary*, 137–38, 142; of gender in modernity, 2; of gender in *Monsieur Vénus*, 145; of gender in "Une Passion dans le désert," 97, 103; of gender in realism, 178–79; of gender in *Seraphita*, 163; of Julien's gender identity, 30; in Lacan, 13, 14, 21, 112–13; in rhetoric of nature, 87–90,

93–94; in *Sarrasine*, 112–14; suppression of, 144; of Vautrin's gender, 95. *See also* Deconstruction; Double trajectory; Opposites; Polarities

Art, 154, 177; and gender in *La Cousine Bette* and *Le Cousin Pons*, 56–57

Artifice: cult of, 144; of fiction, 154; of gender, 169; of language, 167; in *Monsieur Vénus*, 144–45, 153

Auerbach, Nina, 77, 190 n.36

Autonomy: of art and language, 176; of language, 144

B

Bachelard, Gaston, 156

Bad mother: in *Le Lys dans la vallée*, 80–81, 87, 93; in "Une Passion dans le désert," 94–106 passim. *See also* Fallen Woman; Good mother; Mother; Woman

Balzac, Honoré de: castration in, 96–98; and the Civil Code, 183 n.35; creation of reality in, 171; and the family, 18, 42–43, 44, 45–57; his feminine male characters, 40; feminine metaphors in, 76–117; gender identity in, 19, 21; groups of women in, 52; homosexuality in, 185 n.32; landscape symbols in, 158–59; marginal identity in, 47; platonic love in, 84; and rhetoric of gender, 18–19, 44–45; woman in, 51, 76.

INDEX

INDEX

INDEX

oxymoron, 160; and Romanticism, 18; and selflessness, 46; taming power of, 101; as veiling, 173. *See also* Chiasmus; Cliché; Discourse; Language; Metaphor, Metonymy; Textuality

Ricardou, Jean, 126

Ridge, George Ross, 193

Riffaterre, Michael, 193 n.32

Romanticism, 18, 123–43

Rose, Jacqueline, 10, 11, 12, 13, 21, 183 n.25

Rosen, Elisheva, 186 n.46

Rosolato, Guy, 174, 175, 194 n.6, 194 n.10

Rousseau, Jean Jacques, 78, 79, 80, 85, 86, 187 n.7, 189 n.24

S

Sabin, Margery, 76

Samson, and Delilah, 50–51

Sartre, Jean Paul, 122, 134

Saussure, Ferdinand de, 12

Schor, Naomi, 20, 58, 66, 76, 121, 122, 123, 134, 185 n.18, 185 n.20, 188 n.19, 192 n.12, 192 n.14, 194 n.8

Screen memory, 175

Seduction, 95, 101, 108

Sensible, 167, 194 n.48

Shaffer, John W., 44

Shakespeare, 128

Shelley, Mary, 152

Sign, 123–30

Signifier, 124–43; Derrida on, 16; as fetish, 60–61; and gender, 64–65; Lacan on, 9; and money, 60–61

Similarity: danger of, 104–6; and difference, 141; of gender, 138, 169–79; and rhetoric, 116

Simon, Jules, 72

Slave, 46, 79, 98–99

Sleeping Beauty, 67, 186–87 n.49

Smith, Bonnie, 44, 75, 76

Spivak, Gayatri, 193 n.32

Splitting, 16, 166

Stearns, Peter W., 23–24

Stendhal: aporia of gender in, 30–41; battle of sexes in, 26; castration in, 35–42; and church, 27–30, 38, 39–40, 41–42; and class, 18, 24–25, 34, 42; and decapitation, 35–42; double trajectory in, 41–42; family in, 44; his feminism, 185 n.20; and gender, 3, 21, 40–41; gender and class in, 23–42; gender and law in, 30–35, 41–42; gender and the political in, 39; groups of women in, 52, 57; machine of gender in, 35–42 passim, 57; male characters and women in, 25–27; masculinity in, 40; paternity in, 34; and patriarchy, 38; phallocentrism in, 40–41; power in, 27, 41–42; slave in, 46; women in, 25–42, 38–39, 185 n.17

Works:

—*Armance,* 25–26, 34, 40

—*La Chartreuse de Parme,* 24–25, 26–27, 34, 38, 40

—*Lamiel,* 24–25, 27, 34, 38, 40

—*Le Rouge et le noir,* 24–42, 71, 72, 73, 74, 108, 143, 150, 152, 174, 176; decapitation in, 35–42; industrial power in, 27, 35–38, 41–42; politics and gender in, 30

Swedenborg, 156

T

Taming, 99–101, 103–4, 116, 174–75

Textuality; as fiction, 154; fiction, and reality, 112, 130–43, 177; and gender, 9, 156, 167, 186 n.45; grammar, and gender, 119; as machine, 154. *See also* Cliché; Language; Metaphor; Metonymy; Rhetoric

Todorov, Tzvetan, 144, 155, 167–68

Totality, 13, 115, 116, 148, 167

Travel, and gender, 57–58, 68–69

Trompe l'oeil, 170, 176

Truth, 13, 106–17, 158